FOREWORD

Current debate on working-time issues includes reduced working hours, work sharing, capital-operating hours and flexible scheduling of the company labour force. The OECD has combined its ongoing work on labour-market flexibility with the study of new, diversified working-time arrangements. In May 1993, a panel of experts was invited to discuss issues in "Flexible Working-Time Arrangements: The Role of Collective Bargaining and Government Intervention", bringing to a close a project conducted by the Directorate for Education, Employment, Labour and Social Affairs under the OECD's Programme of Work for 1991 and 1992.

The expert meeting assembled delegates of the OECD's Working Party on Industrial Relations, representatives from the business community and labour unions, and the authors of a number of country reports treating recent trends in flexible working-time arrangements. The meeting particularly addressed collective bargaining on working-time issues, different viewpoints of social partners, and the role governments can play.

This book contains the revised national reports, an overview and summary of the issues discussed therein, and a brief account of the meeting's proceedings. It was compiled and edited by Peter Tergeist of the Directorate for Education, Employment, Labour and Social Affairs, and is published on the responsibility of the Secretary-General of the OECD.

FLEXIBLE WORKING TIME

COLLECTIVE BARGAINING
AND GOVERNMENT INTERVENTION

ORGANISATION FOR ECONOMIC CO-OPERATION AND DEVELOPMENT

ORGANISATION FOR ECONOMIC CO-OPERATION AND DEVELOPMENT

Pursuant to Article 1 of the Convention signed in Paris on 14th December 1960, and which came into force on 30th September 1961, the Organisation for Economic Co-operation and Development (OECD) shall promote policies designed:

- to achieve the highest sustainable economic growth and employment and a rising standard of living in Member countries, while maintaining financial stability, and thus to contribute to the development of the world economy;
- to contribute to sound economic expansion in Member as well as non-member countries in the process of economic development; and
- to contribute to the expansion of world trade on a multilateral, non-discriminatory basis in accordance with international obligations.

The original Member countries of the OECD are Austria, Belgium, Canada, Denmark, France, Germany, Greece, Iceland, Ireland, Italy, Luxembourg, the Netherlands, Norway, Portugal, Spain, Sweden, Switzerland, Turkey, the United Kingdom and the United States. The following countries became Members subsequently through accession at the dates indicated hereafter: Japan (28th April 1964), Finland (28th January 1969), Australia (7th June 1971), New Zealand (29th May 1973) and Mexico (18th May 1994). The Commission of the European Communities takes part in the work of the OECD (Article 13 of the OECD Convention).

Publié en français sous le titre :

LA FLEXIBILITÉ DU TEMPS DE TRAVAIL
NÉGOCIATIONS COLLECTIVES ET INTERVENTION DE L'ÉTAT

TABLE OF CONTENTS

INTRODUCTION

Peter Tergeist

Chapter 1
SYNTHESIS REPORT

Gerhard Bosch

Chapter 2
GERMANY: THE CASE OF THE METAL MANUFACTURING INDUSTRY

Rainer Trinczek

Chapter 3

JAPAN: THE CASE OF THE METAL MANUFACTURING INDUSTRY

Yoshio Sasajima

Chapter 4

UNITED KINGDOM: THE CASE OF THE METAL MANUFACTURING INDUSTRY

Paul Blyton

Chapter 5

CANADA: THE CASE OF RETAIL TRADE

Diane Bellemare, Marie-France Molinari and Lise Poulin-Simon

Chapter 6

FRANCE: THE CASE OF RETAIL TRADE

Michel Lallement

Chapter 7

ITALY: THE CASE OF RETAIL TRADE

Giovanni Gasparini

Chapter 8

THE NETHERLANDS: THE CASE OF HEALTH CARE

W.A.M. de Lange and D.H.C. van Maanen

Chapter 9
SWEDEN: THE CASE OF HEALTH CARE

Casten von Otter and Birger Viklund

Chapter 10
PROCEEDINGS OF THE OECD EXPERTS' MEETING ON FLEXIBLE WORKING TIME ARRANGEMENTS: THE ROLE OF BARGAINING AND GOVERNMENT INTERVENTION

Gerhard Bosch and Peter Tergeist

INTRODUCTION

by

Peter Tergeist

Pressure for greater flexibility in industrial relations and labour utilisation is being felt in all OECD countries. Since the 1980s, the OECD Secretariat has carried out a number of studies on this issue, with particular reference to trends in labour flexibility at the enterprise and establishment level [see, *inter alia*, OECD (1986); (1989); (1992), and numerous chapters in the *OECD Employment Outlook*, 1984-1994].

There exists no single model of enterprise labour flexibility. Depending on, *inter alia*, competitive strategies and national legislative frameworks, firms may stress different variants: from the external quantitative type (varying the quantity of employment through hiring and firing) to a functional type of flexibility involving multi-skilling and variation of tasks, and finally to the flexible scheduling of employees' time budgets.

Over the last decade, interest in more flexible ways of scheduling work has increased considerably. This interest has developed alongside the policy concerns with working time reduction and work sharing as means to combat persistent employment. However, it has also taken on a life of its own; to a certain extent, the debate on working hours has changed from the quantitative to the qualitative in that the issue of working time duration is being linked to, or even replaced by, a focus on flexible working time arrangements. In fact, while the trend for a reduction of the standard working week which started in the 1950s, has come to a halt or slowed down in most countries, the diversification of working time patterns has been a growing phenomenon throughout the OECD area.

Previously, the trend towards reduction of weekly working hours mainly went on with unchanged time structures; for example, the change from 48 to 40 weekly hours in principle still implied the 8 hour day. This approach has gradually given way to a stress on more flexible scheduling; in other words, there is now a much closer link between reducing and adjusting working time.

It has been argued that the increasing focus on working time flexibility represents a *quid pro quo* which employers have sought in exchange for granting further overall work time reductions; some observers have also noted that this change came about after the relative failure (at least in relation to initial expectations) of a policy to stimulate job creation by means of such uniform reductions [Treu (1989); Catinat, Donni and Taddei (1990)]. There is, however, a broader societal reason behind the diversification of working time patterns: the long-term need to schedule working hours in ways that, at the same time, ensure economic efficiency and respond to individual worker preferences.

A number of supply side and demand side factors have been singled out in the literature as influencing the trend towards flexible working time patterns [see, for example, Bosch (1989)]. On the supply side, the massive entry of women, in particular of married women with children, into the labour market has played an important part. On the other hand, in most countries the number of one- and two-person households without children has risen considerably and the dependence on a tight family schedule has therefore decreased. Finally, higher standards of living, increased education levels and more opportunities for organising leisure have led to attitudinal changes concerning the relation between working time and free time, including the trade-off between income and leisure.

As for labour demand, companies are interested in flexible working time arrangements as a means of fully exploiting productive capacity, extending plant utilisation time and shop opening hours and of better adapting production to seasonal and demand variations. In addition, increased training needs through new technologies imply longer absences of many core employees. Possible negative effects of such absences may be countered by more flexible scheduling.

Elements of working time flexibility

The notion of "flexible working time arrangements" (also called "flexible time management" or "diversification of work timetables") can be broken down into the following main elements [see also ILO (1986)]:

  a) flexible scheduling of work during the day, week or year: flexitime, daily rest periods, compressed workweeks, staggered hours, annualisation of time and pay, scheduling of annual leave, shift work, weekend work, shop-opening hours;
  b) the multiplication of employment relationships deviating from the full-time, Monday-to-Friday type work contract of indefinite duration which used to be considered the norm: such as part-time work, fixed-term contracts, temporary and agency employment, "on-call" arrangements or telework;
  c) more variable scheduling of work over the lifetime: average age of transition from school to employment, educational, sabbatical and parental leave, pensionable age, phased retirement.

This volume, while touching on most of the items mentioned, will focus in particular on item a), *i.e.* flexible forms of scheduling work during the day, week or year.

The principal actors

There are four principal actors, when it comes to determining flexible working time arrangements: workers, employers, labour unions and governments.

The **modern workforce** is concerned with a more "individualised" balance between work and private life. Different groups of workers – such as older workers, workers with family responsibilities, higher income groups, etc. – have specific, and sometimes conflicting, interests in one or the other form of working time flexibility: work sharing, parental leave, partial retirement, sabbaticals, etc. Workers as consumers may prefer longer shop opening hours which, in turn, will put demands on the flexibility of some of their fellow workers. The same goes for workers as parents and, in a larger sense, as members of civil society, when it comes to time pressures emanating from schools, day care facilities and public services (such as opening hours of municipal offices).

Individual workers' attitudes toward working time arrangements have been measured by means of opinion surveys. A 1989 survey conducted in 11 member countries of the European Community found that a certain number of both full-time and part-time workers were not satisfied with the length of their working hours; comparing the two groups, it was found that for one part-time worker who would have preferred full-time employment, more than three full-time workers (21 per cent in the survey) would have preferred to work part time. By contrast, a 1985 survey in the United States found that only 8 per cent of American workers would have liked to work fewer hours with a corresponding reduction of their earnings [OECD (1994, Chapter 6); *European Economy* (1991)].

Over the last century, **employers** have conceded continuous union demands for a shorter work week, although it has been argued that, due to their concern with capacity or capital utilisation, they tend to prefer wage increases to hours reductions [see White (1987)]. Just to keep plant utilisation time at current levels calls for greater flexibility in scheduling and organisation, as working time is being further reduced. However, it is above all the *extension* of operating hours which has become an issue of growing importance for employers, following rising capital expenditures and increasing concern with the cost of capital in many industries. In addition, changes in national and international markets occur more and more rapidly. In order to ensure an optimal response to market demands which may exist only for limited periods of time, some employers want to be able to extend operating time on a temporary basis.

More flexible scheduling arrangements are therefore actively sought by employers and employer organisations in current negotiation processes. They are, however, confronted with different statutory regulation and varying responses by employee representatives, so that average operating times vary greatly between countries. A 1989 survey by the European Community, for example, found operating hours in manufacturing ranging from 53 in Germany to 77 in Belgium [*European Economy* (1989)].

Shift work and overtime enable a company to extend its operating time, as does the presence of part-time workers and the willingness of core workers to work unusual hours, including weekends. For example, when a company decides to have workers put in, say, 36 hours over a four-day period, while it operates 5 or 6 days, new patterns of time management are required. Another example of new organisation patterns involves special weekend shifts, wherein workers only work Saturdays and Sundays, but then for very long hours (2×12 hours, paid as 36, for example). Traditional overtime work remains an important element in companies' working time practices. Overtime permits a degree of

11

flexibility which is considered essential to adjust to rapid changes in demand. Companies also consider that in a number of OECD countries the costs involved in dismissing workers tend to make hiring additional personnel much more expensive than scheduling overtime work.

Labour unions have historically conceived of their role as that of defending employees' "collective" interests; there is therefore some concern that the trend towards flexibilisation and "individualisation" of working time will weaken solidarity and render union work more difficult. The reduction of the standard working week remains the major demand of most labour unions, at least those operating in Europe. To cite one labour union position paper, the European Trade Union Confederation has noted that "the reduction of working time without loss of wages remains a fundamental demand in a period of unemployment when work sharing is imperative..." [ETUC (1990)]. Among the major arguments put forward for this strategy are, first, the redistribution of the existing volume of work as a way to increase employment and, second, a general improvement in the quality of life through increasing rest and recreation.

In recent bargaining rounds, unions have accepted flexible scheduling as a *quid pro quo* for general working hours reduction. In this respect, the European Trade Union Institute [ETUI (1986)] has noted that organised labour does not oppose flexible working hours, but reserves the right to examine all forms of such flexibility as to whether they lead to an improvement of working conditions and take into account employees' preferences, rather than being a mere tool to reduce wage costs and increase profitability. Collective bargaining, the institute maintains, is the principal instrument to assure such beneficial results. In particular, bargaining has to make sure that new patterns of time management do not result in increased stress and strain at the workplace and do not deviate from rules and regulations on maximum daily and weekly hours.

Labour unions are also willing to accept certain forms of extended company operating time. They tend to warn, however, against the detrimental implications of shift work and night work on occupational health and safety, and question a productivity calculus which does not take into account such results of shift work and "unsocial" hours as increased turnover, absenteeism and accident rates.

Government regulations set the framework within which work time scheduling can occur. The extent of legal regulations varies widely between countries, with maximum weekly hours, weekly rest, annual leave and public holidays being regulated most everywhere. In addition, governments can vary the scope for introducing flexible working time arrangements, *inter alia*, by setting a maximum length of averaging periods, restricting night and Sunday working, or influencing incentives for employers to rely on overtime work through the fixing of overtime wage premia.

While many governments are trying to provide more legislative flexibility, often regulations have not kept pace with changes in practice. Some countries, therefore, are tempted to tolerate practices which violate the letter of the law; others have begun to allow exceptions upon conclusion of a collective agreement. In Sweden, for example, exceptions to the entire Working Hours Act of 1982 may be made through collective agreements if they are approved by the central trade union organisation [ILO (1988)]. As one analyst of international labour law developments has noted, this development seems to result from "a certain helplessness of the legislator towards the new developments (...) an attitude of trial and error, [introducing some] legislation but leaving it to the collective partners to do what they like with it in order to find out which could be the best way for further legislation at a later stage" [Blanpain (1988)].

Governments tend to share the employers' concern about achieving economic advantages from adjusted working time arrangements. In France, for example, the government set up a special investigation committee to put forward proposals for an extension of plant utilisation time. Some of the subsequent Committee recommendations were incorporated into working time legislation [Taddei (1986)]. Later research has indicated that in fact machine running times in France, after having reached an historic low in 1983, are now showing an upward trend [Cette (1990)]. Some governments are also reflecting about a partial wage compensation of reduced working time, if it is combined with higher productivity through increased flexibility and longer operating hours (see the detailed provisions in the French Five-year law on labour, employment and vocational training of December, 1993).

Finally, mention should be made of attempts at **supra-national** regulation of issues concerning flexibility of working time arrangements. Apart from the Conventions and Recommendations of the International Labour Organisation in this area [see Bosch (1992) for a list of respective ILO Conventions and ratifying countries] the European Community has been particularly active. For example, Title 1, point 7 of the Community Charter of the Fundamental Social Rights of Workers laid down the goal of "an approximation of [living and working] conditions as regards in particular the duration and organisation of working time and forms of employment other than open-ended contracts, such as fixed-term contracts, part-time working, temporary work and seasonal work". Consequently, the Commission of the European Communities proposed four draft directives concerning the organisation of working time and the status of the said "atypical" forms of employment. The working time directive which lays down rules on average weekly working hours, minimum rest periods, annual leave, night and shift work, was adopted by the EC-Council in November, 1993; however, it is being challenged by the United Kingdom before the European Court of Justice.

The OECD project

The OECD Secretariat, after discussions in the Working Party on Industrial Relations, has approached the issue of flexible working time arrangements from the angle of collective bargaining and industrial relations. Collective bargaining has, in most countries, been a major instrument for shaping new forms of time management. At the same time, the impact of a country's institutionalised labour relations system becomes evident in the specific interplay between legislation and collective bargaining to regulate working time issues.

An area of special concern for the project has been the trend for decentralised bargaining over working time issues which has altered traditional bargaining patterns. Negotiations have tended to become increasingly concentrated at enterprise and plant levels where positions of employers and union representatives have become more detailed and sophisticated. It is especially the labour unions that seek to retain a degree of control over the process at national or branch level. The interplay between central and decentralised levels in the fixing of working time arrangements has thus been of particular importance.

Eight national reports (on Canada, France, Germany, Italy, Japan, the Netherlands, Sweden and the United Kingdom) on three particular industries (metal manufacturing, retail trade and health services) were commissioned by the OECD to generate comparable information on the subject. All national studies, and a synthesis report, were discussed at a meeting of experts in May, 1993; the revised versions are contained in this volume. National authors were invited to discuss labour/management cooperation, consultation and negotiation patterns on flexible working time arrangements in one of the three selected industries. To assure a measure of comparability, the following list of questions served as a broad guide to the studies:

1. To what extent do firms use flexible working time practices to reduce labour cost or cope with fluctuations in demand for output, as opposed to usage to improve the quality of their workforce? Is there a managerial preference for either flexible scheduling of existing employees or "flexible staffing", *i.e.* resorting to the external labour market? Are flexible working time practices used by firms to develop internal labour markets?

2. Can productivity and cost impacts on firms of flexible working time practices be documented?

3. Do decisions on shift work patterns, flexitime, staggered hours and compressed workweeks belong to the area of management prerogatives, or are they subject to negotiation, consultation and/or co-determination?

4. What are the positions of leading trade unions on the use of working time flexibility? Do they favour flexible scheduling? Do they oppose flexible staffing practices, and how effective has their opposition been?

5. Are central trade union policies consistent with local union activities? To what extent are local works councils or enterprise committees independent actors in this area?

6. What are the main government regulations referring to flexible working time arrangements? To what extent are derogations possible through collective agreements? Do the regulations facilitate or limit the use of flexibility practices? How firm is the interdiction of Sunday work? Is the maximum extent of overtime tightly regulated?

7. Can examples both of successful and failed trade union or works council negotiation for working time flexibility be documented? Demonstrate, for example, a company's implementation of a new shift work system, focusing on the accompanying negotiation, consultation and/or co-determination processes.

8. Has there been a *quid pro quo* in negotiations between increased scheduling flexibility and work time reductions?

9. How do the parties to collective bargaining handle the linkage between individual working time and company operating hours?

Bibliography

BLANPAIN, R. (1988), "General Report", in R. Blanpain and E. Köhler, eds., *Legal and Contractual Limitations to Working Time in the European Community Member States*, Deventer: Kluwer.

BOSCH, G. (1989), "Reducing Annual Working Time and Improving Schedule Flexibility – Causes, Effects, Controversies", in A. Gladstone, ed., *Current Issues in Labour Relations: An International Perspective*, Berlin-New York: de Gruyter.

BOSCH, G. *et al.* (1992), "Working Time in Fourteen Industrialised Countries: An Overview", Institut Arbeit und Technik, Working paper IAT-AM 05.

CATINAT, M., DONNI, E. and TADDEI, D. (1990), "Réorganisation-réduction du temps de travail", in: *Travail et Société*, Vol. 15, No. 2.

CETTE, G. (1990), "Durée d'utilisation des équipements: l'inversion d'une tendance longue", in *Economie et Statistique*, April.

EUROPEAN ECONOMY (1989), "Working Hours and Plant Operating Times", Supplement B, No. 11, November.

EUROPEAN ECONOMY (1991), "Developments on the labour market in the Community", No. 47, March.

ETUC (European Trade Union Confederation) (1990), *Guideline declaration on collective bargaining*, April.

ETUI (European Trade Union Institute) (1986), *Flexibility of Working Time in Western Europe*, Brussels.

ILO (International Labour Office) (1986), "Flexibility in Working Time", *Conditions of Work Digest*, Vol. 5, No. 2, Geneva.

ILO (International Labour Office) (1988), *Working Time Issues in Industrialised Countries*, Geneva.

OECD (1984), *Shorter Working Time. A Dilemma for Collective Bargaining*, Paris.

OECD (1986), *Flexibility in the Labour Market. The Current Debate,* Paris.

OECD (1989), *Labour Market Flexibility. Trends in Enterprises*, Paris.

OECD (1992), *New Directions in Work Organisation: The Industrial Relations Response*, Paris.

OECD (1994), *The OECD Jobs Study. Evidence and Explanations*, Paris.

TADDEI, D. (1986), *Des Machines et des Hommes. Pour l'emploi, par une meilleure utilisation des équipements*, Report for the Prime Minister, Paris: La Documentation Francaise.

TREU, T. (1989), ''Introduction to Chapter III on Working Time Arrangements'', in A. Gladstone, (ed.), *Current Issues in Labour Relations: An International Perspective*, Berlin-New York: de Gruyter.

WHITE, M. (1987), *Working Hours. Assessing the Potential for Reduction,* International Labour Office, Geneva.

Chapter 1

SYNTHESIS REPORT

by

Gerhard Bosch

A. ELEMENTS OF NEW WORKING TIME ARRANGEMENTS

A comparison of the eight national chapters on flexible working time arrangements in three different sectors of economic activity reveals many interesting common features. All chapters indicate long-term structural changes that are leading to the creation of new types of flexible working time arrangements. The differences in the time arrangements described in the reports lie first in the specific characteristics of the various national institutions. Second, they arise out of the particular features of the sectors investigated in the reports. Third, and finally, in a situation in which time arrangements are being restructured, the different strategies adopted by employers, firms and trade unions are also playing a role.

It is not possible, therefore, to speak of "flexible working time arrangements" as such, since they take completely different forms depending on national regulations, the sector involved and the flexibility strategies adopted. In other words, it is possible to discern not only "societal effects" [Maurice *et al.* (1982)] but also "sectoral" and "strategy effects". The latter are important for the future because today's strategies may determine tomorrow's structures. The old question of whether "strategy follows structure" or "structure follows strategy" [Chandler (1962); Ansoff (1976)] – the subject of much debate in management theory – will be settled here in diplomatic fashion: while in the short term, structures – *i.e.* societal and sectoral effects – determine time arrangements, in the long term, strategic behaviour becomes increasingly important.

The diverse forms of flexible working time arrangements revealed by international comparison can, therefore, be grasped only by combining various levels of analysis:

- it is necessary first to investigate the changing interests of firms and employees that are leading to the creation of new time arrangements;
- second, the influence of the various national regulatory systems (legislation, collective agreements, company agreements) and of "national time customs" must be analysed;

- third, we must seek greater understanding of the factors influencing the development of sector-specific flexibilisation structures;
- fourth, the actual shape of flexible working time arrangements at establishment level, as well as practical experiments with various time management strategies, have to be investigated.

Many analyses of flexible time arrangements base their arguments on only one of these four levels. This is not in itself a problem, provided one is aware of the limits of such analyses. However, it becomes a problem when a single level of analysis is assumed to take account of the whole picture and leads to hasty generalisations.

Working time and operating hours

In speaking of time arrangements, a distinction has to be made between working time and operating or opening hours. Flexibility may apply to both sets of arrangements, but this is not necessarily the case. Thus firms' operating hours, for example, may remain constant, but may be combined with a wide range of different working time arrangements (*e.g.* with part-time rather than full-time shifts). Working time and operating hours can be shortened or lengthened, standardised, varied (*e.g.* seasonally fluctuating working time) or differentiated (*e.g.* part-time versus full-time working, or different operating hours in various parts of a factory).

The distinction between working time and operating hours, in itself trivial, forces us to specify more precisely whether the dynamic of time arrangements is the product of changes in operating and opening hours or of changes in work schedules. The eight Country chapters in this volume show that the dynamic has its origins in both sets of arrangements and that the different interests of firms and employees play a role on both sides.

Flexible working time arrangements are actually nothing new. Overtime is a long-established way of extending operating time and working hours to meet firms' requirements. Shift, night and weekend working are equally familiar. Everybody who has looked in detail at the reality of firms' time arrangements in the past is well aware of the wide range of formal and informal arrangements that exist in order to create the flexibility needed to match working time and operating hours to the needs of firms and individuals. A typical example are holidays taken for local festivals. Also, working time and operating hours have always been negotiated at local level. This short look back shows that one has to be more precise about what is actually new in today's working time arrangements.

B.   FIRMS' INTERESTS WITH REGARD TO NEW TIME ARRANGEMENTS

Firms' interests with regard to new time arrangements – the eight chapters contain a great deal of evidence in this respect – run along the following lines:
- an extension of operating hours in order to make better use of existing capital stock;

- improved adjustment of working time and operating hours to fluctuations in orders;
- the replacement of expensive forms of organising working time with cheaper forms.

The extension of operating and opening hours

In recent years, plant utilisation time has been considerably extended in most industrialised countries [Anxo *et al.* (1995); Bosch (1991); Foss (1984); Cette (1990)]. The reasons for this increase in operating hours are primarily increasing capital intensity and the accelerating pace of technical change. As capital intensity increases, firms can considerably reduce capital unit costs by extending operating hours. Furthermore, the capital employed is amortised more rapidly, with a consequent reduction in the risks associated with large-scale investments. Longer operating hours also allow firms to avoid having to invest when demand rises. From a business management point of view, extended operating hours make sense even when demand is stagnating or falling, since firms can concentrate production on the most efficient machines. However, firms have to allow for higher maintenance and wage costs, because of night and weekend bonuses [van Deelen (1987)].

The more capital-intensive production becomes, the greater the reductions in unit costs when operating hours are extended. This gives firms the option of increasing their returns while at the same time offering employees additional compensation for night or weekend working [Taddei (1986)].

In the past, operating hours were usually varied by introducing second or third shifts for full-time employees. Firms are now seeking to extend the range of instruments available to them. They want to be able to measure out the extension of operating hours more precisely in order to deal with situations in which there is not sufficient demand to justify the introduction of new shifts.

This fine tuning comprises a range of new instruments, including working through breaks, staggered operating hours on expensive machines, a combination of full-time and part-time shifts, variation of annual shut-down times (holidays, extra days off between two public holidays or between a public holiday and a weekend) and multiple job holder systems. By combining these instruments in various ways, firms are able to define in detail the desired operating hours without having to choose between fixed alternatives as they had to in the past. However, all the instruments listed above are difficult to modify in the short term, since they all (with the exception of staggered working times) involve changes in the number of employees. As a result, overtime is still the main instrument used to cope with short-term variations in operating hours.

The new instruments make firms' personnel planning more complicated. The homogeneous time structures and stable work groups typical of traditional time arrangements are broken up. Firms in the German metal industry, for example, which are still sticking to the 8-hour day and the 40-hour week despite the reduction in working time from 40 to 36 hours, have to give each worker about 35 shifts off per year. If 30 days vacation are added on, it is not difficult to understand why such a method of time management gives rise to communication and quality control problems. It is therefore no coincidence that new time arrangements are today being increasingly combined with group work systems intended to ensure better communication, social interaction and improved quality of work. Multiple job holder systems, in which the number of employees is greater than the number of jobs, are one way of achieving these goals. The various work groups can either agree among themselves on how working times are to be allocated, or the allocation proceeds in accordance with fixed rules (*e.g.* rolling days). Depending on the numerical ratio and combination of full-time and part-time employees, a wide variety of permutations becomes possible [Hoff and Weidinger (1988)]. Chart 1.1 presents a model widely used in both manufacturing and service industries.

The economic advantages of extended operating hours cannot be easily transferred to the service sector. There are certainly individual examples that point in the same direction, for example the increased utilisation of expensive operating theatres in hospitals (*cf.* the chapter on health care in Sweden). However, operating hours in public services are mostly determined not on economic but on social grounds. In private services, such as retail trade, any extension of opening hours initially entails increased costs, mainly for staff, without any significant cost reductions by way of compensation. These increased costs can be justified only if sales rise proportionally, or by even greater amounts.

Chart 1.1. **Model of a multiple job holder scheme**

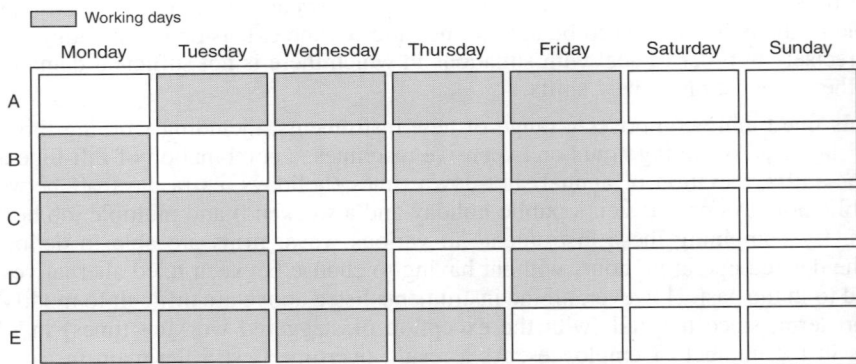

5 workers (A, B, C, D and E) hold 4 jobs. With daily working time set at nine hours, each worker works four nine-hour days per week, *i.e.* 36 hours per week. At the same time, operating hours are increased from 40 to 45 hours per week., *i.e.* by 12.5 per cent. Each worker has an extra day off per week and also has an "extra long" weekend every 5 weeks, from Thursday evening to Tuesday morning.
Source: Van Deelen (1987), p. 83.

Most studies of the retail trade assume that any extension of opening hours leads to a redistribution of the existing volume of sales among the various categories of firms. Thus increased opening hours significantly intensify competition between retail outlets [Cette *et al.* (1992)]. Unlike firms in the manufacturing sector, traders in the retail sector cannot use additional returns created by falling unit costs to offer compensation for night and weekend working. From a purely economic perspective, the following conclusion can be drawn: if both operating hours in manufacturing industry and opening times in private services are to be extended, market conditions will lead to considerable divergence in the social quality of new time arrangements, particularly as far as compensation for unsocial working hours is concerned.

Fluctuating operating hours

In a historical analysis of the increasing use of continuous operating hours in the course of industrialisation, Deutschmann (1985) refers, among other things, to the development of storekeeping techniques (in addition to the mechanisation of energy sources, the organisation of the labour process and the development and expansion of markets). Storekeeping used to enable firms to protect their production process from short-term market fluctuations. This is becoming increasingly less possible today, when just-in-time supply systems increasingly require just-in-time production.

The ability to react quickly, which has become a decisive parameter in competitiveness, requires firms to analyse their daily, weekly, monthly and seasonal fluctuations in demand much more precisely than in the past and to adjust their time planning accordingly. It has long been standard practice in the service sector to match working time to variations in customer volume (*cf.* the three chapters on retail trade in Canada, France and Italy). It is only recently that such fluctuating working times are also being implemented in the manufacturing industry (see the chapter on the United Kingdom). The principal new element in today's time arrangements is the instruments used to implement them. Thus, expensive alternations between short-time working and overtime (as in Europe) or between temporary lay-offs and overtime (as in the United States and Canada) can be avoided by incorporating foreseeable fluctuations into annual shift plans, which eliminates the cost of overtime pay and additional expenditure for short-time working or lay-offs.

Even fluctuating working time and operating hours can be more easily managed by means of multiple job holder systems or group working. Work groups, for example, may be required to guarantee the presence of a minimum number of workers and to decide for themselves on the allocation of free time, including the use of flexitime systems. Incentive systems can encourage work groups to adapt their working hours to suit the firm's needs, for example by requiring 45 minutes' work at busy times in exchange for each hour of free time taken during slack periods (see the chapter on Swedish health care).

The substitution of cheaper forms of working time organisation for expensive ones

In many cases, new time arrangements have nothing to do with the introduction of interesting and innovative working-time models, but are merely attempts to reduce wage costs by replacing expensive forms of working-time organisation with cheaper ones. This is indeed the purpose behind most annual hours schemes. The Country chapters offer many examples of this, often involving the replacement of full-time workers by part-time and casual workers. As a result, work can be intensified and absenteeism reduced; the labour force, divided into smaller units, can be adjusted to fluctuations in demand; overtime pay can be avoided; weekend working and work on demand are easier to organise; and in some countries wages for part-time workers can be lower than those for full-time employees.

Often only marginal workers are subject to this type of flexibility, since firms fear it may lead to a general collapse of motivation among other employees, with negative consequences for product or service quality. On the other hand, it is hardly surprising that this variant of working-time flexibility is being introduced particularly in the labour-intensive service sector, where it is being further reinforced by other forms of flexibility, such as temporary employment or fixed-term contracts, also intended to reduce labour costs. Since wages account for such a high proportion of total costs in the service sector, considerable savings can be achieved through such strategies.

In the case of permanent workers, the flexible scheduling of working hours can be made cheaper by weakening protective regulations. One example frequently discussed in France and Germany is the reinstatement of Saturday as a normal working day in manufacturing, for which no bonuses would need to be paid (bonuses for Saturday work are not usually paid in the service sector). However, these proposals have rarely been implemented because they are a potential source of conflict.

C. EMPLOYEES' INTERESTS WITH REGARD TO NEW TIME ARRANGEMENTS

Employees also have a considerable interest in more flexible working hours, which, however, do not necessarily coincide with those of firms. The increased interest in flexibility on the part of employees is the result of:

- increasing labour market participation by women;
- an increase in the number of people combining education or training with work; and
- increasingly diverse lifestyles.

At the same time, workers are less willing to accept unsocial working hours. In general, therefore, employees' wishes in respect of working time are becoming important constraints on employers' strategies.

The desire for greater control over working time

Women's employment has increased very rapidly in all OECD countries in recent decades. Since women are, as a rule, still responsible for a greater share of child care and housework, their labour market availability is restricted. As a result, the supply of labour for part-time jobs, particularly in the service sector, has significantly expanded.

Women's working time preferences are strongly influenced by the availability or non-availability of child care facilities. In Scandinavia, there is usually a comprehensive network of day nurseries underpinning a high female participation rate as well as increasingly long hours of part-time employment [OECD (1990), Chapter 5]. Schools in France and Belgium provide education from the age of three years and are open all day, but since most are closed on Wednesdays, many women work four days a week; by contrast, children's clothes departments in the retail sector are extremely busy on Wednesdays. Schools in Germany and the Netherlands are, as a rule, open only until lunch time, so that most women are able to work only in the mornings. In Sweden, both men and women can take extended parental leave, with a right to return to their old job. This obvious correlation between women's working hours and a country's child care and school system shows the extent to which working time is influenced by widely differing national social institutions outside the world of work [Ebbing (1992)].

To a certain extent, the OECD countries have long had differing objectives with respect to women's work and have been pursuing different strategies for integrating women into the labour force. The Scandinavian countries have been the most enthusiastic advocates of women's integration into the labour market and have made available a wide range of options for both men and women such as parental leave, temporary reduction in working hours, etc. [see Näsman (1992)]. In other countries, such as the United Kingdom, the United States, the Netherlands, Germany and the southern European countries, reconciling work and family life has until now been largely a private matter.

However, as female participation rates have risen in OECD countries, it has become increasingly evident that a large part of women's interests in flexible working time arrangements remain unfulfilled. The introduction of parental leave and increased state nursery provision, for example, are now key issues on the domestic agenda both in Germany and in the United States. In the long term, therefore, firms will have to reckon with women's desire to stabilize their employment patterns. There is virtually no area that better demonstrates the importance of welfare state arrangements for work time schedules than the connection between women's working hours and child care and education institutions. The experience of the Scandinavian countries and those of France and Belgium are proof that structure can follow strategy.

In all industrialised economies, the number of those enrolled in higher education has increased rapidly. In Western Germany, for example, there were only 232 000 university students in 1961. By 1990, that figure had risen to 1.6 million. While in the past, university education or other types of schooling beyond the minimum leaving age were largely restricted to the children of the better off, who were financially supported by their parents, many students today have to work. As a result, there is a huge additional pool of labour that is interested mainly in part-time work and can often work only outside school and university hours (evenings, weekends and holidays). Since students are often insured through their parents' health insurance schemes or those run by universities, they are willing to forego insurance contributions, which reduces employers' labour costs. Certain labour markets – e.g. in the retail trade, restaurants and catering – are partially structured on this basis, a phenomenon that has not really been acknowledged in discussions on flexible working time arrangements.

Family situations have grown increasingly diverse. In all industrialised countries (except Japan) the plurality of life styles has increased considerably. Many couples have no children or fewer children than was once the norm. Many workers no longer live in large families, but either alone or with one other person. In Western Germany, for example, the proportion of one and two-person households increased between 1950 and 1990 from 45 to 65 per cent. This goes hand in hand with a decline in traditional ties and the individualisation of social attitudes. The less restricted nature of individual life styles means that individual wishes with regard to time arrangements can be more clearly articulated. Increased incomes enable some of these workers to express and implement those wishes, even if they have to forego income in doing so (as with sabbaticals, for example).

The increasing rejection of night and weekend work

With the expansion of the service sector and the extension of operating hours in manufacturing industry, demand for workers available at night and on weekends is growing. At the same time, however, willingness to work at such times has decreased. A representative survey of European firms carried out by the European Foundation for the Improvement of Living and Working Conditions in Dublin shows that 38 per cent of the firms surveyed in five European countries (Belgium, Germany, Italy, Spain and the United Kingdom) had experienced difficulties in the past in finding workers for Saturday work. Despite high levels of unemployment in some areas, 68 per cent expected to experience such difficulties in the future [Infratest (1989)].

A representative survey of employees in the European Community found that only 21 per cent of those questioned were prepared to work on Sundays and 22 per cent to work nights, even for higher pay. A larger group – 44 per cent of those surveyed – was said to be willing to work on Saturdays, but the survey did not distinguish between the Saturday morning shift, which is more widely accepted, and the Saturday afternoon or late shifts, which are not acceptable to the majority of people (cf. Table 1.1).

The free weekend became widespread throughout Western Europe in the 1960s and 1970s, and even earlier in North America, and is considered, together with the avoidance of shift-work, as an indicator of affluence that employees are reluctant to give up without a struggle [Henckel et al. (1994)]. The manager of a German textile factory described the situation in the following terms: ''Our arguments about the need for night and weekend work go virtually unheeded by workers who, on their way to work on Friday at midday, meet office workers, tennis rackets in hand, who have made use of flexitime arrangements to leave work as early as 1.00 or 2.00 p.m.''.

However, the surveys also reveal considerable differences between countries. In the United Kingdom and France, there is greater willingness to work Sundays and nights for extra pay than in Germany or Italy. There may be very different reasons for this: lower

Table 1.1. **Employees' working time preferences**

(European Community Survey)

Question: Would you be willing to work different hours if you were offered higher wages or additional leisure time?

| | New schedules implying | | | | | | | | | | | | | | |
| | Early or midday shifts | | | Night shifts | | | Saturday work | | | Sunday work | | | Variable working time | | |
	Yes	No	No response	Yes	No	No response	Yes	No	No response	Yes	No	No response	Yes	No	No response
Belgium	51	34	15	19	67	14	42	44	14	24	62	14	52	34	14
Denmark	63	29	8	24	70	7	41	52	7	31	63	7	34	58	8
Germany	45	51	4	10	85	5	33	62	5	10	85	5	34	61	5
Greece	61	39	0	4	96	0	8	91	1	2	98	0	24	76	0
Spain	72	20	8	28	64	8	40	52	8	19	73	8	47	42	11
France	68	25	7	30	62	8	56	40	4	30	66	4	74	21	5
Ireland	67	25	8	32	62	5	58	35	7	30	63	7	61	31	8
Italy	57	43	0	10	90	0	51	49	0	12	88	0	66	34	0
Netherlands	60	35	5	10	90	0	9	91	0	1	99	0	17	88	0
Portugal	56	31	13	3	84	13	2	85	13	0	87	13	26	61	13
United Kingdom	69	31	0	39	61	0	56	44	0	39	61	0	55	45	0
Total	61	35	4	22	74	4	44	52	4	21	75	4	52	44	4

Source: European Economy, No. 47, March 1991, p. 148.

25

real wages and higher unemployment in France compared to Germany; more stable family and kinship structures in Italy; or different national traditions. We should, however, hesitate before making hasty generalisations about a larger or lower degree of employee flexibility in various countries: for example, few firms in the United Kingdom succeed in manning the Friday night shift, an evening many people value highly as leisure time.

In Germany, there are no problems in keeping a factory open in the summer, while in the United Kingdom, France and Italy the annual shutdown is seen by workers as something they are entitled to. German factories close down for annual holidays for an average of only 0.4 weeks per year, compared with 1.4 weeks in France, 1.8 weeks in the United Kingdom and 2.4 weeks in Italy [*European Economy* (1991)]. All societies need their collective leisure time, which can of course be taken at very different times. It may even be the case that differences within countries are greater than those between countries. In large urban areas with a "service sector culture" it is becoming more and more difficult to obtain workers for shift work on production lines. This is true of both the BMW assembly plant in Munich and the Peugeot plant at Poissy, in the Greater Paris region.

These various trends in worker preferences cannot be easily summarised, since there are several different trends running counter to each other. First, there is a growing pool of labour (women, students) prepared to accept more flexible working hours. Second, permanent workers are on the whole becoming less willing to work unsocial hours. Third, working time preferences are becoming increasingly individualised, so that a minority of workers, sufficient to meet firms' needs, is prepared to work unsocial hours. Finally, high unemployment is reducing individuals' chances of having their own working time preferences fulfilled.

D.   THE NEGOTIATION OF WORKING TIME ARRANGEMENTS

Both employees and firms have a growing interest in new time arrangements. Undoubtedly there are happy circumstances in which the interests of employees and firms coincide. For example, if demand fluctuates and the slack periods happen to coincide with the periods when employees want to have time off (*e.g.* in the summer or after Christmas), agreement can quickly be reached. Frequently, however, the interests of the two sides diverge. This applies above all to weekend and night work, but also to all strategies for replacing expensive forms of time flexibility by cheaper ones. Thus the scheduling of working hours offers considerable potential for conflict that can be mitigated only through the negotiation of reasonable compromises.

The working time arrangements described in the eight Country chapters show two things. First, there are considerable differences in the extent to which employee interests are taken into account in individual countries and sectors. Second, time arrangements are a "moving target", with negotiating processes constantly being transformed in reaction to changes in political circumstances, workers' time preferences, and competitive situations.

26

Differing negotiating processes

There are many examples, particularly in capital-intensive parts of the manufacturing industry, that indicate that the corridor of common interests is being extended through compromises acceptable to both sides. There are good structural reasons for this: the predominantly male work force in such sectors is highly unionised, wage costs are relatively less significant than capital costs and the extension of operating hours gives firms a range of options for financing attractive compromises (*cf.* the examples of Rover and BMW in the chapters on the United Kingdom and Germany). The compromises may take the following shape: working hours are reduced in exchange for night and weekend working; reduced working hours require an increase in the number of shift teams; this in turn makes it possible to reduce the number of nights and weekends that each individual has to work and to offer workers long weekends at regular intervals; furthermore, some new schedules also imply higher wages. Sometimes these compromises are so attractive that firms have more applicants for new shift systems than they require. This was the case, for example, with the introduction of a night shift at Opel's assembly plant in Bochum (Germany) in 1990. Opel paid night-shift workers a monthly premium of about DM 800 and gave them an additional five days' holiday per year [Lehndorff and Bosch (1993)].

Firms and, in many cases, works councils or trade union organisations frequently smooth the path for these compromises by adopting selective strategies. They do not try to persuade the entire work force to work nights and weekends, preferring rather to recruit volunteers from within the firms or from outside. In this way they can avoid conflict with the permanent work force and make use of the sufficiently large minority of employees willing to work weekends or nights. In France and Belgium, this principle of selective recruitment for unsocial working hours has even been enshrined in legislation. In these two countries, Sunday working for economic reasons is permitted only if the workers involved have been specially recruited for weekend work (*équipes de suppléance*) [Bloch-London and Butel (1992)].

By contrast, in many parts of the labour-intensive service sector (except banking, insurance and financial services), new working-time arrangements are introduced above all in order to reduce wage costs. The work force in many firms in this sector is predominantly female, poorly unionised and at a relative disadvantage in the labour market because of inadequate skills and discontinuous work histories. It is in service industries that flexible time arrangements are frequently associated with a worsening of existing standards. The chapter on Canada, for example, indicates that part-time workers are less well paid than full-time employees and are also more likely to work unsocial hours.

This contrasting situation between different sectors of the economy is leading to increasing divergence in working conditions. The repercussions on the labour market are revealed by the chapters on the retail trade and the health care sector in this volume: the reputation of these sectors in the labour market is declining, and even with high levels of unemployment they are experiencing recruitment difficulties.

Industrial relations and working time arrangements

Industrial relations in individual countries and sectors have a considerable influence on the organisation of working time arrangements. The chapters reveal two differences between countries and sectors of particular importance. The first is the existence or absence of a mechanism ensuring a general application of certain minimum standards for working time. Such a mechanism may either consist of legal regulations or be laid down in collective agreements with broad applicability. The second is the existence or absence of an institutionalised system for the representation of interests within firms that gives the various parties power to negotiate on issues relating to working time (*e.g.* works councils).

In North America and Japan as well as in the United Kingdom, there are few legal or sector-wide regulations on working time. In these countries, new time arrangements are negotiated mainly at establishment level. As a consequence, there are great differences in time arrangements between companies and plants. The often exemplary compromises between the interests of firms and those of employees agreed in individual plants cannot be easily transferred to other establishments or firms.

In industrial relations systems that have long been decentralised, such as in the United States, Canada and Japan, there seems to be little serious debate on flexible working hours at national level. Competition between unionised and non-unionised firms gives these systems an in-built deregulatory mechanism in times of high unemployment. Working time and operating hours have not been taken out of competition by comprehensive minimum standards. In the United States, in particular, unionised firms have used concession bargaining to emulate the extension and flexibilisation of working time introduced by non-unionised firms.

In most Western European countries minimum standards on working time are laid down in legislation or collective agreements. However, these standards have changed considerably in recent years. Often, working-time regulation has been made less rigid; in general, space for negotiation has been opened up. In Belgium, France and Sweden, legal regulations can be modified by collective agreements. Notably, it is at plant level that this space has been opened up. As a rule, sectoral agreements only lay down guidelines on working time, with details of time arrangements being negotiated at plant level (*cf.* the detailed discussion in the chapters on Italy and Germany).

However, if there is increasing room for manœuvre at plant level, employee interests can be defended only if there is an effective system of employee representation. This is certainly the case with German and Dutch works councils and Swedish trade union organisations at plant level, but does not apply, for example, to France [Bosch and Lallement (1991)]. The weakness of employee representation at plant level in many countries is a decided Achilles heel in the flexibilisation of working time. It implies that decentralised forms of work scheduling tend to be associated with an increase in employer dominance in the determination of working time.

As plant-level negotiation gains in strength, new areas of conflict within associations emerge. Trade union organisations active beyond plant level are particularly aware of the risks of an increasing break-up of common standards. The more the regulation of working time is decentralised, the more employees are exposed to direct pressure from firms to fit in with their time requirements.

However, trade unions' justified fears in this respect have on many occasions led them to miss out on the opportunity to participate in the determination of flexible working hours. For example, the chapter on the Netherlands shows that unions have not been very active in organising the large mass of part-time employees. Works councils and plant-level trade union organisations often take a more open-minded attitude towards new time arrangements than trade unions at national level. The employers' camp, also, is not free from this type of conflict, even if disputes here tend to be less public. In Germany, for example, plant-level compromises on new working time arrangements have been criticised by employer associations as going too far.

In most Western European countries there has not in recent years been an unambiguous trend towards the decentralisation of negotiations on working time. Rather, there has been a complex reorganisation of the division of labour between state legislation and negotiations at plant, enterprise and industry levels. Plant-level negotiations have certainly increased in importance. However, both governments and the collective bargaining process have also taken on new responsibilities in the determination of working time, for example in the introduction of parental leave or of minimum standards for part-time employees.

There is some evidence to support the argument that collective bargaining will further increase in importance. First, employees in sectors with very flexible forms of working time, such as hospitals, may in the future become more highly unionised and thus better able to articulate their views (see the chapter on the Netherlands). Second, a lengthy phase of plant-level experimentation with new forms of working time has perhaps led to a clearer recognition of how flexibility can sensibly be regulated. At present, the observation by Blanpain and Köhler (1988) certainly still applies: the current situation produces "a certain helplessness of the legislator towards the new developments (...) an attitude of trial and error, [providing some] legislation but leaving it to the collective partners to do what they like with it in order to find out which could be the best way for further legislation at a later stage".

E. THE METAL INDUSTRY: THE EXAMPLE OF CAR MANUFACTURING

One sector in which time arrangements have been changing particularly rapidly is the automobile industry. These changes have been almost exclusively concerned with the extension of operating hours. There are two reasons for this:

- as a result of the car boom at the end of the 1980s, demand increased for a short period to such an extent that the available capacity proved insufficient;
- automation has led to a very rapid increase in capital intensity, particularly in press and body shops.

Furthermore, recent working time reductions in some countries (particularly Germany and Belgium) have given firms an opportunity to reflect on the way they organise time. However, the influence of working time reductions is felt more in the long than in the short term. In 1950, most automobile workers were still working more than 2 000 hours per year. With a two-shift system, this gave operating hours of more than 4 000 per year. With working time now below 1 600 hours in Germany and Belgium, operating hours tend to fall to less than 3 200 per year.

Until a few years ago, nearly all cars were produced in two-shift systems. Japan, North America and the United Kingdom used the day and night shift system, while the early and late shift system prevailed in continental Europe. The traditional two-shift system offers firms advantages worth considering: it leaves adequate time for essential maintenance during the night or between shifts and also offers scope for overtime, which is often needed in order to respond to changing economic circumstances. However, since the end of the 1980s some plants have changed over to shift systems that make it possible to extend operating hours, *i.e.* either to the three-shift system or to so-called long shifts (8.5 to 10 hours per day). In 1992, about 17 per cent of cars produced in member countries of the European Community were made in factories with new shift systems [Lehndorff and Bosch (1993)].

As a consequence, operating hours in Europe today diverge widely. Table 1.2 outlines the situation in 1990. "Top of the league" in the European car industry, with 5 336 hours, is General Motor's Saragossa plant in Spain. "Bottom of the table", with only 3 345 hours in 1990, is Ford Saarlouis in Germany. And yet the Ford Saarlouis plant, with its highly efficient work organisation, is considered one of the most productive assembly plants in Europe. Relatively short operating hours may also indicate that management has succeeded in increasing output without resorting to expensive overtime and shift systems.

New shift systems have been introduced particularly in plants built on greenfield sites. The entire logistics of such plants are designed from the outset around new shift systems. Moreover, such systems are easy to implement with a new work force. All the new car factories currently being built in Europe are planning to introduce a three-shift system or long shifts. It has proved more difficult to change shift systems in "brownfield" plants. In part, such plants have neither the capacity nor the logistical organisation for extended operating hours (for example, there may not be adequate parking space for the output of a third shift). In addition, some work forces have resisted the introduction of longer shifts or of a night shift. In such plants, some firms have been able to use international competition between plants to push through new working time arrangements. Major investment projects have been made dependent on concessions on operating hours. In some instances, reductions in working time and wage increases have been offered in compensation.

There are currently several competing management strategies and concepts of time organisation in the motor industry. Some companies have approved long shifts in which daily working time is increased to more than eight hours. Multiple job holder systems are being introduced. At Peugeot in Poissy and BMW in Munich, for example, five employees share four jobs, with one person always off work in the rolling system. The advantage for employees lies in the change-over to the four-day week, while the disadvantage is the long and tiring daily working hours. For firms, the advantage is that they can still use the night for repairs and maintenance. The disadvantages are increased

Table 1.2. **Working time and operating hours in the European automobile industry, 1990**

Manufacturer	Plant	Shift system	Negotiated working hours	Operating hours excl. overtime[a]	Operating hours incl. overtime[b]
BMW	Regensburg[c]	2 × 9[d]	1 548	4 554	
	Munich[c]	2 × 8.6	1 628	3 948	
VW	Wolfsburg	2	1 608	3 712	3 960[e]
MERCEDES	Sindelfingen	2	1 628	3 984	
FORD	Saarlouis	2	1 628	3 345	3 375
	Köln	2	1 635	3 420	3 420
OPEL	Bochum	2	1 635	5 250	5 280
	Rüsselsheim	2	1 635	3 349	3 458
GM	Antwerp	2 × 9.7[d]	1 565	5 120	5 120
VW	Brussels	3	1 616	5 221	5 221
FORD	Genk	2	1 693	3 557	3 587
FIAT	Mirafiori	2	1 688	3 480	3 510
	Cassino	3	1 688	5 220	5 260
	all others	2	1 688	3 480	3 510
RENAULT	Flins	2	1 725	3 496	3 640
PSA	Poissy[c]	2 × 9.75	1 733	4 408	
	Sochaux	2	1 740	3 527	3 619
	Mulhouse	2	1 740	3 527	3 757[f]
ROVER	Longbridge[c]	3	1 641	4 925	
VAUXHALL	Luton	2	1 688	3 450	3 572
	Ellesmere Port	2 (day/night)	1 755	3 588	3 713
NISSAN	Sunderland	2 (day/night)	1 788	3 666	3 391
FORD	Dagenham	2 (day/night)	1 778	3 650	3 666
FORD	Valencia	2	1 720	3 441	3 503
GM	Saragossa	3	1 725	5 336	5 434
SEAT	Zona Franca	2	1 768	3 632	3 672

a) Including short breaks, but excluding meal breaks.
b) Based on "collective" forms of overtime only (*e.g.* special shifts).
c) Recalculated as if the present shift system had applied over the whole year in 1990.
d) Plus early shift on Saturday.
e) Including reduced night shift, weighted with capacity effect.
f) 1989.
Source: Interviews and own calculations; see also Lehndorff and Bosch (1993).

illness and labour turnover because of the long shifts. Employees who work long shifts tend to be unprepared to do overtime as well, although there is some indication that this may not necessarily be the case in the United States (*cf.* the Saturn project).

Since the eight-hour day seems strongly established as a norm in the consciousness of employees, they have to be offered a great deal before they will agree to exceed the eight-hour limit by any significant amount. Despite a threat to close the plant, General Motors in Antwerp were able to introduce 10-hour shifts only in exchange for a reduction in weekly working time to 34 hours. In exchange for 9-hour shifts, BMW in Regensburg offered a 1.5 hour reduction in weekly working hours. As a result, long shifts are considered more expensive than night shifts. Companies have drawn lessons from this: the "second generation" of long shifts only slightly exceeds the eight-hour limit (8 hours, 35 minutes at the BMW Regensburg plant) and have proved less costly to introduce.

The introduction of a three-shift system does have the merit of avoiding exhaustingly long shift times. Moreover, shorter shifts mean that workers are more willing to work overtime on Saturdays. The establishment of a permanent night shift avoids conflict with the regular work force. The disadvantages for employers lie in the fact that there is no spare time for maintenance work and the cleaning of paint shops. As a result, maintenance and repair work has to be done during the night shift. This means that the introduction of a night shift in the motor industry tends to increase output by only about 25 per cent rather than by 50 per cent.

It is above all in Japanese transplants in Europe (*e.g.* Nissan Sunderland) and the United States, that the traditional two-shift system is maintained, on the grounds that it is both simple and flexible. These plants tend to schedule an above-average amount of overtime work. They reject any attempt to combine production and maintenance work or to mix work groups by introducing multiple job holder systems. Japanese management seems afraid that such systems lead to a loss of control over workers and a blurring of responsibilities for quality. English managers working at Rover with Honda managers sum up this attitude by pointing out that "the Japanese do not like complications" [Lehndorff (1992)].

The situation in Japan contrasts sharply with the widely divergent working times and operating hours observed in Europe (see Table 1.3). All assembly plants and body shops in Japan still operate the traditional day and night shift system. Each manufacturer uses the same shift systems in its various plants. Permanent work groups and shift teams are formed in order to encourage group cohesion and to ensure responsibility for quality. If they fall sick, workers tend to take holiday leave, and companies also exert strong pressure on employees not to take their full holiday entitlement. As a result, 95 per cent of employees are present at any one time (compared with 75-80 per cent in Europe), which ensures group stability.

Plants are closed down for significantly shorter periods in the course of a year than is the case in Europe, since holidays are taken on an individual basis and are not combined with plant shutdowns. Public holidays are taken in blocks (*e.g.* the so-called "golden week") in order to create time for the shutdowns required when models are changed or major repair work has to be done. Overtime is an integral part of the Japanese productive system, and the amount worked is far higher than in Europe or the United States. As a result, operating hours are considerably higher than 4 000 hours. Such long operating hours can be achieved in Europe only by introducing new shift systems. Furthermore, the Japanese can reduce their operating hours by about 20 per cent without having to dismiss workers.

Table 1.3. **Working time and operating hours in the Japanese automobile industry, 1990**

Manufacturer	Shift system	Negotiated working hours [a]	Actual working hours [b]	Operating hours
Toyota	2 (day/night)	1 808	2 323	4 850
Nissan	2 (day/night)	1 808	2 357	4 858
Honda	2 (early/late)	1 800	1 938	4 144
Mazda	2 (day/night)	1 800	2 392	4 912
Mitsubishi	2 (day/night)	1 800	2 364	4 946
Isuzu	2 (day/night)	1 808	2 386	4 902
Fuji	2 (day/night)	1 816	2 274	4 700
Daihatsu	2 (day/night)	1 808	2 299	4 756
Hino	2 (day/night)	1 808	2 475	5 110
Suzuki	2 (day/night)	1 824	2 319	4 782
Yamaha	2 (day/night)	1 816	2 187	4 510

a) Includes the full holiday entitlement (in contrast to the standard Japanese method which does not include the holiday entitlement in the calculation of negotiated working time).
b) Production workers.
Source: Data supplied by Japan Automobile Workers Union and Toyota Motors Union; see also Lehndorff and Bosch (1993).

Of course there are also differing concepts of management in Japan. The exception in the motor industry is Honda. Honda operates the continental European early and late shift system which has no scope for overtime between shifts but avoids the need to pay expensive night shift bonuses. Honda sets greater store by the intensification of work and has the shortest allowed times in the Japanese motor industry [Lehndorff and Bosch (1993)].

F.   RETAIL TRADE

Shop opening hours are more tightly regulated in most countries than operating hours in manufacturing industry. The legislation in question goes back in some instances to the last century, when it was passed for three main reasons. First, Sunday was to be protected for religious reasons. Second, working time and shop opening hours were closely coupled, so that a reduction in the extremely long working times in manufacturing industry could be achieved only by restricting shop opening hours. Until recently, the opening hours of Italian retail shops even corresponded closely to the working time of full-time employees (see the chapter on Italy). Third, this compulsory harmonisation meant that shop opening hours were taken out of competition, thus protecting businesses from ruinous competition. Since the 1950s, as a result particularly of the spread of large retail chains, a fourth reason has been added. By restricting shop opening hours, small shops are to be protected from competition from the large chains. This aspect is particularly important in Italy and France.

Whereas operating hours in manufacturing industry are determined through the market and, increasingly, through international competition and cost considerations, opening hours in retail trade have until now been set by national regulation. This has led to the development of very different shopping habits in the various countries. Foreign nationals, for example, have some difficulty getting used to shop closing times in Germany and Switzerland. As a rule, shop opening hours are not subject to the same pressure of international competition. There is still a great deal of scope for countries to determine their own shop opening hours, and it is therefore to be expected that national traditions in this area will be maintained for longer and be more prominent in this area than in manufacturing. For example, according to an investigation carried out by the European Community, there are considerable differences in the length of shop opening hours in the various European Community member states (Table 1.4). Exceptions are to be found in certain border regions, such as between Canada and the United States, where cross-border competition has led to increased harmonization in the legal regulation of shop opening hours (*cf.* the chapter on Canada).

In most countries, legal restrictions on shop opening hours have been relaxed in recent years. This has led to an extension of opening hours, which are now far longer than individual working hours. There are also sharp fluctuations in demand during the day, week, month and year. Firms' manpower planners have to try to match staffing levels to these various fluctuations. In doing this, they are constrained by the need to maintain a minimum number of staff on duty at all times during opening hours. The retail trade is one of the most labour cost-intensive sectors. And since increasingly tough competition has at the same time exerted downward pressure on prices, the sector is dominated by strategies for reducing staffing costs. In most countries, the retail trade is one of the sectors with the lowest pay levels, and working time flexibility is achieved primarily by employing part-time workers, who are deployed to fit in as closely as possible with fluctuations in demand. In general, the compensation for unsocial working hours is not particularly generous.

The retail trade employs a disproportionately high number of women, particularly in sales jobs, since it is difficult to recruit men for the precarious, low-paid jobs so often encountered in the sector. In Germany, for example, women's share of total employment in the sector has risen continuously, from a mere 17 per cent in 1882 to over 52 per cent in 1970 [Willms (1983), p. 123]. More than virtually any other sector, the retail trade has to adjust to the availability of its female work force, which is determined to a large extent by the child-care facilities available.

Compared with manufacturing and other service industries (*e.g.* banking and insurance), the retail trade is a particularly heterogeneous sector. There is a multiplicity of different types of enterprise, ranging from small independent traders to large groups. Since it is difficult to reduce the interests of such a wide variety of enterprises to a common denominator, employer organisations in virtually all countries are very unstable. Many employees work in small businesses. Such workers, and those in precarious jobs, are a tough proposition for trade union organisers.

In many countries (such as Canada) this combination of unstable employer organisations and weak trade unions gives individual enterprises far-reaching opportunities to shape working time in accordance with their own interests. In some countries, however, it

Table 1.4. Opening hours and working time in retail trade

(European Community Survey)

Questions: 1. What are the average opening hours per week in your retail business?
2. What are the average contracted weekly working hours for a full-time employee in your retail business?

	Average weekly opening hours of premises									Contracted weekly working hours of a full-time employee						
	< 45	46-50	51- 55	56-60	61-65	66-75	76+	No answer	Average	> 35	35-38	38-40	40-42	42+	No answer	Average
Belgium	12	7	79	0	0	0	0	2	51	0	87	10	1	0	2	38
Germany	37	27	16	4	10	0	0	6	48	0	12	83	0	1	4	39
Spain	57	23	6	6	4	2	1	1	45							43
France	12	17	17	17	17	16	2	3	56	6	11	78	4	1	0	38
Italy	33	7	57	3	0	0	0	0	49							38
Netherlands	19	19	44	7	1	2	7	1	52	2	12	52	17	10	7	40
Portugal	2	32	32	31	1	0	2	0	51	0	0	0	0	44	0	44
United Kingdom	13	15	22	17	8	11	14	1	58	1	24	44	7	5	19	39
Total	24	31	26	11	8	7	5	2	53	2	19	60	5	4	9	39

Source: European Economy, No. 47, March 1991, p. 134.

35

has been possible through legislation (France) or collective agreements (Italy) to lay down at least a few minimum standards for flexible working time arrangements. In France, for example, the collectively agreed minimum weekly working time is 16 hours. In Germany, a 50 per cent supplement is paid on top of the hourly rate for work after 6.30 p.m.

As in other sectors, considerable differences can be observed in management strategies. Some businesses compete only on price and seize every opportunity to reduce costs, with negative consequences for working conditions. Other firms are laying increasing emphasis on quality of service and are seeking to increase their employees' attachment with permanent employment contracts. However, changes of strategy in both directions can be observed, as the chapter on France demonstrates, using the example of the Euromarché supermarket chain.

Different management strategies, variations in the availability and opening hours of childcare facilities, and the different minimum standards on working time laid down in collective agreements or in law, mean that there are wide disparities in time arrangements from firm to firm and from country to country. France is an example of a country where working time flexibility in retail trade is at least partially regulated, with a high proportion of full-time employees, part-time workers generally working more than 20 hours per week and interesting experiments being conducted with semi-autonomous work groups. Canada and the United Kingdom, on the other hand, are countries where flexibility is largely unregulated, with a high proportion of part-time workers working very short hours.

G. HEALTH CARE

Because they have to provide care around the clock, hospitals never close their doors, and their employees have always worked at nights and weekends. Thus in contrast to the retail trade or the car industry, the question here is not so much that of changing existing time arrangements in order to extend operating or opening hours, but rather of attempting first, to use more flexible working hours in order to deploy staff more economically and second, to make the exceptionally high proportion of unsocial working hours more acceptable to employees. The extension of utilisation times is relevant only in the case of operating theatres. Chapters 8 and 9 on health care in the Netherlands and Sweden both mention efforts to make more intensive use of these increasingly expensive facilities.

The health care sector is extremely labour intensive. Because of the intense financial pressure, attempts to reduce costs usually begin with personnel costs. One important starting point is the flexibilisation of working time. The demand for patient care fluctuates enormously over the course of a day. If working times remain rigid, therefore, organisations also have to finance those periods when staff are under less pressure. In consequence, they try to reduce these slack periods by introducing various forms of flexible working hours.

The health care professions have a bad image virtually everywhere, due to a combination of comparatively low pay, inconvenient working hours and high workload. Low pay affects doctors, who are frequently men, much less than nurses, most of whom are women. Nurses are also least satisfied with their working conditions. As employees become increasingly reluctant to work unsocial hours, the relative position of hospitals in the labour market has deteriorated; they are increasingly complaining of high turnover and serious recruitment problems. In organising their working time, therefore, hospitals are being forced not only to pursue their own interest in reducing costs but also to go some way towards accommodating the wishes of their employees, in order to make careers in health care attractive again.

The hospitals' need to reduce costs and their employees' desire for more attractive working conditions can be only partially reconciled. The elimination of slack periods, which employees tend to regard rather as well-earned breaks after periods of hard work, increases workloads. Some fairly promising models of working time organisation are being blocked on grounds of cost. The introduction of part-time work reduces absenteeism and turnover, but it may be that the growing interest in part-time work is a consequence of the increased workload and not simply a reflection of the desire of a largely female work force to be able more easily to combine work and family life.

The Swedish Time Bank Model is a noteworthy attempt to reconcile the differing interests of hospitals and their employees. The success of this model is based on two generalisable principles. The first is the introduction of group work; employees agree working times with each other, which reduces the employer's organisational burden and gives each individual an opportunity (and a sense of achievement) to articulate their own interests. The second is that each group is supposed to contain members of the various categories within the work force (part-time/full-time, with children/without children, etc.). In this way both employers and employees are able to turn the divergent interests of the different categories to good advantage, since such a mix makes it easier to agree on working times.

Since the various European health care systems are largely financed by the state, or at least out of public funds (through para-fiscal health insurance schemes), employers and trade unions are joined at the negotiating table by a third and highly influential partner, namely the government. In the Netherlands, the negotiating parties are obliged to remain within the health care budget, which is announced by the government before the bargaining process gets under way. This is one of the main reasons why pay bargaining in this sector is very highly centralised. However, there is a strong trend towards a more flexible division between centralised and decentralised bargaining. In order to alleviate recruitment problems, efforts are being made (in the Netherlands, for example) to match pay more closely to local conditions. More flexible working time arrangements, in particular, can only be managed at local level, since the needs of individual hospitals and their work forces vary widely in this respect.

Both the Swedish and the Dutch trade unions have great difficulties in dealing with flexible working hours, since their policies have for many years been determined largely by the concerns and interests of male full-time workers. This has clearly changed in recent years. Part-time workers in the Dutch health care sector have now become unionised, although the rate of trade union membership has otherwise declined in that country. Thus, the public health care sector offers greater opportunities for trade unions than the private service sector, although the problems are comparable. As a result, full-time and part-time workers in the Netherlands are now treated equally (except in respect of overtime supplements). Trade union membership in the Swedish health care sector has long been very high, and the unions exert considerable influence over the centralised pay bargaining process. The Swedish unions obviously fear that the decentralisation of pay bargaining will lead to a loss of influence. Thus the debate on the decentralisation of pay bargaining is taking place in both countries against a background of a high degree of central regulation, reflecting efforts to create greater room for manœuvre at the plant or local level.

H.   CONCLUSIONS

The eight country chapters that follow show that the term "flexible working time arrangements" denotes a wide range of different phenomena. First, it refers to new forms of working time, such as part-time work, multiple job holder systems, annual working times, etc., that supplement but in no way replace the "old" forms of flexibilisation, such as overtime. Second, it denotes new compromises between employees and employers, in which employees working unsocial hours are compensated more generously (or at least differently) than in the past with additional time off and redesigned shift patterns. Third, however, the term also signifies the loosening of regulations intended to protect workers and/or the substitution of expensive forms of time management for cheaper ones.

Both firms and employees are interested in more flexibile working hours. Often, however, their interests do not coincide. This divergence of interests is dealt with in very different ways in different countries and sectors. In the capital-intensive sectors of manufacturing industry, firms seek to reduce their capital costs by extending operating hours and are able to offer attractive compromises to their highly unionised work forces. By contrast, in the labour-intensive service sector, flexible working time arrangements are intended to reduce staff costs which, in a sector dominated by small firms and price competition and with a high proportion of women workers, may lead to unattractive time arrangements for employees. Thus, clear sectoral effects can be discerned in working time arrangements.

These sectoral effects are overlain by societal effects whose influence can be discerned in two main tendencies. The first of these is the existence of legal or collectively agreed and generally applicable minimum conditions that have to be taken into account in the determination of time arrangements. The second is the existence or non-existence of a plant-level system of employee representation endowed with real power. In countries with legal or collectively agreed minimum conditions and effective employee representation much greater account has been taken of employees' interests than in countries characterised by *laissez-faire* policies.

It is not the degree of working time flexibility that distinguishes one country from another, but rather the way in which that flexibility is regulated. Unregulated flexibility means that the interests of firms predominate, with trade unions forced to react defensively because of their lack of opportunity to participate in the determination of working time. Regulated flexibility, on the other hand, can create a balance between the interests of employees and those of firms. It increases the acceptance of flexible time arrangements and avoids negative consequences for individual sectors, such as persistent recruitment problems in sectors with unfavourable working-time regulations. There are also opportunities for governments and the social partners to act strategically in order to influence the future regulation of working time flexibility (strategic effects). Such strategic action depends on interaction between legislation and collective agreements. Without legal support, collective bargaining will hardly be able to ensure the effective representation of interests at plant level.

Bibliography

ANSOFF, H.I. (1976), "Managing surprise and discontinuity – Strategic response to weak signals", in *Zeitschrift für betriebswirtschaftliche Forschung*, Vol. 28, pp. 129-152.

ANXO, D., BOSCH, G., BOSWORTH, D., CETTE, G., STERNER, T. and TADDEI, D. (eds.) (1995), *Work Patterns and Capital Utilisation: An international comparative study*, Deventer: Kluwer.

BLANPAIN, R. and KÖHLER, E. (eds.) (1988), *Legal and Contractual Limitations to Working Time in the European Community Member States*, Deventer: Kluwer.

BLOCH-LONDON, C. and BUTEL, M. (1992), "Weekend-shifts: in pursuance of flexibility", in: Ebbing, U. (ed).

BOSCH, G. (1989*a*), "Reducing Annual Working time and Improving Schedule Flexibility – Causes, Effects, Controversies", in Gladstone, A. *et al.*, (eds.), *Current Issues In Labor Relations. An International Perspective,* Berlin/New York: de Gruyter, pp. 193-218.

BOSCH, G. (1989*b*), *Wettlauf rund um die Uhr. Betriebs- und Arbeitszeiten in Europa*, Bonn: J.H.W. Dietz.

BOSCH, G. (1991), "Operating Hours: An International Comparison", Paper presented to the 4th International Symposium on Working Time, Gelsenkirchen (published in German as "Betriebszeiten im internationalen Vergleich", in *WSI-Mitteilungen*, No. 7).

BOSCH, G. and LALLEMENT, M. (1991), "Emploi et temps de travail dans la grande distribution alimentaire allemande", in *Formation Emploi*, No. 36, October-December.

BOSCH, G. and LALLEMENT, M. (1991), "La négociation collective sur le temps de travail en France et Allemagne", in *Travail et Emploi,* No. 49, pp. 31-45.

BOSCH, G., DAWKINS, P. and MICHON, F. (eds.) (1993), *Times are Changing: Working time in 14 industrialised countries*, International Institute for Labour Studies, Geneva.

CETTE, G. (1990), "Durée d'utilisation des équipements: L'inversion d'une tendance longue", in *Économie et Statistique,* No. 231, April.

CETTE, G. *et al.* (1992), "Ouverture dominicale: impact macroéconomique", in *Futuribles,* April.

CHANDLER, A.D. (1962), *Strategy and Structure*, Cambridge, Mass.: MIT Press.

DEUTSCHMANN, C. (1985), *Der Weg zum Normalarbeitstag. Die Entwicklung der Arbeitszeiten in der deutschen Industrie bis 1918*, Frankfurt/New York: Campus.

EBBING, U. (ed.) (1992), *Aspects of part-time work in different countries*, Arbeitspapier 1992 – 7, Arbeitskreis sozialwissenschaftliche Forschung, Gelsenkirchen.

EUROPEAN ECONOMY (1991), *Developments in the Labour Market in the Community*, No. 47, March.

FOSS, M.(1984), *Changing utilization of fixed capital. An element in long-term growth*, American Enterprise Institute for Public Policy Research, Washington and London.

GREGORY, A. (1992), "Part-time working and patterns of working hours in large-scale grocery retailing in Britain and France", in Ebbing, U. (ed.).

HENCKEL, D., HOLLBACH, B. and RINDERSPACHER J.-P. (1994), "The World on the Weekend. An Attempted Summary", in RINDERSPACHER, J.-P., HENCKEL, D. and HOLLBACH, B. (eds.), *Die Welt am Wochenende. Entwicklungsperspektiven der Wochenruhetage – Ein interkultureller Vergleich*, SWI Verlag, Bochum.

HOFF, A. and WEIDINGER, M. (1988), *Innovative Arbeitszeitgestaltung. Chance für Unternehmen*, Bonn.

INFRATEST (1989), *New Forms of Work and Activity*, 5 volumes, Munich.

LEHNDORFF, S. (ed.) (1992), "Flexibilisierung der Betriebs- und Arbeitszeiten in der Automobilindustrie. Dokumentation der Gelsenkirchener Arbeitstagung des Instituts Arbeit und Technik", Arbeitspapier IAT-AM 06, Gelsenkirchen.

LEHNDORFF, S. and BOSCH, G. (1993), *Autos bauen zu jeder Zeit. Arbeits-und Betriebszeiten in der europäischen und japanischen Automobilindustrie*, Berlin: Sigma.

MAURICE, M., SELLIER F. and SILVESTRE, J.J. (1982), *Politique d'éducation et organisation industrielle en France et en Allemagne. Essai d'analyse sociétal*, Paris: Presse Universitaire française.

NÄSMAN, E. (1992), "Parental Leave in Sweden – A Workplace Issue", in Ebbing, U. (ed.).

OECD (1990), *Employment Outlook*, Chapter 5, "Child Care in OECD Countries", Paris.

TADDEI, D. (1986), *Des machines et des hommes. Pour l'emploi, par une meilleure utilisation des équipements*, Rapport au Premier Ministre, Paris: La Documentation française.

VAN DEELEN H. (1987), *Kosten optimaler Arbeits- und Betriebszeiten. Zusammenhänge, Methoden und Anwendungsbeispiele*, Berlin: E. Schmidt Verlag.

WILLMS, A. (1983), "Zur Entwicklung des Verhältnisses von Frauenarbeit und Männerarbeit in Deutschland 1892-1980", in Müller, W. *et al.*, *Strukturwandel der Frauenarbeit 1880-1980*, Frankfurt/New York: Campus.

Chapter 2

GERMANY: THE CASE OF THE METAL MANUFACTURING INDUSTRY

by

Rainer Trinczek

A.   INTRODUCTION

Since the early 1980s, more flexible working hours have, as elsewhere, been a controversial subject of discussion among the general public in the Federal Republic of Germany.[1] It is no accident that this discussion started precisely in that period; in fact, such a development was encouraged at the time by a combination of different factors.

One important background factor was the change in direction of the Federal Government's economic, social and legal policy after the Schmidt Government was replaced in 1982 by Helmut Kohl's Conservative-Liberal cabinet. In characterising this change in policy, leading representatives of the new Federal Government repeatedly used the slogans "more market" and "deregulation". Two objectives were connected with these terms. First, the Government expected deregulation measures to produce a new growth dynamic in the economy. Second, it wished to dissociate itself from political opponents who, in the words of the then Economics Minister, would like to "organise life according to German industrial standards ("DIN-Norms"), because they do not trust people to look after their own interests in a responsible way and want them to conform to pre-determined behavioural patterns" [Bangemann (1988), p. 141].

Applied to working time policy, this meant tackling the allegedly (over-) rigid structures in this field, and pursuing more flexible strategies. It also meant taking a critical look at the attitudes particularly prevalent in the trade unions, where standardisation of norms was still preferred. Not without reason did the new Government soon announce that the 1938 Working Time Act was to be reviewed, in order to meet the new economic and social needs for a more flexible organisation of working time.[2]

Another factor was that, during the metal industry collective bargaining round of 1984, in which the aim of IG Metall was to obtain a reduction in working hours, the employers had made the demand for more flexible working time into the main plank of their counter-strategy. They considered (and still do) that flexible working hours are an integral part of a bargaining policy responding to the new international competitive conditions and to increased pressures on the utilisation of modern and increasingly capital-intensive production systems. The relative competitive disadvantages of German firms, mainly caused by the comparatively high wage level and short working hours, would be at least partly offset – according to the metal industry employers – by more flexible working time arrangements [see Schoenaich-Carolath (1988); Gesamtmetall (1988); and Lindena (1989)].

The intensive debate among academics, widely taken up in the media and in the political arena, concerning ongoing changes in social values, the differentiation of life-styles, and the accelerating trend towards individualisation in modern societies is a third major factor which promoted flexible working hours as a topic [see, *inter alia*, Beck (1986)]. In this context, temporal flexibility was approached in a quite different context, not as an economic or social policy concern of government or as a desire by employers to bolster their international competitiveness, but as a subjective concern of employees. Assuming that the social trends described above are correct, an increasing range of individual working time preferences, unsatisfied by standardised working time arrangements, can be expected. The wish for greater autonomy with regard to personal time budgets would therefore – according to the frequently expressed view – result in additional pressure for a relaxation of current working time regimes.[3]

The discussion on flexible working hours in Germany is situated in the broader context of a debate about more flexible employment conditions in general and what is currently referred to as the "end of the normal employment relationship" [*cf.* Mückenberger (1985); Bosch (1986); Hinrichs (1989)]. The increasing variety of employment conditions and labour contracts is an important phenomenon characterising German labour markets. This chapter, however, will concentrate on the flexible management of working hours within German metal manufacturing firms.

The plan of the chapter is as follows: section B discusses the various regulation levels and formal regulation modes in the organisation of working hours; empirical findings on the dissemination of flexible working time practices are presented in section C; and finally, the chapter findings are summarised in a general conclusion (section D). Since this topic can be meaningfully discussed only against the backdrop of the specific structure of industrial relations and the functioning of internal and external labour markets, the appropriate indications will be given as required.

B. THE REGULATION OF WORKING TIME

Apart from the individual employment contract, three main regulation levels can be distinguished with regard to the organisation of working time: 1) the government regulation level; 2) the collective agreement regulation level; and 3) the plant regulation level.

Government regulation

Legislation influences the organisation of working time in companies, and accordingly the possibilities of making working time more flexible, in two ways: through procedural and through substantive provisions.[4] As far as the procedural aspect of government regulation is concerned, the Works Constitution Act has given the works councils statutory co-determination rights with regard to the scheduling of working hours (see further below).

On the substantive side, the government intervenes directly or indirectly in the organisation of working time by means of a large number of statutory provisions [see, for example, Peters (1989)].[5] In Germany working time regulation traditionally falls in the domain of labour protection legislation. Minimum legal provisions are laid down to prevent employed persons from being monopolised for such long periods by their work that they do not have enough time to recuperate and meet their family and social obligations. The Federal Labour Tribunal once summarised the legislator's intentions by stating that legal provisions on working time "should ensure that employees are not excessively worn out and, for the sake of their human dignity and the development of their personalities, give them the opportunity to enjoy free time and leisure" [Judgement of 25 July 1957, quoted by Peters (1989), p. 21].

For over half a century, the main legal source for working time regulation was the Working Time Act of 1938. It regulated daily working hours for all employed persons beyond the age of 18 and contained a number of provisions of relevance for flexible working time arrangements.[6] Standard working time was defined as an eight-hour day over a six-day week, *i.e.* a 48-hour week. In certain circumstances, daily working time could be extended to ten hours, which means a maximum working week of 60 hours. To define such circumstances, the Act referred – in addition to fluctuating workloads – to "special" operational situations (such as maintenance work). In addition, it expressly mentioned the possibility that the collective bargaining parties voluntarily agree to a regular working time of up to ten hours. The Act considerably restricted fluctuations in individual working time, which had to be evened out within a period of only two weeks at most.[7]

The Act has therefore legally prescribed a framework for the organisation of the working day. Considering the changes in the organisation of work which have occurred since the 1930s, it is not surprising that both labour and management have repeatedly pressed for new working time legislation, albeit with different intentions. The unions have been mainly intent on obtaining legal protection for the standard working week (five days, at forty hours from Monday to Friday) which had long since been accepted under collective agreements in large sectors of the economy, and on curtailing the possibilities of stretching daily working time, which they believe to be too extensive. What has mattered most to employers, is to obtain a relaxation of those provisions which they see as a threat to their increasing flexibility needs. Another major concern for employers is the possibility of extending company operating hours, involving in particular the legal limits to Sunday work, which are considered too restrictive and incompatible with a modern economy geared to the world market and exposed to international competition.

In this context it is important to note that Sunday and holiday rest periods are expressly protected by constitutional law provisions both in the Basic Law and in the *Länder* constitutions. Exemptions must therefore be specially justified and are subject to quite specific conditions, the principles of which are set out in the Industrial Code

(Gewerbeordnung). Apart from inspection, cleaning and maintenance operations, the Code basically limits industrial work on Sundays to cases where equipment must be kept running round the clock because of the physical nature of the production process (as in some parts of the chemical and steel industries). The prevalent legal view is that economic considerations in themselves are not a sufficient reason for abolishing the Sunday rest period guaranteed by the Basic Law [Richardi (1988)].

In late 1992 the Federal Ministry of Labour and Social Affairs submitted a working time Bill which assembled the most important provisions on working time within a single instrument. While the Bill largely disregarded the trade unions' wishes, it did not completely meet the employers' interests either. On the whole, however, the Bill can be described as more "employer-friendly" than the previous Working Time Act. Disregarding average working hours laid down in collective agreements, the new law is still based on a six-day working week with a standard daily working time of eight hours and a daily maximum of ten hours.[8] An extension of the daily working period from eight to ten hours is facilitated by the fact that it is no longer tied to any substantive conditions, except for the obligation to even out the time worked. The Act extends the maximum evening-out period from 2 to 16 weeks, which largely meets the employers' flexibility needs. At the same time, it contains a broad waiver clause which, among other things, now explicitly allows trade unions and employers to extend the evening-out period for as long as they wish by collective agreement. The Federal Government considers that "the framework for flexible and individual working time patterns will be improved" through the new Act and that "the scope for a more intelligent distribution of working time will be extended" [BMAS (1992)], an assertion which is challenged in particular by the trade unions. For example, a Board Member of the German Metal Workers union publicly called the new Bill "something of a give-away to German employers". With some amendments, mainly referring to work on Sundays, it was passed by both houses of parliament during 1994.

To sum up, the legal provisions are limited to setting a relatively loose minimum framework for the organisation of working time at company level, within which there is comparatively wide scope for flexibility. This remains true after the passage of the 1994 Working Time Act. The broad terms of the waiver clause reduce the mandatory core of the Act – apart from the restrictions on Sunday work – to limiting maximum daily and weekly working time to, respectively, 10 and 60 hours.

Regulation by collective agreement

While government regulations in the area of working time mainly aim at preventing people from working for excessively long periods, collective agreements determine the practical framework within which firms fix the length of the working week, and negotiate changes in its duration and distribution.

As far as collective bargaining on flexible working hours is concerned, the year 1984 was a turning point for the German metal manufacturing industry. In the bargaining round at that time, the employers countered the unions' wish for shorter working hours with their own demand for more flexible working time arrangements. The dispute came to an end after the most extensive strike action in Germany's post-war history, with an arbitration ruling accepted by both parties which basically combined both demands.[9]

The ruling established a basis for compromise between employers and trade unions which marked all subsequent bargaining rounds in the metal industry: from 1984 onwards, IG Metall could not obtain any reductions in working time unless it was prepared to compromise on flexibility issues. This juxtaposition of shorter and more flexible working hours is therefore found in all subsequent collective agreements on further reductions in working hours, *i.e.* in the agreement concluded in 1987 on the 37.5- and 37-hour week, and the settlement approved in 1990 for the 36- and 35-hour week.

The main flexibility components in collective agreements for the German metal industry consist of the possibilities of *differentiating* and *varying* working time. Differentiated working time means the option under a collective agreement of assigning differing regular weekly working hours to individual employees or employee groups. This provision allows companies to increase or reduce the amount of time worked by certain employees, leading to a more flexible personnel utilisation.

Over the years, provisions on differentiated working hours have been modified. In the 1984 and 1987 agreements the possibility of using differentiated working times was tied to the obligation of arriving at the "standard working time" under the current collective agreement, as expressed by the average working hours for all full-time employees.[10] If a firm was interested in having some employees work longer than the average, an under-average working time had to be simultaneously approved for other employees. Detailed implementation was delegated to the parties within the firm who had to negotiate a separate agreement on implementing the collective agreements concluded at branch level.[11]

Metal industry employers used the 1990 bargaining round to have a new differentiation rule adopted: the so-called "13/18 per cent rule", which provides that – depending on the district[12] – a working time of up to 40 hours which exceeds the standard time laid down in the collective agreement can be accepted under an individual arrangement for up to 13 per cent (excluding employees not within the regular pay scale), or up to 18 per cent of a company's employees (including those not within this scale). In addition, the obligation to even out the number of hours worked within the firm was abolished.

From the employers' viewpoint, this rule had some advantages compared with the original provisions on differentiated schedules. One major aspect was that, according to the new rules, no agreement at plant level – considered as "burdensome" by employers – was any longer required on how the terms of the collective agreement were to be implemented by the firm. While the collective agreements of 1984 and 1987 still required such an agreement between management and works council, with the new collective agreement only the individual employee has to reach agreement with management on a change in his employment contract; the works council no longer takes part in this negotiation process. Management simply has to inform the works council of the number of employees not working normal hours so that it can monitor observance of the percentage clauses in the collective agreement.

The second important flexibility component in the metal industry collective agreements since 1984 is the possibility of varying working time, *i.e.* of distributing fixed amounts of working time unevenly within a given period. The 1984 collective agreement contained such a time-varying option in that it allowed employees' regular working hours to be distributed unevenly over days or weeks – provided that they were evened out within a given period. This evening-out period was originally set at two months, but was then extended to six months in the 1987 collective agreement and to one year in the 1994 agreement. An extended evening-out period of up to two years was approved for employees who came under the "13/18 per cent" provision.

In addition to these "new" flexibility components, the metal industry's collective agreements also include provisions concerning the "traditional" flexibility instruments, such as overtime. But while overtime pay is clearly defined, provisions on the amount of overtime tend to be loosely formulated in that they specify a "standard case" from which more or less clearly defined exemptions are possible at company level. For instance, in most districts, the maximum number of overtime hours has been set at 20 a month, but at the same time there is the possibility of agreeing at company level to a higher number of overtime hours in exceptional circumstances.

IG Metall has so far managed to prevent Saturday work from being recognised as standard working time in collective agreements: usually, despite various moves by employers, regular weekly working time must run from Monday to Friday. Almost invariably, however, collective agreements allow certain exemptions, although in such cases a co-determination right of the works council has been stipulated in the collective agreement.

To sum up, collective agreements in the German metal industry treat mainly three aspects of working time regulation. First, they define the duration of a full-time employee's working week; since 1990, a range of possible working hours has been fixed, according to which there is a "standard" working week for the vast majority of employees (36 hours as from 1 April 1993; 35 hours as from 1 April 1995) and a "differing" working week of up to 40 hours for a maximum of 13 per cent or 18 per cent of employees.

Second, since the mid-1980s "new" forms of flexible working time arrangements have been made possible under collective agreements by using the "differentiated" and "varied" working time formulae. Finally, the settlements traditionally include rules concerning the more "conventional" flexibility instruments (shift work, overtime, etc.), in which payment for these types of work is regulated in detail and maximum limits are laid down for the amount of time employees can be made to work, although some scope for flexibility remains.

Regulation at establishment level

As is well-known, issues concerning co-determination at establishment level are covered in Germany by the Works Constitution Act, which defines the works councils' spheres of action and influence as well as possible methods for resolving conflicts, all of which are to be settled amicably. The works councils' rights are usually broken down into pure information rights, participation rights, objection rights and (mandatory) co-determination rights. In areas where the Act gives the works council mandatory co-determination rights, its approval is needed for all measures taken by the firm; if such approval is refused, the only alternative is for a ruling by a conciliation board. Thus, some spheres of action are removed from unilateral management prerogative.

The organisation of company working hours is one of the subjects that are listed in the Works Constitution Act under mandatory co-determination rights:

"*§87 Co-determination rights: where a regulation by law or collective agreement does not exist, the Works Council shall have co-determination rights in the following matters:*

(...)

2. the start and end of the daily working period, including breaks, as well as the distribution of working time over the various days of the week;

3. temporary shortening or lengthening of the company's usual working hours".

These provisions ensure that no measure introducing more flexible working time arrangements (whether overtime, introduction of shift work, new shift work arrangements, short-time work, staggered working hours or new rules on breaks), can be decided and implemented without the participation of the employees' representatives.[13]

The more flexible working time arrangements become a central issue in negotiations, the more important is the place of the establishment level within the industrial relations system. One purpose of making working time more flexible is to adjust it to the varying amount of labour input required by different plants; for this reason, the plant is almost "automatically" the main bargaining arena when it comes to implementing flexible working time arrangements. The settlements in the metal industry since 1984, whose implementation required separate negotiations at company and establishment levels have confirmed this trend towards decentralised regulation.

It is an important feature of the German industrial relations system that the body set up to represent the employees' interests within the firm is in strictly legal terms independent of the trade unions. The links between trade unions and works councils are largely informal: although the works council is committed by law to observing the collective agreements in force and to organising its work "in conjunction with the trade unions represented in the firm" (Works Constitution Act), this does not mean it has to follow a specific line of action. Neither is it a trade union body, which as such would be bound by trade union positions, nor do trade union regulations recognise the works council as union bodies. It is a legal entity in its own right and is entitled to act independently of any trade union.

In reality trade unions and works councils are, however, closely connected, with regard to both staff and function. For example, the works council is usually the centre of trade union work in a firm; it is responsible, to a large extent, for the recruitment of members, it guarantees the flow of information from the company to the trade union, and forms the central recruitment pool for future trade union officials. In turn, works councils benefit from the backflow of information, from trade unions' education arrangements, and from the legal aid and active support which unions can give in cases of conflict. Usually a practical relationship is thus formed between works councils and trade unions, which is reflected, *inter alia*, in the fact that members of works councils are frequently honorary trade union officials.

The power of a trade union to censure works councils for not following trade union policies is, however, comparatively small because of the latter's legally guaranteed independent status, and is frequently limited to "moral pressure". Since works councils are tied into a structure of conflicting interests which forces them continually to reconcile the positions of the firm, the employees and the trade union, some tendency towards "company syndicalism" cannot be avoided.

This course taken by the works councils, which tend to gear their action to the interests of "their" plant and its employees, has become apparent, *inter alia*, in the case of flexitime systems. These were introduced in a large number of metal manufacturing companies in the 1970s and early 1980s with the consent and sometimes even at the express wish of the works council, although IG Metall's attitude to this scheme was quite negative until the mid-1980s. In addition, the works councils have not consistently followed IG Metall's standards when implementing collective agreements on shorter and more flexible working hours at company level. On the one hand, they have sometimes been confronted with the specific wishes of "their" employees (*i.e.* also their electors), and on the other they have sometimes felt that it was not appropriate to show too much opposition to the management's flexibility demands in order to protect the company's competitiveness.

For example, there have been various cases in the car industry where the works councils have agreed to the introduction of Saturday work against the will of "their" trade union. Such "concessions" which by-pass the trade union – especially in the case of controversial topics such as week-end work – are sometimes the result of threats by management to shift certain production lines to another location.

The Opel works council and management in Kaiserslautern, for example, reached an agreement providing for regular work on Saturdays, after the works council realised that the Kaiserslautern plant no longer appeared in the long-term investment plan of Opel's parent company General Motors. According to the works council, the workforce was exposed to competition between the firm's establishments in different countries, so that, for example, they were competing for future shares in production with GM's Saragossa plant in Spain, where comparatively long operating hours were routine. Since it was a matter of protecting "its own" workforce in the medium term, the works council said it could not take into account the union's misgivings, although basically it entirely agreed with them.

The metal workers' union fears that, as a result of such individual agreements, pressure will gradually build up in the metal manufacturing industry as a whole and that, with the example set by the Opel works in Kaiserslautern, other works councils will be prevailed on to accept Saturday work. As a consequence, the standard five-day working week from Monday to Friday might be gradually undermined.

In sum, the analysis of the legal framework conditions for flexible working hours shows the typical mix of the German industrial relations system. Substantive norms are combined with the procedural obligation of employee participation, through the representative body of the works council. This ensures that some balance of interests is achieved between the firm and its employees, which, in turn, has a positive effect on the acceptance of company policy – and accordingly on social integration.

C. EMPIRICAL FINDINGS ON THE SPREAD OF FLEXIBLE WORKING TIME ARRANGEMENTS

Preliminary comments

The analysis of the basic legal framework for flexible working hours in the German metal industry has shown that this area is extensively regulated, but not in a fashion that necessarily leads to operational rigidities. This seems to be due first to the specific mix of substantive and procedural regulation under the German system, and second to the co-operative spirit of the participants. Both employers and trade unions consider that a "spirit of fruitful co-operation" has contributed decisively to Germany's economic success, which in turn has been reflected in a comparatively high standard of working and living conditions for employees. Since all participants have benefited in some way or other from this "positive sum" arrangement, the German industrial relation system has been able to achieve a surprisingly high degree of stability.

However, the prevalent political culture of "give and take", and the shared decision-making between sectoral collective agreement and company level, have not allowed any radical moves towards more flexible company working hours. Employers have resigned themselves to this arrangement by adopting a "middle course" strategy which is not simply intended to force through company interests "at any price", but accepts, to a certain extent, the validity of employees' interests and tries to resolve differences as far as possible by means of compromise.[14]

This pattern is also reflected in companies' flexibility policies: active "flexible staffing", *i.e.* regulating fluctuating company demand for labour primarily by recruiting or shedding labour on the external labour market, does not play a central role in the metal manufacturing industry. It seems rather that a pattern has been set up which provides for flexible staffing at the increasingly frayed edges of internal labour markets, but tries to absorb fluctuations in the volume of work mainly through flexible scheduling of the main core of personnel on "standard" contracts.

The results of labour market research referring to the "closure" of internal labour markets as a principal strategy taken by firms [Hohn (1988)], fit in with this picture. They suggest that, especially in large firms, the predominant aim in company employment policy is to achieve the greatest possible stability in employment conditions, relying on a core of "insiders" in the company labour market [Sengenberger (1987)].[15]

On the other hand, an increasing number of "quasi-outsiders", meaning those without a regular, "standard" employment contract (workers from temporary employment agencies, employees on fixed-term contracts, etc.), have in recent years formed an outer ring around this core. This group of employees represents the basic "flexibility component" in a consensual company employment policy involving management, employee representatives and the large group of insiders.

"Flexible staffing" in the quasi-outsider segment of the company labour market, and "flexible scheduling" among the insiders seem to increasingly represent the standard method of absorbing fluctuations in the volume of work.[16] If such fluctuations occur, first, temporary employees are usually withdrawn and fixed-term contracts allowed to run out;

second, if necessary, the labour input in the firm or in certain departments is further reduced by phasing out overtime, introducing short-time work or lengthening holiday periods; and third, natural attrition is no longer offset by replacements. Should lay-offs be unavoidable despite these measures, firms tend to rely on employees "volunteering" to leave – under more or less pressure from the company – in return for financial compensation guaranteed by welfare schemes ("social plans"). In this system, redundancies are seen only as a last resort.[17] While as a rule all other steps can be undertaken more or less consensually, redundancy decisions – except in times of a severe economic crisis – usually jeopardise the basis for consensus in corporate policy and may lead to social conflict, which management will tend to avoid since it usually involves high costs.

The model outlined above of a corporate flexibility policy obviously contains a marked syndicalistic element. "Insider" labour is protected to the detriment of "outsiders" on the labour market. As an organisation defending employees' interests both within and outside the firm, a trade union cannot completely endorse such a concept. Leading representatives of IG Metall take the view that firms have a basic social obligation to provide a constant level of employment despite seasonal or cyclical fluctuations. The union therefore accepts flexibility strategies only in so far as they, to the extent possible, rule out flexible staffing and keep to non-excessive use of flexible scheduling.

Moreover, IG Metall considers current working time practices as providing sufficient flexibility for companies. In its view, the German metal industry, in principle, does not need new instruments for greater working time flexibility over and above those it already has under the consensual system of labour relations and employment policy.

Plant-level implementation of the new flexibility provisions: differentiated and varied working hours

The way the new flexibility options contained in the branch agreements have been actually implemented at plant level broadly confirmed the trade union's view that the long-standing possibilities for flexible working hours were already sufficiently great. In 1984/85, the process of implementing the 1984 collective agreement on shorter and more flexible working hours had already produced the unexpected result that firms made surprisingly little use of the "new" possibilities for both differentiated and varied working time.[18] Differentiated working hours were used in fewer than 15 per cent of the firms concerned; in all, only about 5 per cent of the employees covered by collective agreements in the German metal industry worked hours that deviated from the standard times fixed in those agreements. The varied-hours formula permitted by the 1984 settlement was used to an even lesser extent.

The view was repeatedly expressed at the time that, in the area of flexible working hours, firms were possibly passing through an incubation phase, and that they would first try out the new working time formulae on a small scale, before extending them to other parts of their activities. The results of the plant-level implementation of the second round of collective agreements on working time concluded in 1987, however, proved the contrary [see Ellguth et al. (1989)]: the use of the varied-time formula remained at an extremely low level although the basic conditions had been made more advantageous for employers with the extension of the evening-out period from two to six months. In addition, management's interest in differentiated working times even dwindled, probably due to the restrictive provisions on this issue in the 1987 collective agreement.[19]

Even the 13/18 per cent rule in the 1990 agreement, which was again more advantageous for employers, did not lead to a notable increase in differentiated working hours. According to a survey conducted by IG Metall in the autumn of 1991, about 18 per cent of the some 3 700 firms in the survey had taken advantage of this new differentiation possibility. Among all employees covered by the survey (around 1.9 million), only 2 per cent were affected by the possibility of working longer (up to 40) hours [Promberger *et al.* (1992)].

Two main reasons can be identified for the surprisingly limited use of the new options for more flexible working hours in metal industry firms. First, some opposition had been expressed by employees or employee representatives against excessive use of flexible working time arrangements. However, a more decisive factor was that the firms themselves showed only limited interest in using the new flexibility provisions.

As already suggested above, the main explanation for this limited interest by company managers seems to be that the arrangements in metal manufacturing firms had already allowed a comparatively high degree of flexibility prior to the 1984 collective agreement.

The picture suggested publicly by the employer association in the run-up to the collective dispute at the time, according to which company working hours were too rigid, had never really corresponded to reality. Companies have always had recourse to the extension or withdrawal of overtime, the introduction of short-time work, flexitime systems, etc., in order to absorb fluctuations in the volume of work. These options which a majority of company management representatives considers adequate[20] also have the advantage of being an established company policy instrument and of being reasonably acceptable, and relatively uncontroversial to management, employees and works councils.[21]

Use of "other" possibilities for more flexible working hours

In the debate on working time arrangements, the catchword "flexibility" usually covers all attempts by firms to relax existing measures. However, such efforts are often directed at two quite different strategic goals. The first consists of responding to externally generated, market-induced demands for flexibility by means of a more flexible system of working hours. The other is to arrive at an improved utilisation of the increasingly capital-intensive production apparatus by extending the actual periods during which the plant is used. Apart from the general intention that available resources should be used more economically, the two goals have hardly anything in common. Measures which promote the second goal frequently contribute nothing to achieving the first – and vice versa.

A number of new working time formulae are directed at the extension of company operating hours. Complex shift work formulae and staggered working hours and/or breaks have a prominent place in the discussion.[22] The importance to many firms of increasing plant utilisation time is shown, *inter alia*, by the working time system used by the BMW assembly plant in Regensburg. Under this system, the firm offered the employees a 36-hour working week (*i.e.* at the time this system was introduced, considerably less than the standard week), but was able to increase company operating hours considerably by programming the reduced individual working periods in a specific way. The plant works on the basis of two nine-hour shifts, with Saturday included as a regular working day. The employees therefore have a four-day work week, with a shifting four-day duty period each week (*e.g.* Monday to Thursday during the first week, Tuesday to Friday during the second week, etc.).

Benefits from this working time formula accrue to both sides. The employees benefit through shorter working hours, but in return agree to work longer shifts and Saturdays; and although labour costs for the firm have increased, they are more than offset by the extended plant utilisation times.

Various other metal manufacturing firms are trying to extend plant utilisation times by introducing night shift work on especially capital-intensive or key types of machinery. Because of the reduction in weekly working hours, this is increasingly resulting in the introduction of a four-shift system, partly including regular Saturday work. In one foundry, for instance, it is stipulated that, in the course of a twelve-week period, each employee has to work 58 eight-hour shifts, including 18 early, 19 late and 21 night shifts. By means of a computer programme, the members of the four shift teams receive in advance every quarter their duty roster which is optimised in each case in terms of free-time periods, etc. For the employees involved, the reduction in weekly working hours is mainly reflected by an increase in the number of free shifts.

For many employers, the movement towards the 35-hour week has put into sharper focus the issue of company operating hours. Since 1984 increasing efforts have been made to systematically extend operating hours at least in capital-intensive sectors. According to a survey conducted by the employer federation Gesamtmetall in 1988, among about 4 300 firms 15 per cent had used the reduction of working hours to introduce or extend shift work; 14 per cent had introduced or extended staggered working hours; 10 per cent had gone over to operation of equipment during breaks; and 10 per cent of firms had re-organised their shift plans [Gesamtmetall (1989)].[23]

These figures are broadly consistent with those from IG Metall surveys which have, in particular, confirmed the increase in shift work in metal industry firms. According to a survey, conducted in 1989, of over 5 000 such firms [IG Metall (1989)], shift work in one or more forms was practised in just under 55 per cent of firms; two-shift patterns or a combination of two and three shifts predominated (respectively 53.8 and 39.9 per cent of all shift work firms). On the other hand, firms with a three-shift or continuous-shift system were the exception – although, according to the 1989 microcensus, over 10 per cent of employees in this sector had to work nights, and of these over two thirds had to do so on a continuous or regular basis [Seifert (1992)].

The weekend still seems to be widely regarded as non-standard working time in the German metal industry. According to the IG Metall survey of 1989, Saturday was included in standard working time in less than 3 per cent of firms and for only 0.7 per cent of employees; overtime was, however, already being worked more or less regularly on Saturdays in about 20 per cent of the firms and by 4 per cent of employees. According to our own empirical findings and the statements of various trade union officials, an increasing number of firms, especially large firms, are at present experimenting with complex shift formulae in which Saturday is included as a regular working day. Firms often try to reward participation in such shift work by offering additional reductions in working hours.

The introduction of staggered working hours also aims at increasing plant utilisation time, while shortening working hours for individual employees. Staggered working hours either concern staggered break periods, which guarantees that workplaces are continuously manned, or the distribution of daily working hours more generally, in which case the aim is to fill the organisational gap between single-shift work and conventional multi-shift work. Even if the total workforce covered by staggered hours in the German metal industry is still extremely small – around 1 per cent in 1988 [Ellguth *et al.* (1989), p. 157] – there is a notable increase in the number of firms which use this formula. While staggered hours were identified in just under 18 per cent of firms in a survey in 1985 [Bosch *et al.* (1988), p. 89], the figure rose to about 30 per cent by 1988 [Ellguth *et al.* (1989), p. 155]. The main objective of firms seems to be to raise plant utilisation time in areas in which traditional shift work would be difficult to organise. This applies particularly to non-manual jobs, and among these especially to cost-intensive CAD workstations as well as marketing or sales.

Apart from the issue of extending operating hours, German metal manufacturing firms usually attempt to adjust working hours to cyclical fluctuations by means of various well-known measures which have already been referred to above. Importantly, flexitime systems (*gleitende Arbeitszeiten*), which are used to absorb short-term peaks in the volume of orders, are increasingly appearing alongside the traditional strategies of overtime, short-time work and changing shift work patterns. Flexitime, which has spread considerably over the last few years, seems to be developing into a general strategy which can reconcile a company's flexibility needs with the way in which employees want to organise their time budgets [*cf.* Bosch *et al.* (1992)]; as a rule, neither employers nor employees are willing to do without flexitime systems once they have been introduced.[24]

D.   CONCLUSIONS

Flexible working hours can be properly discussed only in connection with the system of industrial relations on the one hand, and the structure of internal and external labour markets on the other, since a company's flexibility potential is to a large extent influenced by them. Against this background, this Chapter has shown that the flexibility demands on German metal manufacturing companies in the last few years could be met to a large extent within the framework of the existing industrial relations system. It is not only that both the dual system of workers' representation and the structure of internal labour markets show a considerable flexibility potential, but in addition, a pattern for regulating company working time has evolved over several decades which has already allowed a considerable amount of flexibility with regard to working hours.

With overtime, short-time work and the adjustment of shift work in order to adapt to fluctuations in the volume of work, German companies have been able to use a well-established pattern for the flexible management of operating hours. The real "novelty" in this respect in the last few years seems to be that these "traditional" instruments of company working time policy have been handled in an increasingly innovative way (*e.g.* new shift plans or staggered working hours), or alternatively have been carefully extended (flexitime systems). That the existing possibilities for flexible personnel utilisation are largely considered adequate by the industrial parties concerned is shown by the fact that little use has been made of the new flexibility provisions in different collective agreements since 1984.

By contrast, in view of increasing costs for fixed capital, employers are genuinely interested in extending plant utilisation times. This is shown in particular by the increase in shift work, although the proportion of weekend work is, despite a recent considerable increase, still quite limited. Future initiatives by employers might therefore be expected in this area, rather than in the flexible adjustment of working time arrangements to demand fluctuations.

Notes

1. In united Germany there are obviously considerable differences between the old and new federal states (*Länder*), especially with regard to collective agreements. In the medium term, however, collective agreement standards in the east will be brought into line with those in the west. This chapter refers exclusively to the present situation in the "old Federal Republic".

2. It took over 10 years before a new act came into effect. The dilatory behaviour concerning the amendment of the Working Time Act seems indicative of the Kohl government's general attitude to deregulation. Without wishing to play down the importance of the corresponding legal changes, the Federal Government – particularly in an international comparison – has pursued a very cautious deregulation policy [see, for example, Lecher (1987), or Kastendiek (1987)].

3. Some experts and collective bargaining specialists have concluded that more flexible working time arrangements could meet the needs of both employers and employees [*cf.* Teriet (1977)]. However, this assumption has been frequently criticised, since according to empirical findings, employees' and employers' preferences concerning working time flexibility are not easily compatible [*cf.* Smentek (1991); Hinrichs (1992)].

4. While this section looks at the legislative side, the courts, and the labour law tribunals in particular, clarify and interpret the law in numerous individual decisions. As decisions are reached, "prevalent opinion" emerges concerning what is intended by the law or how it is to be applied. As the judgement of the Federal Constitutional Court of January 1992 concerning night work for women shows, the courts may in certain cases give binding instructions that working time regulations be amended or redrafted by the legislature.

5. Japan obviously has a similar tradition of state intervention in working time matters (*cf.* Chapter 3), whereas in the United Kingdom the traditional "voluntaristic" approach still seems prevalent (*cf.* Chapter 4).

6. In addition to these provisions, the Act also covered other subjects, such as breaks and rest periods between shifts, overtime pay, etc.

7. This comparatively restrictive provision, however, is no longer applicable in the German metal manufacturing industry, since the evening-out period has, in the meantime, been extended under a collective agreement, following a lengthy period in which the admissibility of such a measure under labour law was contested. In practice, the provision had already been eased for some time by flexi-time agreements which usually provide for an evening-out period of at least a month.

8. Night workers whose daily working time may not exceed nine hours are an exception. Special protection rules for night workers were necessary because of a judgement by the Constitutional Court which, on grounds of equality of the sexes, repealed the original ban on industrial night work by women. At the same time the court categorically stated that "night work is basically

detrimental to any person'', and committed the legislator to minimising the possible damage to night workers through appropriate statutory provisions. Accordingly, the Act provides, *inter alia*, for a shorter evening-out period of at most four weeks in the event of fluctuating working times, for regular medical examinations and exemptions from night work for health and family reasons.

9. Such a trade-off shorter working hours for more flexibility – is no German speciality (*cf.* the comparative overview in Chapter 1). But obviously there are major national differences as to where management typically seeks more flexibility. Whereas in the Japanese and the German metal industry, employers demand more flexible working time arrangements in exchange for shorter working hours, management in the United Kingdom, against the background of a traditionally less flexible organisation of work, is pressing for more functional flexibility (*cf.* Chapters 3 and 4).

10. The range of differentiation was originally between 40 and 37 hours in the case of the 38.5-hour week and, as from January 1989, between 39 and 36.5 hours in the case of the 37-hour week.

11. This devolution of responsibility for negotiations from the branch agreement to the company level has frequently been interpreted as evidence that the increasing economic pressure for greater flexibility might also lead to a change of structure in the German system of industrial relations, *i.e.* to what has at times been referred to as its ''decentralisation'', ''Japanisation'' or ''Americanisation''.

12. There is no national-level bargaining in the German metal manufacturing industry, but only decentralised negotiations at district level. However, as a rule a so-called ''pilot contract'' is concluded in one of these districts, which serves as a framework for agreements in other districts, so that there is considerable uniformity among individual agreements.

13. There are some exceptions to this regulation although they are legally contested. One example is the previously-mentioned 13/18 per cent arrangement in the 1990 settlement, where the metal workers and employers had agreed to settle the relevant measures by individual contract. Many labour law specialists, however, take the view that the works council, in principle, could latch onto the negotiation between employers and employees because it has to assent to the time at which work starts and finishes.

14. The suggestion here is not that such a style is the predominant or even the only type of company management policy. However, it does seem typical of the German metal industry and particularly of large metal manufacturers [see also Weltz (1977)].

15. Such a personnel policy obviously requires a workforce with comparatively wide basic skills and on absence of rigid job demarcations, which allow firms to develop an internally flexible labour market, where, for example, employees can be transferred or new kinds of work can be assigned without difficulty. Such a flexibly organised company labour market in itself reduces the need for flexible staffing.

16. The insider/quasi-outsider formula for company labour markets differs from the conventional formula of key and peripheral personnel in that it is not primarily based on qualification characteristics but on employment status.

17. Large Japanese companies seem to have developed a similar pattern of adjusting labour input in times of reduced demand (*cf.* Chapter 3).

18. In addition to our own surveys [Schmidt and Trinczek (1986*a* and *b*)], see the statistical study by the FIAB/WSI Research Group [Bosch *et al.* (1988)].

19. As already mentioned, in 1987 the range of differentiated working times was narrowed to 37 to 39.5 hours for the 37.5-hour week and to 36.5 to 39 hours for the 37-hour week. This meant

that for every employee the firm wished to use for 39.5 hours a week, for example, four employees had to be placed on 37 hours. As a result, the problem of selecting those employees who were to work less than the average number of hours per week laid down in the collective agreement became more acute since these employees were increasingly identified as under-achievers. In addition, the rule in the new collective agreement on adjustment payments to employees working less than the average number of hours was improved to the employees' benefit, so that the attractiveness of differentiated working times for management was further reduced.

20. This rather "conservative" attitude of managers towards "new" options in the field of working time flexibility seems also prevalent in the United Kingdom (*cf.* Chapter 4).

21. In addition, the use of the new collective agreement provisions involved high personnel management costs, which seemed scarcely justifiable to many managers considering the comparatively limited advantages of the new flexibility options.

22. Many of these formulae show that more flexible utilisation of equipment by the company does not necessarily mean flexible working hours for the employees. Thus staggered working hours or shift formulae may very well be connected with more rigid working time arrangements for the individual employee.

23. Unfortunately there are no official statistics on changing working time patterns by industrial sector. Neither do other representative studies on working time trends break down their data by sector [for example, see the otherwise comprehensive survey by Gross *et al.* (1991)]. This is why surveys by the employer federation and the metal workers union are used.

24. It was not least for this reason that IG Metall came out in support of flexitime in the 1980s – after they had long been opposed to this formula, mainly on the grounds that flexitime was overtime by another name and subjected working hours to the employers' dictates. Despite the negative attitude of the union, flexitime agreements, which to a large extent were welcomed by the employees concerned, had been concluded between management and works councils in various metal industry firms since the start of the 1970s and increasingly in the early 1980s.

Bibliography

BANGEMANN, M. (1988), "Deregulierung zur Belebung der Marktkräfte", in *Bulletin der Bundesregierung*, 3 February, Bonn.

BECK, U. (1986), *Risikogesellschaft, Auf dem Weg in eine andere Moderne,* Frankfurt: Suhrkamp.

BIEHLER, H. and BRANDES, W. (1981), *Arbeitsmarktsegmentation in der Bundesrepublik, Theorie und Empirie des dreigeteilten Arbeitsmarkts,* Frankfurt/New York: Campus.

BISPINCK, R./WSI-TARIFARCHIV (1990), *Arbeitszeitregelungen und arbeitsbezogene Zuschläge, Eine Analyse von Tarifverträgen aus zehn Wirtschaftszweigen* (WSI-Tarifarchiv – Elemente qualitativer Tarifpolitik, No. 12), Düsseldorf.

BMAS (1992), "Neues Arbeitszeitgesetz", *Pressemitteilung des Bundesministers für Arbeit und Sozialordnung,* 18 September, Bonn.

BOSCH, A. *et al.* (1992), "Gleitzeit: Wieviel Zeitautonomie ist gefragt?", in *WSI-Mitteilungen,* Vol. 45, pp. 51-59.

BOSCH, G. *et al.* (1988), *Arbeitszeitverkürzung im Betrieb, Die Umsetzung der 38,5-Stunden-Woche in der Metall-, Druck- und Holzindustrie sowie im Einzelhandel,* Köln: Bund.

BOSCH, G. (1986), "Hat das Normalarbeitsverhältnis eine Zukunft?", in *WSI-Mitteilungen,* Vol. 39, pp. 163-176.

ELLGUTH, P. *et al.* (1989), *Betriebliche Arbeitszeitentwicklung zwischen Kontinuität und Bruch. Die Umsetzung der 37,5-Stunden-Woche in der metallverarbeitenden Industrie der Region Nürnberg/Fürth/Erlangen,* IPRAS-Schriftenreihe zur Arbeitszeitforschung, No. 5, Erlangen.

GESAMTMETALL (1988), Sonderdruck Gesamtmetall (special advertising section) in *Frankfurter Allgemeine Zeitung,* 12 January.

GESAMTMETALL (1989), *Ergebnisse der Verbandsumfrage zu den ab 01.04.1988 geltenden Arbeitszeitregelungen in den Betrieben der Metallindustrie,* Köln: Gesamtmetall.

GROSS, H. *et al.* (1991), *Arbeitszeiten und Betriebszeiten 1990. Ergebnisse einer aktuellen Betriebsbefragung zu Arbeitszeitformen und Betriebszeiten in der Bundesrepublik Deutschland,* Berlin: Institut zur Erforschung sozialer Chancen.

HEGNER, F. and KRAMER, U. (1988), *Neue Erfahrungen mit beweglichen Arbeitszeiten, Beispiel-Sammlung aus der Metallindustrie,* Köln: Gesamtmetall.

HEGNER, F. *et al.* (1992), *Betriebliche Zeitgestaltung für die Zukunft 2005, Gründe – Schritte – Beispiele,* Köln: Gesamtmetall.

HINRICHS, K. (1989), "Irreguläre Beschäftigungsverhältnisse und soziale Sicherheit: Facetten der 'Erosion' des Normalarbeitsverhältnisses in der Bundesrepublik", in *Prokla,* No. 77, pp. 7-32.

HINRICHS, K. (1992), "Zur Zukunft der Arbeitszeitflexibilisierung: Arbeitnehmerpräferenzen, betriebliche Interessen und Beschäftigungswirkungen", in *Soziale Welt,* Vol. 43, pp. 313-330.

HOHN, H.-W. (1988), *Von der Einheitsgewerkschaft zum Betriebssyndikalismus: Soziale Schließung im dualen System der Interessenvertretung*, Berlin.

IG METALL (1989), *Umfrage '89 Arbeitszeitverkürzung. Erste Auswertung des Gesamtergebnisses*, Frankfurt.

KASTENDIEK, H. (1987), "Konservative Wende und industrielle Beziehungen in Großbritannien und in der Bundesrepublik", in Abromeit, H. and Blanke, B. (eds.): *Arbeitsmarkt, Arbeitsbeziehungen und Politik in den 80er Jahren* (Leviathan, No. 8), Opladen, pp. 179-193.

KITTNER, M. (1992), *Arbeits- und Sozialordnung. Ausgewählte und eingeleitete Gesetzestexte*, 18th ed., Köln: Bund.

LECHER, W. (1987), "Deregulierung der Arbeitsbeziehungen. Gesellschaftliche und gewerkschaftliche Entwicklungen in Großbritannien, den USA, Japan und Frankreich" in *Soziale Welt*, Vol. 38, pp.148-165.

LINDENA, B. (1989), "Flexibilisierung notwendiger denn je", in *Der Arbeitgeber*, Vol. 41, pp. 44-45.

LINNENKOHL, K. *et al.* (1992), *Arbeitszeitflexibilisierung: 140 Unternehmen und ihre Modelle (mit Checklisten für Betriebsvereinbarungen)*, Heidelberg: Verlag Recht und Wirtschaft.

MÜCKENBERGER, U. (1985), "Die Krise des Normalarbeitsverhältnisses. Hat das Arbeitsrecht noch Zukunft?", in *Zeitschrift für Sozialreform*, Vol. 31, pp. 415-434 and 457-475.

PETERS, B. (1989), *Handbuch des Arbeitszeitrechts*, 6th ed., Hannover: Klages.

PROMBERGER, M. *et al.* (1992), *Arbeitszeitdifferenzierung in der Metallindustrie 1991/92. Zur betrieblichen Umsetzung der Arbeitszeitbestimmungen in den Manteltarifverträgen der Metallverarbeitenden Industrie aus dem Jahr 1990*, IPRAS-Schriftenreihe zur Arbeitszeitforschung, No. 6, Erlangen.

RICHARDI, R. (1988), *Grenzen industrieller Sonntagsarbeit. Ein Rechtsgutachten*, Bonn: Neue Gesellschaft.

SCHMIDT, R. and TRINCZEK, R. (1986*a*), "Erfahrungen und Perspektiven gewerkschaftlicher Arbeitszeitpolitik", in *Prokla*, No. 64, pp. 85-105.

SCHMIDT, R. and TRINCZEK, R. (1986*b*), "Die betriebliche Gestaltung tariflicher Arbeitszeitnormen in der Metallindustrie", in *WSI-Mitteilungen*, Vol. 39, pp. 641-652.

SCHOENAICH-CAROLATH, A.-F. zu (1988), "Arbeitszeit zu kurz und unflexibel", in *Der Arbeitgeber*, Vol. 40, pp. 292-295.

SEIFERT, H. (1992), "Nachtarbeit Metallverarbeitendes Gewerbe: Bedrohliche Lage", in *Der Gewerkschafter*, Vol. 40, No. 4, p. 12.

SENGENBERGER, W. (1975), *Arbeitsmarktstruktur. Ansätze zu einem Modell des segmentierten Arbeitsmarkts*, Frankfurt/München: Campus.

SENGENBERGER, W. (1987), *Struktur und Funktionsweise von Arbeitsmärkten. Die Bundesrepublik Deutschland im internationalen Vergleich*, Frankfurt/New York: Campus.

SMENTEK, M. (1991), *Arbeitszeit-Flexibilisieurung. Zwischen "kapitalistischer Zeitökonomie" und "sozialer Zeitstruktur"*, Hamburg.

TERIET, B. (1977), "Die Wiedergewinnung der Zeitsouveränität", in Duve, F. (ed.), *Technologie und Politik 8*, Reinbek, pp. 75-111.

WELTZ, F. (1977), "Kooperative Konfliktverarbeitung. Ein Stil industrieller Beziehungen in deutschen Unternehmen", in *Gewerkschaftliche Monatshefte*, Vol. 28, pp. 291-31 and 489-494.

ZWICKEL, K. (1992), "Nur eine 'Steilvorlage' für die deutschen Arbeitgeber", in *Handelsblatt*, 5 October.

Chapter 3

JAPAN: THE CASE OF THE METAL MANUFACTURING INDUSTRY

by

Yoshio Sasajima

A.   INTRODUCTION

In Japan, the movement toward shorter working hours began to get under way around 1986, and hours of work have been reduced in many companies since then. In the process of reducing working hours, flexible working time arrangements have also been promoted, not only as a supplement to working hour reduction, but also to implement a more flexible management of working hours and/or to improve the quality of working life.

Trends in working hours in the metal manufacturing sector (machinery, electrical machinery, transport equipment and precision machinery) have paralleled the trends in the economy as a whole. After first discussing the overall trend toward shorter working hours, and the legal framework for working time regulation, this chapter goes on to outline the framework of industrial relations in Japan. It then analyses the arrangements for flexible working hours in metal manufacturing and the particular case of a new shift work pattern at Toyota Motor Corporation.

B.   THE MOVEMENT TOWARDS SHORTER WORKING HOURS

Until the first oil shock in 1973, hours of work in Japan had been slowly declining, with some fluctuations caused by business cycles. However, the recession and more unstable economic growth in the wake of the first oil shock halted the trend and brought a long period of stagnation. In the mid-1980s, the Japanese economy enjoyed a huge trade surplus, which led to severe trade friction between Japan and its major trade partners. In consequence, economic growth had to be based more on internal than on external demand.

In this situation, the report submitted to the Prime Minister by the Study Group on Economic Restructuring for International Co-operation in 1986, and one by the government's Economic Council in 1987 both highlighted the need to distribute the gains from economic growth more equitably in the form of shorter working hours; they also advocated working time reduction as one of several measures to expand internal demand. More specifically, they proposed the economy-wide implementation of a five-day work week as soon as possible and a reduction in annual working time to about 1 800 hours.

In response to these developments, the Labour Standards Law was amended in 1987 so as to revise the essential part of working hours regulation for the first time since its enactment. The revision included a reduction of normal weekly working hours and an increase in statutory annual paid leave. In parallel to these developments, a five-day work week scheme was introduced into the financial services. For central and local government employees, a new partial five-day work week scheme, in which offices are closed one Saturday in two, was implemented.

Historically speaking, hours of work in Japan have tended to decrease during economic booms while they stagnate during recessions. An economic boom starting in mid-1988 made it possible to reduce working hours from the point of view of corporate management. Many firms, in response to a severe labour shortage, actively reduced their working hours to secure recruitment of school leavers and to attract those wishing to change jobs. In 1992, a five-day work week system was fully implemented in the central and local government sector. In addition, state schools started to close on the second Saturday of each month as a step toward the five-day school week. In the same year, the new government launched the five-year Economic Plan and the Employment Measures Basic Plan which set a target for annual hours of work at 1 800 hours. In order to attain this target, both plans promote the implementation of the 40-hour work week and a reduction in overtime hours.

Since 1991, the Japanese economy has been undergoing a severe recession as a result of the bursting of the so-called bubble economy. Many firms have been taking a variety of measures to reduce the size of labour input, leading to a sharp decline of overtime hours. Major concerns of both labour and management have shifted from a reduction in working hours to employment security. Although the central government is still making a further effort to reduce hours of work, it is certain that the pace of the reduction will be slowed down.

C. WORKING TIME REGULATION AND FLEXIBILITY SCHEMES

Weekly hours of work

The 1987 amendment of the Labour Standards Law reduced the normal working week from 48 to 40 hours. However, a grace period was introduced to help small and medium-sized firms avoid unnecessary problems stemming from the sharp reduction. Thus, normal working hours were first set at 46 hours and reduced to 44 hours in 1991. The aim is now to reach the target of a 40 hour week as soon as possible. The normal daily working time is eight hours.

In 1991, 29 per cent of companies employing at least 30 workers operated a scheduled working week of 40 hours or less. The proportion of workers on such a schedule was 63 per cent. In larger companies with 1 000 employees or more the figures were 81 and 90 per cent, but in smaller companies with 30 to 99 the proportion fell to 21 and 23 per cent. There is hence a large differential in working hours according to the size of the firm.[1]

Annual paid leave

The statutory annual paid leave, which is prescribed by the Labour Standards Law, is between 10 and 20 days depending on years of service. The minimum entitlement increased from 6 to 10 days in 1987. The leave increases by one day with every additional year of service, up to a maximum of 20 days.

The average entitlement was 15.7 days in 1991.[2] The entitlement tends to be longer for larger companies. The problem concerning annual paid leave is that it is not fully used up every year. In 1991 average days actually taken were 8.6. The utilisation ratio has been between 50 and 60 per cent since 1980.

The reasons why the leave is not fully utilised are as follows. First, there is no compulsion to take annual leave. Second, most companies do not make specific arrangements for annual leave. Third, some annual paid leave tends to be reserved for unexpected illness. Fourth, those who do not make full use of their leave entitlement tend to be better treated in terms of promotion and bonus payment through performance appraisal schemes. Fifth, company-based labour unions do not seem strong enough to change the situation.

Overtime hours

According to the Labour Standards Law, an employer can ask employees for overtime and holiday work if and only if management and the workers' representatives (or the labour union) conclude a general agreement and submit it to a local labour inspection office. The agreement is called the ''36 agreement'' after article 36 of the Law. The minimum overtime premium prescribed by the law is 25 per cent.

For women workers other than managerial and professional staff and those in specific occupations, maximum overtime hours are limited by the Labour Standards Law to six hours a week and 150 hours a year in the case of production workers, and 24 hours every four weeks and 150 hours a year in the case of clerical workers. Male workers enjoy no such statutory regulation.

Despite such regulations, overtime work has traditionally been widespread. In consequence, the Ministry of Labour set up a guideline for maximum overtime hours in 1989, in which the maximum was set at 50 hours a month, 140 hours for three months and 450 hours a year. From 1993 on, maximum overtime has been revised to 45, 120 and 360 hours, respectively. The Ministry advises companies based on the guidelines which, however, have no statutory power.

Table 3.1. **Overtime working hours in metal manufacturing**

Production workers

	1985	1986	1987	1988	1989	1990 [a]
	Hours worked overtime per production worker					
Manufacturing [b]	229	212	223	252	253	191
Machinery [c]	318	356	278	340	337	283
Electrical machinery	202	257	198	232	216	244
Transport equipment	368	353	307	392	415	365
Precision machinery	178	187	154	194	190	191
	Overtime as a percentage of scheduled hours					
Manufacturing [b]	11.9	11.0	11.5	13.1	13.3	9.4
Machinery [c]	16.4	18.3	14.4	17.5	17.6	15.0
Electrical machinery	10.7	13.3	10.5	12.3	11.7	13.2
Transport equipment	19.5	18.8	16.3	20.6	22.0	19.5
Precision machinery	9.3	9.7	8.0	10.2	10.1	11.1

a) Figures for 1990 are average of production, clerical and technical workers.
b) All manufacturing.
c) Agricultural, industrial and office machinery.
Source: Ministry of Labour, *Monthly Labour Survey.*

According to a Ministry of Labour survey, only 8 per cent of establishments concluded a ''36 agreement'' allowing for maximum hours above those listed in the guidelines in the case of monthly limitations, and 6 per cent in the case of annual limitation. It is also noted that a majority of establishments set the possible maximum overtime at the same level as the guidelines. The level of overtime hours has been slowly declining, with some variations associated with business cycles. In 1991, average annual overtime hours per worker were 193 hours for manufacturing industries. Table 3.1 shows trends in overtime hours for production workers in metal manufacturing.

Manufacturing establishments offer on average 25.9 per cent overtime premium for working hours beyond 8 hours. With regard to work during weekends and holidays, the average premium is 26.8 per cent [Ministry of Labour (1990)]. The situation in metal manufacturing is similar to that in the manufacturing industry as a whole. According to a survey by the IMFJC (Japan Council of Metal-workers' Unions), the overtime premium for weekdays is 30 per cent, and that for Saturday, Sunday and holidays 40 per cent in most major companies in electrical machinery, automobile and shipbuilding [IMFJC (1992)].

Shift work systems

There is virtually no regulation with regard to shift working in the Labour Standards Law. However, shift work at night – *i.e.* at any time between 10 p.m. and 5 a.m. – must

Table 3.2. **Shift work patterns**

Percentages

| | Proportion of companies operating shift work [a] | | Distribution of workers by shift system | | | | |
| | 1982 | 1989 | 2 shifts | | 3 shifts | | Others |
			2 crew	3 crew	3 crew	4 crew	
Manufacturing [b]	19.8	23.0 (12.3)	49.9	5.4	15.2	25.5	4.0
Machinery [c]	10.9	15.1 (6.3)	78.5	8.7	2.5	2.9	7.4
Electrical machinery	11.9	22.8 (7.4)	62.4	10.1	15.5	8.6	3.5
Transport equipment	23.3	30.3 (22.3)	96.6	1.0	2.3	0.0	0.2
Precision machinery	11.8	18.9 (3.9)	50.5	4.2	26.8	10.6	8.0

a) Figures in brackets show the proportion of shift workers as a percentage of total workers.
b) All manufacturing.
c) Agricultural, industrial and office machinery.
Source: Ministry of Labour, *Survey on Wages and Working Hours.*

be paid with a premium of at least 25 per cent. As can be seen from Table 3.2, the proportion of companies adopting shift work is increasing. The 2 crew/2 shift pattern is the most popular pattern in metal manufacturing. The major reason for the increase in shift work is held to be management's desire to increase operating hours in order to achieve a quick return on capital.

Flexible hours systems

Promotion of flexible working hours was a feature of the 1987 amendment of the Labour Standards Law. The main reasons for promoting flexibility were, first, the expansion of service industries which require more flexible management of working hours, and, second, smoothing the reduction of working hours and compensating companies through a more flexible utilisation of personnel.

In Japan, working time flexibility has largely taken the form of schemes for averaging out working hours. There are four such schemes: flexitime; an averaging scheme for one week; a scheme for one month; and a scheme for three months. These schemes are described below.

Flexitime

Under flexitime schemes, it is laid down in work rules that both starting and finishing time for work are within certain limits, left to a worker's own decision. In a further written agreement between labour and management the number of workers concerned by the scheme, the averaging period and the number of working hours during one averaging period are defined.

Averaging scheme for one week

The scheme is designed to provide a flexible arrangement for industries where business activities fluctuate sharply from day to day and where it is difficult to specify daily working hours well in advance. Thus, the scheme is limited to retail trade and to hotels and restaurants with fewer than 30 employees. In principle, workers must be informed by the end of a week of the work schedules in respect of each day of the coming week. The schedule operates on the basis of an agreement between labour and management in which scheduled hours are set within a maximum of 42 hours a week. Under the scheme, normal daily hours can be extended to ten hours. The agreement must be submitted to a local labour inspection office.

Averaging scheme over a period of one month

Under the scheme, hours of work for every day and every week must be laid down in work rules or a similar document. Once so defined, it is possible to schedule work over and above normal working hours on specific days or during specific weeks.

Averaging scheme over a period of three months

A written agreement between labour and management sets out the usual hours of work for each day and week, giving an average of 40 hours a week. Once so defined, it is possible to schedule work above normal working hours for specific days and/or specific weeks. However, maximum hours are limited to ten hours a day and 52 hours a week, beyond which it is required to pay an overtime premium. In addition, at least one rest day per week is required. Thus, it is possible to arrange twelve straight working days in the schedule. The agreement must be submitted to a local labour inspection office.

It is useful at this point to give some indication about work rules and labour/ management agreements which are necessary for hours averaging schemes. Under the Labour Standards Law any employer with more than nine employees must prepare work rules and submit them to a local labour inspection office. The work rules must cover the following items in relation to working hours: starting and finishing times, rest breaks, rest days, leaves of absence and shift schedules, if any. The Law also states that the employer must solicit the views of a workers' representative when preparing or changing work rules.

The workers' representative involved in preparing an agreement between labour and management is either a trade unionist, if there is a union of which at least half of the workers concerned are members, or an employee who represents at least half of the workers concerned.

Table 3.3 shows the proportion of companies adopting hours averaging schemes. Since the 1987 revision of the Labour Standards Law, the proportion has been increasing, particularly in larger corporations.

A compressed work week scheme has been implemented by a number of companies in metal manufacturing, but there is no sign of any large diffusion. A staggered hours scheme seems rare in the industry. Both schemes have, however, been spreading in the retail trade.

Table 3.3. **Hours averaging schemes**
Percentages

	Proportion of companies operating averaging schemes	Flexitime	Scheme for 1 month	Scheme for 3 months
Manufacturing[a]				
1989	11.3	1.4	9.6	0.6
1990	14.0	2.2	11.5	0.6
1991	20.8	2.8	17.2	1.8
1992[b]	30.1 (39.6)	3.9 (11.1)	25.9 (26.9)	1.4 (1.6)
Machinery[c]				
1989	12.1	2.4	9.4	0.6
1990	15.9	3.4	12.8	0.7
1991	23.5	4.1	18.9	1.9
1992	31.0 (32.4)	5.0 (9.8)	24.9 (20.5)	2.4 (2.1)
Electrical machinery				
1989	15.1	3.4	12.8	0.7
1990	18.9	3.1	15.7	0.6
1991	23.7	3.6	19.6	2.6
1992	38.1 (51.5)	7.6 (21.1)	32.0 (28.4)	0.3 (1.8)
Transport equipment				
1989	15.2	1.9	13.2	1.1
1990	19.5	3.4	15.8	1.2
1991	20.8	4.7	16.9	0.5
1992	30.1 (53.6)	4.7 (13.9)	24.2 (37.6)	2.7 (2.1)
Precision machinery				
1989	19.0	1.6	17.4	0.1
1990	17.3	2.6	14.9	0.1
1991	20.3	3.3	17.5	0.7
1992	22.4 (37.3)	6.6 (11.8)	16.9 (24.1)	0.4 (1.4)

a) All manufacturing.
b) Figures in brackets show proportion of workers in the schemes in 1992.
c) Agricultural, industrial and office machinery.
Source: Ministry of Labour, *Survey of Wages and Working Hours.*

Flexible counting of hours worked

It is difficult to determine the number of hours worked by those working outside their workplace, since they are not under direct control of their managers. Typical examples include travelling salespersons and news reporters. It is also inappropriate to measure in the usual way the number of hours worked by those whose occupations imply special working patterns like, for example, laboratory researchers. For such cases, the

1987 amendment of the Labour Standards Law introduced a clause for the flexible counting of hours worked. Accordingly, labour and management need to determine in advance the number of daily working hours required for jobs under the scheme. The agreement is due to be submitted to a local labour inspection office.

The Ministry of Labour gives examples of jobs falling under the flexible counting scheme. They include research and development for new products and technology, analysis and design of information systems, news reporting and editing, and product designing. Flexible counting schemes allow more flexibility than flexitime and make it possible to set up working hours including overtime.

Companies adopting flexible counting schemes represent a much smaller percentage than those with averaging schemes. The flexible counting scheme for those working outside company premises is adopted in 4.4 per cent of companies with 30 employees and more, 2.3 per cent of workers being under the scheme in 1991. The figures are respectively 0.7 and 0.1 per cent in the case of the flexible counting scheme for those with special working patterns.

The future direction of working hour regulation

In 1992, the new five-year Economic Plan for the period from 1992 to 1996 was put forward in which the government called for the 1 800 hour working year. The call was repeated in the Basic Plan on Employment Measures.

In response to both the new Economic Plan and the Employment Measures programme, a Ministry of Labour study group on the Labour Standards Law (an advisory body to the Labour Minister) proposed to move to a 40 hour work week starting in April 1994, an increase in overtime premiums and an averaging scheme over a period of one year. Also proposed was the expansion of job categories falling under the flexible counting scheme for those with special working patterns, which is intended to increase the flexibility of working hours for white collar employees. The proposals made by the study group were fully implemented in the revision of the Labour Standards Law of 1993 and are to be put into effect in 1994.

D. FLEXIBLE WORKING HOURS AND INDUSTRIAL RELATIONS

In order to better understand how flexible working hours have been introduced into individual companies, it is necessary first to understand the Japanese system of industrial relations. This section outlines labour union organisation, the structure of collective bargaining and joint consultation and the positions adopted by the trade unions on working time issues. Although this report is concerned with metal manufacturing, the situation it depicts is broadly in line with Japanese industry overall.

Trade union organisation

As is well known, the basic structure of Japanese trade unions is enterprise-based. Each union is thus organised solely by the workers in the enterprise concerned. In most cases, workers of each enterprise are organised by one union.

Most enterprise-based unions are members of an industrial federation. The major industrial federations in metal manufacturing include: *Jidosha Soren* (Confederation of Japanese Automobile Workers' Unions, 764 000 members); *Denki Rengo* (Japanese Electrical, Electronic & Information Workers' Union, 740 000 members); *Zenkin Rengo* (Japanese Federation of Metal Industry Unions, 328 000 members); *Kinzoku Kikai* (National Metal & Machinery Workers' Union of Japan, 203 000 members); and *Zosen Juki Roren* (Japan Confederation of Shipbuilding & Engineering Workers' Unions, 129 000 members). Industrial federations usually join one of two national confederations: *Rengo* (Japanese Trade Union Confederation, referred to hereafter as JTUC) representing 61 per cent of union members, and *Zenroren* (National Confederation of Trade Unions) representing 7 per cent. The remaining 32 per cent are not affiliated with any national confederation.

Most trade unions accept only regular full-time workers as union members. Thus, part-time and/or temporary workers in the same company are in general not members of the union concerned. Blue- and white-collar workers are organised in the same enterprise-based union as long as both are regular full-time workers. Enterprise-based unions tend to have a free hand in their internal management and budget. In other words, industrial federations and national confederations do not control decisions and activities of the local unions which are free to follow or ignore their advice and guidelines.

Collective bargaining

In line with the structure of labour unions, collective bargaining on labour conditions is held at enterprise or at local establishment level. Negotiations on working hours are usually held at enterprise level for matters relating to the total workforce of the company, and at the establishment level for matters related to local workers.

Negotiations concerning institutional changes in working hours systems, such as an increase in annual paid leave, a cut in scheduled working hours, an increase in overtime or shift premiums, etc., are held during the annual negotiation round in spring, the so-called spring offensive. Other working time matters, such as reduction in overtime hours, an increase in the utilisation of annual paid leave, the introduction of flexitime, changes in shift work patterns, etc., are settled through joint consultation rather than through collective bargaining. This is because these latter matters are not directly related to the overall level of contractual working hours, but rather to production and personnel planning and sales activity.

Joint consultation

While the system of joint labour-management consultation is not required by law, it is a widespread practice among Japanese companies. Since most trade unions are company-based, union and management representatives in the joint consultation process tend to be broadly the same people as those involved in collective bargaining and the matters discussed are broadly similar. In many cases, the joint consultation system is based on and regulated by the collective agreement. Thus, systems vary considerably between companies.

According to a survey carried out by the Japan Productivity Center (1986), about 40 per cent of companies make a clear distinction between collective bargaining and joint consultation, so that matters taken up and discussed in each are different. On the other hand, about 30 per cent discuss and decide bargaining matters in the joint consultation machinery, and about 40 per cent make use of the joint consultation machinery as a preliminary discussion forum before going into formal bargaining.

Matters taken up in the consultation machinery are defined by collective agreement in 45 per cent of establishments, by work rules in 16 per cent, by other documents in 10 per cent, by past practice in 1 per cent, and not defined at all in 15 per cent of establishments.

The present state of the joint consultation system in Japan is described below, based on the 1989 Ministry of Labour Survey on Communication between Labour and Management.[3] Table 3.4 shows the extent to which joint consultation is used in Japan. The proportion of firms adopting joint consultation is 78 per cent among companies with a recognised trade union. In 57 per cent of the cases, the arrangement is based on a collective agreement, in 20 per cent on work rules and in 8 per cent on other documents.

Fourty-four per cent of establishments with consultation machinery have several permanent sub-committees under the main body, where both labour and management discuss specific issues in detail. A safety and health committee is set up in 91 per cent, a rest days and working hours committee in 23 per cent, a workers' welfare committee in

Table 3.4. **Characteristics of the joint consultation system**

Percentages

Employees	Proportion of establishments with consultation system	Employee representatives[a]		
		Union delegates	Elected workers	Designated workers
5 000+	73	83	18	1
1 000-4 999	68	88	14	5
300-999	67	76	20	5
100-299	50	39	44	23
50-99	51	33	56	16
Total	**58**	**59**	**34**	**11**
Unionised	78	88	14	3
Non unionised	39	–	75	27

a) On account of overlapping categories, totals may exceed 100.
Source: Ministry of Labour, *Survey on Communication between Labour and Management*, 1989.

39 per cent, and a productivity committee in 29 per cent of these establishments. Depending on the situation of each company, there may be other special committees dealing with such questions as ageing, personnel policy, overseas affairs, etc. *Ad hoc* sub-committees may be set up if required.

Where a trade union is organised, workers' representatives for joint consultation are nominated by the union in 88 per cent of establishments, elected by workers in 14 per cent, and designated by the employer in 3 per cent. In non-unionised establishments they are elected by workers in 75 per cent, and designated by the employer in 27 per cent of the cases (see Table 3.4; due to overlapping categories, totals exceed 100). Representatives tend to be designated by the employer in the smaller companies.

Table 3.5.   **Matters discussed by joint consultation**

Percentages

Matters discussed	Proportion of establishments consulting on issues		Extent of worker involvement			
	Unionised	Non-unionised	Explanation[a]	Opinion[b]	Consultation[c]	Approval[d]
Management issues						
Management policy	61	48	78	9	12	2
Production/sales plan	62	54	66	13	19	3
Management organisation	65	48	61	13	19	6
New technology/ rationalisation	59	49	39	19	38	5
Personnel management						
Recruitment/job assignment	55	45	42	21	29	7
Transfer/secondment to subsidiaries	65	45	42	21	29	7
Lay-off, dismissal	67	51	11	8	56	25
Labour conditions						
Working system	82	75	11	12	58	19
Working hours/holidays	84	90	9	10	56	25
Safety/health	86	84	12	18	62	9
Compulsory retirement age	71	67	13	7	48	32
Wages/bonuses	72	65	16	4	53	27
Retirement benefits	68	61	17	6	50	28
Other issues						
Education/training	62	67	41	19	33	8
Fringe benefits	82	80	15	20	57	8
Recreation activities	72	74	17	22	53	8

a)   Explanation to workers.
b)   Opinion solicited from workers.
c)   Consultation with workers.
d)   Approval needed from workers.
Source: Ministry of Labour, *Survey on Communication between Labour and Management,* 1989.

Table 3.5 indicates the type of issues discussed during consultation and the extent of worker involvement. The column "explanation" implies that the matters are reported and explained, but that workers' representatives are not asked to take any position. "Opinion" implies that the matters are reported and explained, and that worker's representatives are asked to give their opinion. "Consultation" implies that both labour and management exchange their views and opinions on the matters under discussion with a view to reaching agreement, although the final decision is made by management. "Approval" implies that a decision cannot be made without a consensus between labour and management.

Joint consultation and shorter working hours

Eighty-six per cent of establishments make it a rule to take up matters related to working hours, rest days and leave of absence under their joint consultation arrangements. For example, changes in shift work patterns are often discussed in the production committee which is one of the regular sub-committees under the joint consultation system. Matters relating to the company as a whole are generally taken up in the consultation machinery at company level, while matters relating to a local establishment are taken up at the level of the establishment concerned.

In 1991, Denki Rengo requested member unions to demand and set up labour-management consultation machinery targeted at a reduction in working hours. The request was designed to speed up the reduction of working hours, since the reduction was not proceeding as the federation had planned. As a result, 182 out of a total of 200 company-based member unions succeeded in setting up such machinery. Since most companies were already equipped with a joint consultation system, an *ad hoc* group was set up under the existing consultation machinery and treated as one of its sub-committees.

Trade union positions on flexibility, overtime and shift working

National confederation

Rengo (JTUC) has proposed a target of 1 800 hours (including overtime) as the average number of annual working hours per worker, with overtime being no higher than 150 hours a year. In addition, it has pressed for the raising of overtime premiums.

With regard to the flexibility of working hours, Rengo maintains that flexibility should not be linked to the reduction of working hours until the 40 hour work week had been fully implemented. It opposes an averaging scheme over a period of one year, which was proposed by a study group on the Labour Standards Law (see above), since it fears the abuse of the scheme. However, it is taking a favourable attitude towards flexitime, which is supported by many union members.

With regard to shift work systems, Rengo proposes that the total number of workers under a shift work schedule should be kept as small as possible, and that the working hours of workers on shift work schedules should be shorter than those of regular daytime workers. It also advocates a 5 crew/3 shift system for continuous shift operations, and proposes that total night work hours should be kept below 40 hours in any three week period.

Industrial federations

Zosen Juki Roren (Japan Confederation of Shipbuilding and Engineering Workers' Unions) is ready to accept some degree of flexibility in exchange for the reduction of working hours. In a special report presented at the 21st annual convention in 1990, *Five-year Plan for Shorter Working Hours*, the Confederation made the following statement:

"In order to attain 1 800 hours a year, it is necessary to make a distinction between the operating hours and working hours of an individual worker, and to accept flexibility in daily working hours and working days. In other words, we should accept a work pattern such that individual working days become less on the one hand and operating days more on the other. In addition, we should consider flexitime and shift work arrangements in a constructive way so as to improve efficiency."

With regard to overtime, the same report shows the union's position as follows:

"Overtime work is to some extent inevitable in view of the characteristics of our industry and its contribution to employment stability. Thus, average overtime hours are targeted to 150 hours a year, but maximum overtime hours of the '36 agreement' should be set at 40 hours a month for the time being, and move to 30 hours a month at the earliest possible time."

Denki Rengo (Japanese Electrical, Electronic & Information Workers' Union) has set out its basic position on working hours in the *Second Medium-term Directives on Working Hours*, adopted in 1989. A reduction in working hours in the electrical machinery industry has been promoted on the basis of these directives. In relation to the reduction of overtime, the directives suggest the following measures:

"We should make efforts to reduce overtime hours through productivity gains via the expansion of labour-saving investment and an increase in the number of workers in the case of blue-collar workers, and through flexible working hours arrangements such as flexitime systems in the case of white-collar workers. With these efforts, we should attain 200 overtime hours on average by 1993."

Jidosha Soren (Confederation of Japanese Automobile Workers' Unions) adopted a *New Medium-term Plan for the Reduction of Working Hours* in 1991 stating, *inter alia*, that:

"Maximum overtime hours of the '36 agreement' should be 30 hours a month, flexitime should be actively introduced for white-collar employees, and the reduction of working hours should be reflected in the company's production, sales and personnel planning through joint consultation."

Jidosha Soren considers that shift work is inevitable in view of the characteristics of the industry. Its basic position concerning shift working is hence that the labour conditions of those under the shift work pattern should be improved; the number of employees working through midnight should be reduced; and the day/night 2 shift work pattern should be replaced by a continuous 2 shift pattern.[4]

75

E. CORPORATE MANAGEMENT AND THE FLEXIBILITY OF LABOUR INPUT

Demand for output is not always stable. Production and sales activities tend to fluctuate according to the business cycle. In response to these fluctuations, it is necessary for a firm to adjust the size of labour input to its output level, in order to reduce labour cost. Thus, flexibility in working time arrangements is a concept of great interest for the company.

Response to changes in demand

Japanese manufacturing companies have at their disposal a range of labour input adjustment measures to respond to changes in demand. Although the measures and the way to use each measure vary substantially between companies, a general pattern followed by large corporations to reduce labour input during recessions can be observed.

The most frequently used measure is a reduction in overtime hours followed by a reduction or freeze in hiring. Other measures, in order of priority, include: a transfer within the company; termination of contract for fixed-term and part-time workers; dismissal of fixed-term and part-time workers; transfer to subsidiaries and/or related companies. Temporary shut-downs may take place as well. As a last resort, voluntary resignations of full-time regular workers are sought, and finally collective dismissals may take place if the voluntary resignation scheme proves insufficient.

Since temporary workers, such as fixed-term and part-time workers, are in general not members of a company-based union, management may terminate the contracts of these workers or dismiss them without prior consultation with the union. Many large corporations in the manufacturing sector employ such workers who contribute to labour input flexibility. The number of temporary and part-time workers employed in metal manufacturing is shown in Table 3.6.

Table 3.6. **Part-time and temporary employment in metal manufacturing, 1990**[a]

Thousands

	Machinery	Electrical Machinery	Transport Equipment	Precision Machinery
Regular workers[b]	1 081	1 995	977	292
Temporary workers	35	91	52	14
Total	1 116	2 086	1 029	306
of whom:				
Part-time workers	68	264	58	30

a) Data refer to companies with 5 employees and above. They include both production and non-production workers.
b) Regular workers are defined as those with indefinite-term contracts, temporary workers those with fixed-term contracts and part-time workers those whose scheduled working hours are shorter than the normal hours of the company concerned.
Source: Ministry of Labour, *Employment Trend Survey.*

76

Economic effects of flexible working time arrangements

With regard to the effectiveness of implementing flexitime schemes in metal manufacturing, 12 per cent of companies surveyed by the Japan Productivity Center described them as effective, 79 per cent as reasonably effective, and 4 per cent as having little or no effect [Japan Productivity Center (1992)]. The benefits of these schemes were reported as follows: better adjustment of working hours to individual job; a reduction of overtime hours; improvement in time-keeping and efficiency; avoiding rush hours while commuting, and increased motivation. Similar results were also reported by surveys conducted by the Ministry of Labour (1990) and Rengo (1992).

Positions of employer organisations with regard to flexible working time arrangements

Nikkeiren, the Japan Federation of Employers' Associations, pointed out in 1992 in its report, *Seeking New Socio-economic and Industrial Relations*, that shorter working hours were the most important issue at present. The association proposed that individual employers take the following steps towards achieving shorter working hours:

- The reduction should be realised through the distribution of productivity gains as in the case of wage increases.
- Both labour saving and efficient management should systematically be promoted.
- Targets should be set for total hours of work.
- The reduction should be promoted through labour-management negotiation and co-operation, and not through initiatives of the government.

It also noted that parent and other related companies should support the reduction of working hours in small and medium-sized companies where it is often difficult to implement. As regards other concrete measures, the report advocated *inter alia* a cut in overtime hours, further promotion of the five-day work week, programmed use of annual paid leave, full use of flexible working hours such as hours averaging schemes and flexitime, and the introduction of a long-service award in terms of a vacation bonus.

To give another example, Tousho, the Tokyo Chamber of Commerce and Industry, noted in its *1992 Proposition Paper on Labour Policies* that averaging schemes for longer periods, for example six months or one year, should be introduced, and that the legal requirements for implementing flexibility in working hours should be simplified.

These examples show that employer organisations are very active in promoting flexible working time arrangements as a corollary to the reduction of total working hours. They are, however, opposed to any increase in overtime premiums. The report now turns to one particular example of changing working time arrangements in the Japanese automobile industry.

F. INTRODUCTION OF A NEW SHIFT WORK PATTERN AT THE TOYOTA MOTOR CORPORATION

Reform of the working hours system

In 1989, Toyota set up a Study Committee on Working Hours (referred to as the SCWH hereafter), with representatives from both labour and management. It was placed under the Toyota joint consultation system and was composed of eight representatives from management (representing personnel management, production, engineering and production technology), and eight representatives from the labour union (with a vice-president, the secretary-general and other executive committee members).

The SCWH examined ways to reform the current working hours system with three basic principles in mind: to reduce the working hours of each employee, to secure the necessary operating days and hours for business activities, and to improve the vitality of the corporate organisation and its workers. As a result of the examination by the Committee, various new working time arrangements have been introduced. They include a modified working calendar, individualisation of long holidays, flexitime for white collar workers, a 3 crew/2 shift work pattern and half-day paid leave.

Examination of a new shift work pattern

The SCWH set up a sub-committee to examine the possibility of shorter working hours in the production department and develop a new shift work pattern. Members of the sub-committee include the director, production director and production technology director (for management), and the vice-president for production and working hours and the secretary general (for the union).

The sub-committee was asked to look into the possibility of introducing a 3 crew/2 shift system in place of the 2 crew day and night shift system. A first proposal was made by management, after the personnel department had exchanged views with the production department, the production technology department, and other related departments. Both labour and management discussed the proposal and a modified version was returned to the various departments concerned so as to obtain their views and identify problems; the employees affected by the proposal were also asked to express their views through union channels. This process was repeated several times and finally resulted in a sub-committee proposal. The proposal was then presented to and approved by the SCWH. The resulting new shift pattern at Toyota is presented in Chart 3.1.

Economic effects of the new pattern

As mentioned above, Japanese automobile companies have traditionally responded to product demand fluctuations through changes in overtime hours. In addition, the practice of hiring and shedding temporary workers has also contributed to the flexibility of output. The proportion of fixed-term temporary workers among total production work-

Chart 3.1. **Previous and new shift work patterns at Toyota**
Three week period

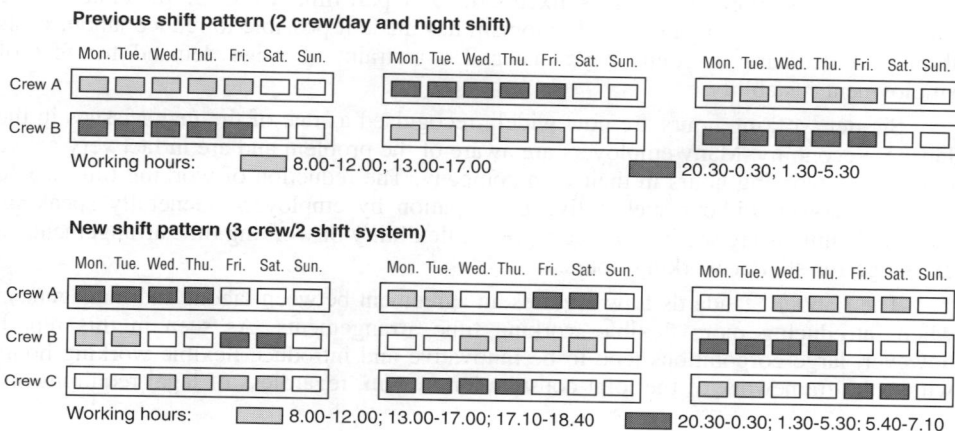

Previous shift pattern (2 crew/day and night shift)

Mon. Tue. Wed. Thu. Fri. Sat. Sun.   Mon. Tue. Wed. Thu. Fri. Sat. Sun.   Mon. Tue. Wed. Thu. Fri. Sat. Sun.

Crew A

Crew B

Working hours: ☐ 8.00-12.00; 13.00-17.00   ■ 20.30-0.30; 1.30-5.30

New shift pattern (3 crew/2 shift system)

Mon. Tue. Wed. Thu. Fri. Sat. Sun.   Mon. Tue. Wed. Thu. Fri. Sat. Sun.   Mon. Tue. Wed. Thu. Fri. Sat. Sun.

Crew A

Crew B

Crew C

Working hours: ☐ 8.00-12.00; 13.00-17.00; 17.10-18.40   ■ 20.30-0.30; 1.30-5.30; 5.40-7.10

Source: Toyota Motors Corporation.

ers varies from company to company, and also according to economic conditions. A rough estimate based on interviews with trade unions suggests about 10 per cent on average in 1992.

There are two shift patterns for overtime work. In the case of the 2 crew/2 shift pattern, overtime work can be done between shifts by widening the time between shifts. Another method is to work on Saturdays and Sundays. The 3 crew/2 shift pattern reduces production flexibility firstly by reducing the time span for overtime work since the time zone between shifts becomes shorter, and secondly by requiring Saturday work, as can be seen from Chart 3.1.

Since the introduction of the 3 crew/2 shift pattern in Toyota is aimed at reducing working hours, it requires an increase in the number of workers to keep production levels constant, especially in labour-intensive sections such as assembly, coating and welding. On the other hand, the sub-committee found that the new pattern can reduce the need for new investment through an increase in operating hours in capital-intensive sections: annual operating days increased from 245 to 297 days, and scheduled operating hours from 3 920 to 5 643 hours.

G. CONCLUSIONS

In the Japanese manufacturing sector, overtime hours have been playing a significant role in the adjustment of labour input. This is also true for metal manufacturing. Although

79

it was not mentioned explicitly above, it should be noted that the rather low premiums for overtime working have contributed to some extent to the heavy dependence on overtime hours by management.[5] Another important source for labour input adjustment has come from temporary workers, such as fixed-term and part-time workers. In addition, the Japanese system of company-based unionism has made it possible to reduce labour costs through a decrease in bonus payments and a restraint of wage demand for fear of employment instability.

Shorter working hours are now widely recognised as one of the major issues in the Japanese economy. Many employers are aware of the problem and are in fact very active in reducing working hours in their own company. The reduction of working time would be much slower without such active participation by employers. Generally speaking, most trade unions are willing to accept greater flexibility of working time arrangements in exchange for shorter working hours.

The Labour Standards Law requires an agreement between labour and management when introducing more flexible working time arrangements. As seen in this report, however, large corporations tend to be innovative and introduce flexible working hours within the framework of the joint consultation system, regardless of legal requirements.

Notes

1. Unless otherwise specified, statistics relating to working hours in the text are quoted from Ministry of Labour, *Survey on Wages and Working Hours*.
2. In many companies, workers are entitled to special leave other than annual paid leave and national holidays. This includes year-end and New Year holidays, special summer vacation, May Day and company anniversary day. An average worker was entitled to 8.2 days of special paid leave in 1991.
3. This Survey covered 4 000 establishments with 50 regular employees and more, in the private sector.
4. A typical day/night 2 shift work pattern is designed with the first shift from 8 a.m. to 5 p.m. and the second from 8 p.m. to 5.30 a.m. A typical continuous work pattern has the first shift from 6 a.m. to 2.45 p.m. and the second from 2.45 p.m. to 11.30 p.m.
5. In fact, the effective premium rate for overtime hours is negative in view of the fact that bonus payments, which account for a fairly large portion of total annual wages, are not taken into account in the calculation of overtime pay. The effective premium rate of 1992 was estimated at minus 7 per cent for the manufacturing industry [see Sarajima (1992); (1993)].

Bibliography

DENKI RENGO (1992), *Rodo Jikan Taisaku Manyuaru* (A Manual for Working Hours Measures).

IMFJC (1992), *Labour Conditions of Member Unions in 1991*.

JAPAN PRODUCTIVITY CENTER (1986), *The Role of the Personnel Department and the Future of Industrial Relations*.

JAPAN PRODUCTIVITY CENTER (1992), *Survey Report on Flexitime Working*.

JIDOSHA SOREN (1992), *Fukusi Seisaku Tosin Essensu-shu* (Summary of Reports of Welfare Policy Committee).

MINISTRY OF LABOUR (1990), *Opinion Survey on Shorter Working Hours*.

RENGO RODO JIKAN TANSHUKU SENTA (1992), *Kotai Hensoku Kinmu no Rodo Jikan Tanshuku* (Reduction of Working Hours for Shift and Irregular Working), Rodo Kyoiku Senta.

ROMU GYOSEI KENKYUSHO (1992), *Saisin Rodojikan Jijo* (The Latest Situation of Working Hours).

SASAJIMA, Yoshio (1991), *Contemporary Labour Problems in Japan, Chuou-Keizaisha*.

SASAJIMA, Yoshio (1992), ''Recommending 100 per cent for overtime premiums'', in *Toyo Keizai*, 20 June.

SASAJIMA, Yoshio (1993), ''The Japanese Labour Market and its Institutions and Performance'', in Hartog, J. and Teeuwes, J. (eds.), *Labour Market Contracts and Institutions*, Amsterdam: North Holland.

SATO, Katsumi (1991), *Shoteigai Rodo Sakugen no Susume* (Promotion of Reducing Overtime Hours), Romu Gyosei Kenkyusho.

Bibliography

Chapter 4

UNITED KINGDOM: THE CASE OF THE METAL MANUFACTURING INDUSTRY*

by

Paul Blyton

A.   INTRODUCTION

The issue of flexibility has been a central and recurring theme in discussions on work and employment in the United Kingdom over the past decade. Despite the empirical and conceptual shortcomings of the term, flexibility has come to represent, among other things, a summary of managerial attempts to recruit, reward and deploy labour in the workplace more freely than in the past, by reforming and re-negotiating existent patterns of employment, job structures and working practices.

Within this search for a less constrained and more malleable labour force, working time has to some extent been "rediscovered" as a potential source of greater flexibility. The essence of this flexibility lies in the scope for varying the working period, though some commentators tend to use the notion of working time flexibility more broadly to encapsulate a range of developments in working time patterns designed to improve the productive use of the working period, rather than its variability *per se*. The objectives behind recent developments in temporal flexibility are far from new. Varying the working period via overtime, temporary shifts, short-time working, etc., is long established. So too is the practice of operating different working hours arrangements at different points in the production process to accommodate varying maintenance requirements, production pressures, etc. What is different about the recent period, however, is the more detailed consideration being given by management to the arrangement and utilisation of working time, resulting in a greater prominence of working time issues in negotiations between management and employee representatives.

---

* To assist in the preparation of this report, a number of companies supplied information on their current working time arrangements. Particular thanks are due to individual managers in British Aerospace, Hitachi, Peugeot Talbot, Rolls-Royce, Toshiba, Vauxhall, and Volvo for their co-operation.

In the metal manufacturing sector,[1] this greater interest in the organisation of working time is associated partly with recent collective agreements to reduce the length of the working week. Outside these agreements, however (which cover less than half of the employees in the sector overall), a number of other working time developments are also evident, most notably the introduction of new shift-work patterns and the development of seasonal hours arrangements. In combination, the various changes in the arrangement and utilisation of working time raise important issues concerning the changing experience of work, the balance between duration, arrangement and intensity of working time, and the extent to which the managerial search for greater efficiency and increased temporal flexibility takes sufficient account of the attitudes and interests of employee groups towards the organisation of working time.

While it is important to highlight the types of developments occurring in particular contexts, however, it is nevertheless true that the overall degree to which working time flexibility has been pursued in the metal manufacturing sector remains comparatively modest, both in terms of the proportion of firms making changes and the depth of changes being introduced. For example, certain working time innovations which are evident elsewhere – such as "flexitime" arrangements, annual hours systems and the use of various part-time schedules – are much less apparent in the metal industries (though examples do exist, such as the annual hours scheme in operation at the washing-machine manufacturer Hotpoint, and flexitime arrangements for some grades of staff within British Aerospace). More generally, the working time arrangements in the majority of firms in the sector (a substantial proportion of which are small and medium size) appear characterised more by continuity than change – or at least, the variability which exists appears to be of similar magnitude to that present in earlier periods.

Further, the recent period of working time development coincides with significant changes in the structure of employee relations in the United Kingdom, with considerable reductions in trade union density and collective bargaining coverage, and a shift in bargaining level from industry to enterprise. Hence, before considering the types of changes being introduced into working time patterns and the way those changes have been agreed and implemented, it is appropriate first to review briefly both the contextual factors influencing the general pattern of working time in the metal sector, and the developments occurring in the overall pattern of collective bargaining in which negotiations over working time changes are situated.

B.   THE CONTEXT OF WORKING TIME CHANGE IN THE UNITED KINGDOM

In terms of the relevance for the pattern of working time change, four factors are worthy of particular attention: the nature of statutory regulation; the pattern of overtime working; the traditional pattern of job controls in engineering; and the impact of recessionary conditions in the early 1990s.

Statutory regulation of working hours

The United Kingdom is virtually unique in Europe in having no general legislation limiting the overall duration or arrangement of working time. There is no statutory regulation, for example, governing the maximum length of the working day or minimum rest periods and holidays. Earlier legislation restricting the hours of women and young people was repealed under the Sex Discrimination Act (1986) and Employment Act (1989) [Horrell and Rubery (1991), p. 1]. The little statutory regulation which continues to exist is confined to particular groups and occupations such as mining and lorry driving [Hepple (1988)]. Thus, the main aspects of working time are determined either by management action or by collective bargaining.

This absence of statutory regulation, coupled with the high level of overtime working (see below), has been one factor accounting for the British Government's continued opposition to the European Community's draft Directive on Working Hours. Employers in the metal manufacturing sector have similarly been highly critical. Commenting on the draft Directive, the Engineering Employers' Federation (EEF) maintained that the limitations on working time, particularly the restrictions proposed on night-working, could have "disastrous consequences" for engineering firms in Britain (quoted in the *Financial Times*, 14 September 1990).

Overtime working

Levels of overtime working have remained persistently high in the United Kingdom. In 1991, over half (52 per cent) of the full-time male manual work-force (and 26 per cent of full-time female manual workers) worked some overtime. In 1991 – a year of marked recession – over one-third of operatives in manufacturing industry worked an average of more than nine hours overtime per week. The latest figures available, for May 1993, show almost 37 per cent of operatives in manufacturing working an average of 9.4 hours overtime per week. This high level of overtime has persisted despite criticism from national employer and trade union bodies, the former critical of costs and the under-utilisation of "standard" hours, the latter critical of long work hours, the possible negative effects on job creation and the potential for employers to use the availability of overtime as a means to suppress basic pay rates.

At the local level, however, high levels of overtime have persisted partly because of the absence of statutory regulation (for example, no restrictions on Sunday working) and also the weakness of voluntary controls. In engineering, for example, the voluntary code of six hours maximum overtime per week, agreed between employers and unions at national level, is regularly breached and appears widely ignored at the local level. For local management, overtime represents a means of both extending the working day, and utilising shift patterns which do not coincide with agreed weekly hours, without requiring additional labour to be engaged. In addition, overtime can provide a vehicle for earnings to be increased without conceding a general wage rise. Similarly, for many employees, overtime payments represent a crucial component in overall earnings. The regularity of much of the overtime worked results in income deriving from overtime being incorporated into routine expenditure patterns. Hence, overtime working represents a means of extending standard hours, which is used widely by management and is actively sought by many in the work-force, particularly those in lower-paid jobs.

While, as we discuss below, in some work settings the desire to reduce overtime costs is acting as a stimulus to working time change, in other contexts the presence of overtime and its utility for both local management and work-force, diminishes the desire to replace overtime working with other forms of temporal flexibility. As one manager put it in an interview with the author, "overtime payments lubricate the wheels of employee relations".

The pattern of job controls

The higher proportion of craft skills in engineering, compared to other branches of manufacturing, and the traditional strength of craft unionism in the United Kingdom, have resulted in workers' job controls being comparatively strong in that industry. This has been particularly true in relation to aspects of work organisation such as job boundaries (demarcation), labour deployment (for example manning levels), and job hierarchies. The traditional strength of these job controls, coupled with a weakening in the power of unions during the 1980s and 1990s, has resulted in a growing employer offensive against workers' job controls. For example, a marked tendency in collective agreements over flexibility issues in recent years has been to focus particularly on questions of job demarcation and labour deployment to a greater extent than other potential sources of flexibility such as working time changes. In their study of flexibility agreements, for example, Marsden and Thompson (1990) found that in the 56 agreements they analysed from the engineering and vehicles sector, labour deployment issues were mentioned in 37 agreements, skills demarcation in 23 and grading issues in 20. In contrast, only 10 (18 per cent) of the agreements contained reference to working time changes.

A similar pattern emerges in the negotiations over a shorter working week in 1990-91 (discussed below). While during the course of negotiations, employers made frequent reference to increasing the variability of working time, in the event, the agreements reached placed more emphasis on achieving increased task flexibility (for example, production workers undertaking a broader range of tasks, including minor maintenance work). Where working time was mentioned, it was more in relation to the utilisation of the working period than in terms of flexibility *per se*. The general impression is one of many managers identifying task-related flexibility as a more easily achieved and/or more productive source of flexibility, efficiency and lower costs, than moves to extend the degree of working time flexibility.

Recession

By 1993, the United Kingdom had experienced three years of recession, the longest period of decline in aggregate output in its post-war history. Levels of business failure, redundancy and unemployment increased markedly between 1989 and the end of 1992. This difficult economic climate appears to have exerted a marked influence on the extent to which firms have been actively pursuing innovations in working time practices, including more flexible working time arrangements. Several of the companies contacted in connection with the preparation of this chapter, for example, indicated that in the context of slack product demand, the only working time change being contemplated was short-time working.

While recessionary conditions have characterised the metal manufacturing sector as a whole during the early 1990s, the over-capacity and lack of demand appear particularly evident in the vehicle production and aviation industries. During 1992, for example, major redundancies and short-time working were announced at Ford, Jaguar, Rolls-Royce and British Aerospace. In vehicle manufacture, with the exception of Rover, other producers indicate working time flexibility not to be a foremost priority. Thus, no other companies have so far followed Rover's introduction of 24 hour, seven-day assembly in parts of its production process (discussed below). Elsewhere in the vehicle sector, the established pattern remains one of production taking place on double-day shiftwork, with maintenance carried out during the non-assembly periods.

Yet, despite the continuing influence of high levels of overtime working, the greater emphasis on securing task, rather than temporal, flexibility and the effects of recession, the engineering industry nevertheless contains a number of significant developments in the area of working time, some of which have been introduced to increase the degree of temporal flexibility in working patterns. We will turn to these following a brief review of collective bargaining developments in the United Kingdom, and of the extent and ways in which working time issues figure in the bargaining process.

C. COLLECTIVE BARGAINING AND THE REGULATION OF WORKING TIME ISSUES

The 1980s and early 1990s have witnessed a number of significant changes in the overall pattern of employee relations in the United Kingdom, primarily caused by shifts in the structure of economic activity, in particular the decline in employment in heavily unionised manufacturing and extractive industries. Between 1979 and 1992, the overall density of unionism fell from 55 per cent to below 38 per cent of the work-force. This decline is also reflected in the extent of union recognition for collective bargaining purposes within establishments. The 1990 Workplace Industrial Relations Survey [Millward et al. (1992)], for example, indicates a drop in the proportion of establishments where unions were recognised for collective bargaining from 64 per cent in 1980 to 53 per cent in 1990. In private sector manufacturing, the decline in union recognition was even sharper, from 65 per cent of establishments in 1980 to 44 per cent in 1990. This fall in recognition in the manufacturing sector partly reflects the scale of decline in union recognition in the engineering and vehicles industries. This appears due in part to the ending of national bargaining arrangements in engineering in 1989 (discussed below), which appears not to have been replaced by alternative bargaining arrangements by many smaller employers. Thus, while union recognition remained stable within larger unionised establishments, recognition fell in smaller workplaces, particularly ones with less than

200 employees. As a result, overall union recognition for bargaining purposes fell from just over half of engineering establishments in 1984 to around a third in 1990 [Millward *et al.* (1992), p. 72].

In those establishments where collective bargaining does take place, however, the same national survey indicates that the issue of working time in general, and the reorganisation of working hours in particular, rank higher in terms of the extent of negotiation between management and trade unions than any other non-pay issue (including physical working conditions, redeployment, redundancy, staffing levels and recruitment issues). Overall, in nearly 80 per cent of workplaces with recognised unions for manual workers, managers reported that the issue of reorganisation of working hours was subject to joint regulation. In the private manufacturing sector and nationalised industries, this proportion was considerably higher (88 per cent and 98 per cent respectively). Further, in those private sector manufacturing establishments with recognised unions, 68 per cent indicated that the reorganisation of working hours was negotiated at establishment level; this compared with 60 per cent in the nationalised sector, 33 per cent in private services, and 26 per cent in public services [Millward *et al.* (1992), p. 251].

The prominence of establishment bargaining over aspects of working time in private sector manufacturing is consistent with a further development in collective bargaining arrangements: the decentralisation of bargaining activity. This includes the shift away, in some sectors at least, from industry-level, multi-employer bargaining towards single employer bargaining [Marginson *et al.* (1988); Purcell (1991); Sisson (1987)]. Further, as Purcell (1991) observes, in a number of larger companies – including major concerns in the engineering sector such as Lucas and Perkins Engines – there has been a move to decentralise collective bargaining arrangements further, away from corporate level down to operating divisions and establishments. In case studies of this decentralisation, such as undertaken in the steel industry [Blyton (1992*b*)], it is clear that such decentralisation can have important consequences for the conduct of the bargaining process, not least the extent to which management is able to focus the bargaining agenda more directly onto the specific issues of plant performance and labour productivity.

The most significant decentralisation of bargaining activity in the United Kingdom in recent years has been the withdrawal from national bargaining by the engineering industry's employers' representatives in 1989, during a protracted dispute with the Confederation of Shipbuilding and Engineering Unions (CSEU) over a shorter working week. Following unsuccessful negotiations over shorter hours, after which the unions embarked on a campaign of selective strike action at targeted plants, the Engineering Employers' Federation (EEF) abandoned its national bargaining role. Though many larger firms were not members of the Federation and had developed independent bargaining machinery at corporate and/or local levels, nevertheless the EEF's withdrawal from national bargaining signalled a further significant decentralisation of bargaining activity (and, as noted above, at the same time appears to have brought about an overall reduction of collective bargaining coverage in the industry).

The ending of the EEF's bargaining role changed the nature of working time agreements in metal manufacturing. Prior to 1989, a typical pattern was for basic weekly hours to be negotiated centrally (either by the EEF and CSEU or at corporate level in those companies who were not members of the Federation), while operational issues such as shift patterns were subject to local agreement. In the late 1970s, for example, the widespread strike action over reducing the 40 hour working week in engineering led to an industry-wide settlement between the employers' association and the union confederation to implement a basic working week of 39 hours by 1981. Similarly, from the mid-1980s onwards, discussions over a shorter working week were led by a sub-committee formed from the employers' association and the national unions.

At the same time, even in the past, local bargaining played an important role in the determination of actual working time practices, such as the extent and pattern of shift-working, the distribution of overtime and short-time working, and the determination of breaks. The difference since 1989, however, is that the industry association has ended its role of negotiating with the unions over basic working hours. Thus, since that time, negotiation over the basic working week has shifted further to corporate and plant levels (or in the case of an increased number of smaller companies, has been replaced by management decision).

Among many larger employers, such as the major vehicle producers, it remains the general practice for working hours to be negotiated centrally at corporate level (usually as part of wider negotiations over pay and conditions, rather than as a separate agreement over hours), supplemented by local agreements on operational issues such as shift patterns. At Vauxhall Motors, for example, the current working week (39 hours) is based on a company agreement reached in 1981. Local agreements, however, detail specific arrangements over shift patterns. At Vauxhall's Luton plant, the four main shift patterns (double day, day, day and night and a three shift system for maintenance crews) are detailed in a local plant agreement. Changes in the shift pattern are subject to local negotiation; for example, the Luton agreement states that if the double dayshift or three shift system is no longer to operate "this will be subject to 10 days notice for purpose of negotiation and an additional 90 days notice of change".

Overall, the pattern of negotiations over the duration and organisation of working time in the metal manufacturing sector is both varied and changing. National surveys indicate a comparatively high degree of collective bargaining over the organisation of working time as a whole, with a significant amount of establishment level bargaining. The collapse of industry-wide bargaining since 1989 has further encouraged a decentralisation of bargaining at larger unionised establishments. At the same time, the withdrawal of national-level bargaining machinery covering hours and other basic terms and conditions appears to have resulted in a growth in the number of establishments where those terms and conditions are now subject to managerial decision rather than joint regulation.

D. DEVELOPMENTS IN THE FLEXIBILITY AND UTILISATION OF WORKING TIME

Agreements linked to the reduction of the working week

Following the campaign of industrial action over a shorter working week in 1989-90 (for more details see Blyton, 1992a), a significant proportion of firms in the metal goods sector reached agreements on the introduction of a 37 hour week. By early 1992, the engineering unions announced that 37 hour agreements had been reached covering 600 000 workers. Among the companies agreeing reductions were key employers in the industry such as British Aerospace and Rolls-Royce. Throughout the negotiations, the union side, particularly the representatives from the largest union, the Amalgamated Engineering Union (AEU), indicated a preparedness to accept changes in working practices and working time arrangements to offset the cost of the hours reduction. In practice, many of the agreements reached tie the hours reduction to the acceptance of a variety of other changes. However, rather than securing agreement to introduce greater variability in working hours, as had been put forward by the EEF during earlier industry negotiations (for example, in the proposal for a 1½ hour variation around the agreed standard working week, to take account of fluctuations in demand), the main management priority in regard to working time proved to be a reduction in non-productive work time. In a survey of a hundred establishments by Richardson and Rubin (1992), increases in the utilisation of working time (for example through "bell to bell" working, cuts in or elimination of breaks, and reductions in time allowances for washing) were identified in 78 per cent of agreements – by far the most common area of union concession. Any linkage of the cut in hours to changes in the arrangement of working time was less prominent: Richardson and Rubin found hours cuts linked to new shift patterns in just over one-quarter (26 per cent) of cases. Earlier analyses of agreements also indicate smaller proportions of companies tying the hours cut to other changes in the arrangement of work time, such as the staggering of meal breaks to ensure continuity of production [Industrial Relations Review and Report (1990)].

A more radical change in the arrangement of working time, however, has taken place at Rover, the British car manufacturer. In exchange for a reduction in basic weekly hours from 39 to 37 at all its plants, Rover negotiated a series of working time changes at its Longbridge plant, most notably the introduction of 24-hour, seven-day working in its engine and transmission assembly, based on a five crew system: the first car producer in the United Kingdom to move to round-the-clock production. According to Rover management, the change was intended to meet the demand for a new series of engines by increasing plant utilisation rather than investing in new equipment [Industrial Relations Services (1990)].

This change in working time in exchange for a cut in weekly hours was negotiated with the Longbridge works committee representing the six unions at the plant. Following employee resistance to the company's original plan for 12 hour shift working, a five-crew, seven-day working pattern was devised, consisting of a combination of three-shift working Monday to Friday, together with a 2 × 12 hour, two-crew weekend cycle. For the 1 050 production employees on the five-crew, seven-day pattern, each crew works 18 shifts over a five-week cycle, including one weekend of two twelve-hour day shifts and one weekend of two twelve-hour night shifts (see Chart 4.1). In the course of the cycle, each crew receives 17 days off and works a weekly average over the five-week period of 31.5 hours (though individual weekly hours vary between 24 and 40).

Despite receiving the support of both national union officials and the Longbridge works committee, the engine plant shift system, together with a less radical change in shift patterns in the body and vehicle assembly areas, was initially rejected in a workforce

Chart 4.1. **Shift pattern at Rover Longbridge**

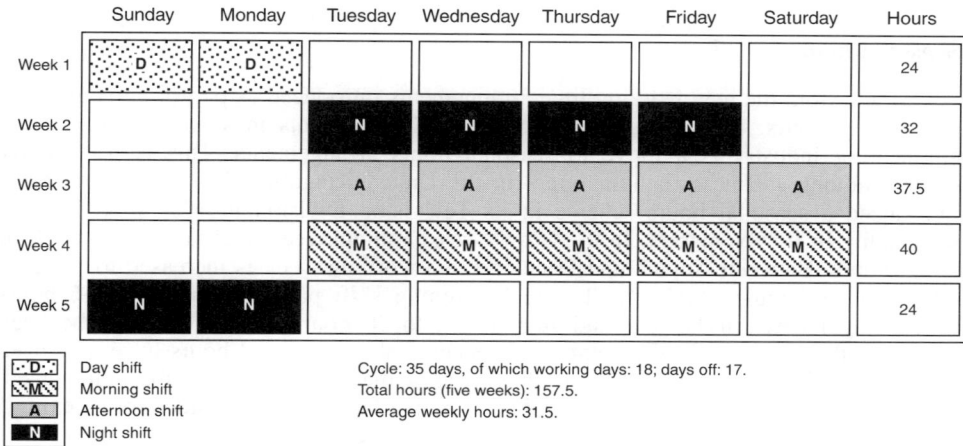

	Sunday	Monday	Tuesday	Wednesday	Thursday	Friday	Saturday	Hours
Week 1	D	D						24
Week 2			N	N	N	N		32
Week 3			A	A	A	A	A	37.5
Week 4			M	M	M	M	M	40
Week 5	N	N						24

D	Day shift
M	Morning shift
A	Afternoon shift
N	Night shift

Cycle: 35 days, of which working days: 18; days off: 17.
Total hours (five weeks): 157.5.
Average weekly hours: 31.5.

Source: IRS (1990).

ballot at the plant in May 1990, possibly reflecting concern over perceived losses in overtime payments, and some resistance to the long weekend shifts. Following more extensive discussion, however (though with no change in the terms of the proposed shift system) a second workplace ballot gained a majority of 21 in favour of the changes [Industrial Relations Services (1990)].

The new shift pattern has extended machine operating times in the power train engine and transmission plant. In the company generally, Rover management has looked to changes such as line speed-ups to offset the cost of reduction in the working week. Earnings for those on the five-crew, seven-day system have remained broadly in line with previous earnings, weekend working being compensated by fewer hours overall and longer blocks of free time.

Both before and after the working hours agreement, Rover management has also been involved in a much wider set of negotiations with trade unions, introducing teamworking and other forms of flexible labour utilisation, and culminating in its so-called "New Deal" agreement which took effect in April 1992, covering such issues as the introduction of single status conditions, the phasing out of "clocking" at the start and end of shifts, a greater emphasis on teamworking, full task flexibility and greater job security [Industrial Relations Services (1992)]. Hence the working time changes may be seen as part of a much broader pattern of work reform in the company. The generally

91

slack vehicle market, however, meant that by 1993 other vehicle producers had not followed Rover's precedent of introducing round-the-clock production. Manufacturers such as Vauxhall continue to assemble mainly using double day shifts, utilising the intervening period for line maintenance.

Seasonal hours

Aside from the new working time arrangements introduced as part of agreements to cut weekly hours, one of the most significant developments in some sections of the engineering industry is a move to seasonal hours arrangements. This is particularly evident among Japanese manufacturers in the United Kingdom. Toshiba, for example introduced a seasonal hours scheme in its Television Division in 1989 to reflect the seasonality in its TV market. In the "low" season, employees work a 4.5 day week of 37.25 hours. Between August and December the working week is increased to a 5 day, 42.5 hours schedule. Similarly, Toshiba's evening shift pattern operates on 16 hours (4 evenings) between January and July, rising to 20 hours over 5 evenings between August and December. In the company's machine shop, seasonal hours have also been agreed regarding the rotating shifts, though as a manager from Toshiba commented, because the shifts follow each other without any overlap, the opportunities for "flexing" upwards or downwards from the standard 39 hours are far more limited.

A similar seasonal hours pattern has been introduced at the Hitachi company in South Wales. Again the scheme was devised to take account of the seasonality of demand for televisions and the company's desire to be less reliant on additional temporary labour and overtime working during its busiest period. Management initially raised its preference for moving to a seasonal hours pattern at the Company Members Board (where representatives are drawn from all segments of the workforce). Having agreed to the scheme in principle, the Board jointly worked out the details of the scheme, which were then discussed by the management with the single union recognised at the plant, the Electrical, Electronic, Telecommunication and Plumbing Union (EETPU). The union agreed to the move to seasonal hours primarily on the grounds that it would help to avoid short-time working and redundancies during the slackest periods.

Employees at Hitachi are paid for 39 hours throughout the year, though actual weekly hours are 42 in the busiest months of August to November, and 37 hours at other times. Some of the cost savings attaching to the scheme are readily identifiable. For example, in the period of extended production during the latter half of 1992, management engaged an additional 50 workers on temporary contracts rather than the customary 200; in addition, less weekend overtime is being worked. Thus, with the seasonal hours pattern, reliance on meeting demand by a mixture of numerical flexibility (temporary workers) and temporal flexibility (seasonal hours and overtime) remains, though the seasonal hours pattern has reduced management's reliance on both overtime and temporary workers. Further, indications to date suggest that possible problems such as higher absenteeism during the longer work-weeks have so far not materialised.

The operation of the seasonal hours scheme at Hitachi is simplified by defining the "pay-back" of longer work-weeks for earlier, shorter ones as a collective rather than an individual pay-back. Hence, whether or not an individual has been absent or has taken his/her holidays in a shorter or longer week has no bearing on their working hours schedule. The system operates simply as a working week of 42 or 37 hours with payment standardised at 39 hours.

It is noteworthy that there was a degree of negative reaction to the seasonal hours scheme among some of the work-force at Hitachi, partly reflecting some resistance to the longer hours worked at basic rates. It is a contractual condition at Hitachi (and is typical elsewhere in U.K. manufacturing) that employees are "available for a reasonable amount of overtime working". In practice at Hitachi, this typically translates into an additional two hours working twice a week, plus periodic Saturday morning working. Normally, these overtime periods attract premium rates (time and a third for the two-hour periods on weekdays, and time and a half for Saturday working). Under the seasonal hours scheme, however, overtime rates at busy times of the year only apply after the 42 "normal" hours have been worked.

Further, since half the work-force is female, problems may arise in relation to fitting the longer hours schedule into patterns of non-work commitments. In addition, the move to seasonal hours has been conceded by employees without gaining any reduction in the basic working week. With only one or two exceptions (such as the construction vehicle manufacturer Komatsu), Japanese companies in the engineering sector continue to work a 39-hour week; this is only likely to change once the bigger Japanese employers (Nissan, Sony, Toyota, Honda) concede a shorter working week.

Other aspects of employee relations introduced into the United Kingdom by Japanese manufacturing companies have influenced changes elsewhere: for example, the development of team-working, total quality management, and single union agreements. It may be anticipated that the seasonal hours patterns recently introduced in a number of Japanese companies will also be seriously considered elsewhere in contexts where demand fluctuates on a regular seasonal pattern. Thus, while fully developed "annual hours" systems remain restricted to a small proportion of companies and sectors (estimates suggest that around 3 per cent of companies in the United Kingdom operated some form of annualised hours system by the late 1980s), seasonal hours potentially represent an intermediate position between standard hours schedules and annualised arrangements. As in annual hours, which have developed principally in process industries such as paper, chemicals, glass and cement manufacture, a primary objective behind the development of seasonal hours is the desire to reduce overtime costs and reliance on temporary labour during the busiest periods.

In addition to its seasonal hours system, Hitachi's working time arrangements demonstrate a number of other features geared to the efficient utilisation of the shift period and the maintenance of operating times. Judging from the management literature and the nature of agreements signed over shorter hours, these features appear to be becoming increasingly common in the engineering sector as a whole. For example, a system of bell-to-bell working operates at Hitachi, whereby employees are required to be at their work area by the time the bell rings to signal the start of the shift. Morning breaks (13 minutes) and lunch breaks (30 minutes) are taken at one of three staggered times to ensure continuity of production. Only the afternoon break (10 minutes) is taken at a common time by all staff. In addition to the contractual requirement to work "a reasonable amount" of overtime, the Company Members Handbook at Hitachi also states that employees "may be required to work on a night shift, double dayshift or three shift system", though the Handbook also states that any shift-working "will be fully discussed and agreed before implementation".

This contractual requirement with regard to overtime and shift-working appears fairly typical of manufacturing in the United Kingdom, although in practice, as in the Hitachi case, it would seem to be a common procedure (in unionised establishments at least) for management to consult over, if not jointly regulate, the practices of overtime and shift-working. According to the most recent Workplace Industrial Relations Survey, 28 per cent of establishments in the vehicles and mechanical and electrical engineering industries operated some kind of shift system in 1990. This was lower than in the manufacturing sector as a whole (42 per cent) and in the overall sample of manufacturing and service establishments combined (37 per cent). This overall proportion of establishments utilising some form of shift system, however, appears to have altered little during the 1980s: 37 per cent of establishments were also found to use shiftwork in the two earlier surveys in 1980 and 1984 [Millward et al. (1992)].

The retention of long working hours

It was noted above how, in some cases, innovations in working hours may be directly attributable to a managerial objective of reducing the extent of overtime working. It was also shown, however, that the flexibility afforded by overtime working has in other cases acted as a brake on the search for alternative sources of temporal flexibility. The general pattern characterising the United Kingdom, of a relatively high amount of overtime, coupled with a significant degree of employee dependence on overtime earnings, is also reflected in the metal manufacturing sector. The annual Labour Force Survey and New Earnings Survey collect information (respectively) on usual hours worked and overtime hours and payments. Table 4.1 shows the spread of normal weekly work hours in the seven main categories within the metal goods/engineering sector.

One of the most striking features of Table 4.1 is the high proportion of workers usually working more than 48 hours per week: in the mechanical engineering industry, for example, more than one in five workers usually has a working week of over 48 hours, while approaching two in five usually have a working week of 45 hours or over. With the 37 or 39 hours as the basic working week in the metal goods/engineering sector, these high actual work weeks reflect a considerable degree of overtime working. As Table 4.2 shows, most of this overtime is undertaken by male manual workers.

Overtime is particularly high in certain industries within the metal manufacturing sector. For male manual workers, for example, average weekly overtime levels in 1992 were particularly high in small tools manufacture (10.4 hours average), machine tools (8.4 hours), fabricated constructional steelwork (8.0 hours), non-ferrous metal foundries (7.7 hours) and mechanical lifting equipment (7.5 hours).

The 1992 New Earnings survey also indicates that in the metal goods, engineering and vehicles sector in April 1992, 55.7 per cent of the full-time manual male workforce received some overtime pay, compared to 27.4 per cent of the non-manual male workforce, 31.9 per cent of the full-time female manual workforce and 20.1 per cent of the non-manual female workforce.

Table 4.1. **Employees' total usual weekly hours in engineering, 1991**

Percentages

	0-16	16-30	31-35	36-40	41-44	45-48	49-59	60+	Average total usual weekly hours
Metal goods	–	4.9	3.7	41.5	16.2	12.8	16.8	–	42.0
Mechanical engineering	2.0	4.3	3.2	37.0	16.3	16.1	17.1	4.1	42.5
Office machinery	–	–	–	35.1	18.2	19.8	13.0	6.0	43.0
Electrical and electronic engineering	1.8	4.9	4.8	41.7	17.1	13.4	12.0	4.3	41.7
Vehicles	–	2.9	–	47.9	17.5	12.1	13.3	3.3	42.1
Other transport equipment	–	–	–	36.1	22.9	17.9	14.1	4.0	43.1
Instrument engineering	–	10.5	–	37.3	13.2	16.4	12.0	–	39.4
All Industries	10.2	13.1	6.8	31.7	12.4	10.3	10.8	4.7	37.4

– Sample size too small to provide a reliable estimate.
Source: 1991 LFS Estimates, quoted by Watson (1992).

95

Table 4.2. **Hours of work of full-time workers in engineering, 1992**

Average weekly hours

	Normal basic	Overtime	Total
Manual males	38.4	5.4	43.7
Non-manual males	37.7	2.0	39.7
Manual females	38.2	2.1	40.3
Non-manual females	37.2	0.7	38.0

Source: *New Earnings Survey* (1992), London: HMSO.

In terms of payment for overtime, there is some variation across the metal industry as a whole regarding the different premium rates. In general, however, overtime worked during the Monday-Saturday period is paid for at time and a quarter, time and a third or time and a half, while Sunday working is typically paid at double time. To give two company examples, the Hotpoint washing machine manufacturer pays overtime at time and a third Monday to Friday, time and a half on Saturday and double time on Sunday. Overtime before or after dayshift working is paid at time and a third, while before or after night shift working it is paid at time and a half [Incomes Data Services (1991), p. 13]. At Otis Elevators, on the other hand, the first two hours of overtime Monday to Saturday are paid at time and a third, rising to time and a half thereafter. Sundays are paid at double time.

In the vehicles sector, it has been the norm for overtime working during Monday to Friday to be paid at time and a third for the first two hours, and at time and a half subsequently. In its 1993 agreement, however, Nissan enhanced this and the first two hours are now paid at time and a half. Assembly-line workers at Nissan currently average around 100 hours overtime a year [Incomes Data Services (1993), p. 28].

E. CONCLUSIONS

Overall, the moves to inject greater variability into working time arrangements in the metal manufacturing sector in the United Kingdom remain comparatively modest. In the recent period this may be accounted for partly by reference to such factors as the continued reliance on securing flexibility via overtime, short-time working, temporary lay-offs, etc.; and the greater emphasis on increasing task flexibility. If anything, the emphasis in working time in recent years has been placed on increasing the utilisation of existing working hours by measures such as bell-to-bell working and the reduction of informal breaks.

Within this general context, however, a number of developments are evident which are designed to make the working period more responsive to production requirements. The replacement of fixed meal breaks by staggered rotas, for example, is designed to ensure continuity of operations. More far-reaching have been the developments in shift patterns to incorporate weekend working, and the introduction of seasonal hours patterns. The Rover case is an example of changing work patterns in the context of an agreed reduction in the working week. The main objective behind the new working pattern was to increase the utilisation of equipment. The main motivation behind seasonal hours arrangements was found to be meeting fluctuating patterns of demand without resorting to high levels of additional labour (through overtime working and temporary employees) at the busiest times. In the Hitachi case, this objective had been achieved to a considerable degree, though not without some employee criticism.

Except from the seasonal hours innovations, however, fluctuations in work pressures are accommodated primarily by overtime working. While clearly the persistently high average levels of overtime indicate that a large proportion is worked on a regular basis (rather than to cover short-term, extraordinary circumstances), the widespread use of overtime and the willingness of many employees to work additional hours to increase their overall earnings, indicate that overtime is a widely available option for many managers to accommodate short-term peaks in demand.

As to the degree of joint regulation of working time, both in terms of its duration and arrangement, several points may be made. On the one hand, in unionised organisations the degree of joint regulation appears high, both within the metal industry and the unionised sector generally. The typical pattern in vehicle production, for example, is for employers and unions to negotiate at corporate level over duration, leaving local negotiations to establish particular work patterns, and procedures for negotiating changes in those patterns. Indeed, a widespread picture in establishments with union recognition is one of joint regulation of operational issues such as shift patterns. In the case of the shift changes at Rover, for example, negotiations were held at local level and the proposed scheme put to a work-force ballot.

Yet, at the same time, the limits to joint regulation of working time must also be recognised. First, recent national surveys indicate a significant reduction during the 1980s in the proportion of establishments where unions are recognised for collective bargaining. In metal manufacturing this decline has been exacerbated by the termination of national bargaining arrangements. It is apparent from the fall in union recognition that many smaller employers have replaced the national bargaining framework with managerial control at local level rather than local joint regulation. Hence, much of the foregoing discussion of joint regulation is more pertinent to the larger establishments with recognised unions.

Moreover, even in establishments where unions are recognised, it remains the case that economic and political factors have weakened union power compared to the 1970s. Hence, while the machinery of joint regulation may remain in place, this is not necessarily a true indication that in the actual processes taking place, trade unions are able to wrest major concessions from management or exercise an effective veto on changes which they disagree with.

Second, for many manufacturing employees, overtime and shift-working are contractual obligations rather than the subjects of individual discretion. Hence, while the specific patterns and arrangements may be subject to consultation and joint regulation, for

97

many individual employees the choice of whether or not to participate in, for example, overtime working, is not available.

Third, the limited nature of employee discretion is also indicated by the lack of development of flexible working hours ("flexitime") systems in the manufacturing sector. Overall, it appears far more common for flexitime arrangements to apply to employees in public and private sector services than in manufacturing (though precise data on the extent of flexitime arrangements in the United Kingdom are not available). Where such schemes have been introduced in manufacturing, they have typically been confined to certain grades of office staff.

Despite the modest level of recent developments in working time flexibility in the metal industry, there are several factors which may result in this issue gaining greater significance in the coming period. First, as employers progressively secure changes in working practices, job boundaries, etc., they are likely to increasingly turn to other potential sources of flexibility to secure productivity improvements. In this context, temporal flexibility may prove increasingly attractive to achieve a better matching of existing staff to changing production and demand conditions, and a means of avoiding over-reliance on temporary working or excessive overtime at particular periods. Pressures to increase capital utilisation are also likely to give rise to new shiftwork systems. In the continuous process sector (*e.g.* chemicals, paper manufacture), there is already evidence of significant compression of the working week taking place, particularly in the form of twelve-hour shifts. Such compression is currently rare in the metal manufacturing sector. However less extreme forms of compression, such as working weeks comprising 4×9 hour shifts, are likely to become an increasingly common feature of working time patterns, particularly if further reductions in the working week are secured by the engineering unions in coming years.

Second, competitive pressures and other factors (not least the European Community's working time Directive) may force more managers to rethink their overtime practices in coming years. This is already occurring in certain sectors and has been an important factor behind the adoption of annual hours systems in some companies [see, for example, Blyton (forthcoming)]. Any sustained move away from the present high reliance on overtime working is likely to occasion a more intensified search for other sources of working time flexibility.

Related to this is a third potential stimulus to change, which is the evidence of an increasing use of formalised seasonal hours arrangements in a number of Japanese companies in the United Kingdom. Given the past tendency for many British managers to imitate personnel practices operated by Japanese inward investors, it might be anticipated that similar consideration will be given to innovations in working time patterns in Japanese companies.

Finally, possible future developments in the labour market (particularly a marked reduction in unemployment) could occasion accelerated change in employers' working time policies. Prior to the growth in unemployment from the end of the 1980s, and in the context of demographic changes reducing the number of young people entering the labour market, there were signs that more firms were introducing new working time patterns in order to attract more women into employment. Thus, the mid- and late 1980s saw increased discussion of arrangements such as career-break schemes and various part-time schedules. This mirrors an earlier period in the 1970s when tight labour market conditions resulted in the introduction of many flexitime arrangements as employers sought to hold on to existing staff and attract new recruits [Blyton (1985)]. In the current labour market conditions of high unemployment and low job security, however, the picture is typically more one of employers seeking greater flexibility for production and cost reasons, rather than to improve the convenience of working time arrangements for employees or the degree of temporal flexibility available to them.

Notes

1. In the United Kingdom, the category of "metal manufacturing" is a less commonly used term than that of "engineering", which embraces the metal goods, engineering and vehicles sector and includes industries such as mechanical and electrical engineering, office machinery, motor vehicles and parts, other transport equipment and metal goods not otherwise specified. In September 1991, there were 2.1 million wage and salary earners in these industries out of a total of around 23 million civilian employees.

Bibliography

BLYTON, P. (1985), *Changes in Working Time: An International Review*, London: Croom Helm.

BLYTON, P. (1992*a*), "Learning from each other: The shorter working week campaigns in Germany and Britain", *Economic and Industrial Democracy*, Vol. 13, No. 3, pp. 417-30.

BLYTON, P. (1992*b*), "Steel: A classic case of industrial relations change in Britain", *Journal of Management Studies*, Vol. 29, No. 5, pp. 635-50.

BLYTON, P. (1994), "Working Hours" in Sisson, K. (ed.) *Personnel Management*, Second Edition, Oxford: Blackwell, pp. 495-526.

HEPPLE, B. (1988), "United Kingdom", in *Legal and Contractual Limitations to Working Time in the European Community Member States*, Blanpain, R. and Köhler, E. (eds.) Deventer: Kluwer.

HORRELL, S. and RUBERY, J. (1991), *Employers' Working Time Policies and Women's Employment*, London, HMSO.

INCOMES DATA SERVICES (1991), *Overtime*, IDS Study No. 496, London: Incomes Data Services.

INCOMES DATA SERVICES (1993), Report No. 634, London: Incomes Data Services.

INDUSTRIAL RELATIONS REVIEW AND REPORT (1990), Report Nos. 461, 464, 466, London: Industrial Relations Services.

INDUSTRIAL RELATIONS SERVICES (IRS) (1990), "Working time arrangements in the European motor industry", IRS Employment Trends No. 471, *Industrial Relations Review and Report*, London, September.

INDUSTRIAL RELATIONS SERVICES (IRS) (1992), "Lean production and Rover's 'New Deal'", IRS Employment Trends No. 514, *Industrial Relations Review and Report*, London, June.

MARGINSON, P., EDWARDS, P.K., MARTIN, R., PURCELL, J. and SISSON, K. (1988), *Beyond the Workplace*, Oxford: Blackwell.

MARSDEN, D., and THOMPSON, M. (1990), "Flexibility agreements and their significance in the increase in productivity in British manufacturing since 1980", *Work, Employment and Society*, Vol. 4, No. 1, pp. 83-104.

MILLWARD, N., STEVENS, M., SMART, D. and HAWES, W.R. (1992), *Workplace Industrial Relations in Transition*, Aldershot: Dartmouth.

PURCELL, J. (1991), "The rediscovery of the management prerogative: The management of labour relations in the 1980s", *Oxford Review of Economic Policy*, Vol. 7, No. 1, pp. 33-43.

RICHARDSON, R., and RUBIN, M. (1992), *The Shorter Working Week in Engineering: Surrender Without Sacrifice?*, Working paper No. 270, Centre for Economic Performance, London School of Economics.

SISSON, K. (1987), *The Management of Collective Bargaining*, Oxford: Blackwell.

WATSON, G. (1992), ''Hours of work in Great Britain and Europe'', *Employment Gazette*, November, pp. 539-557.

Chapter 5

CANADA: THE CASE OF RETAIL TRADE

by

Diane Bellemare, Marie-France Molinari and Lise Poulin-Simon

A.   INTRODUCTION

Modern businesses are increasingly confronted with the globalisation of markets and their survival is more than ever dependent on their ability to respond to contingencies. As one solution to this, Canadian firms are seeking greater flexibility which would allow them to change and adjust their strategies to various market requirements. This is the background against which we shall be examining flexible working time arrangements in the Canadian retail trade, to begin with, from the standpoint of hiring policies and terms and conditions for new employees, worktime planning systems, the programming of leave (*e.g.* parental leave), etc. We shall then be looking at how these practices are determined, *i.e.* whether the employees themselves have any say in this. However, this picture would not be complete if it were confined solely to the internal factors at work within a particular firm, which is why the chapter will also be considering such outside aspects as the economic and legal context, and structural factors such as the composition of subsectors, their growth and their strengths and weaknesses.

B.   THE RETAIL TRADE IN CANADA

The retail sector follows the trend for the economy as a whole. The figures in Table 5.1 show an increase in employment and sales since 1981. However, as a percentage of GDP retail sales have remained relatively stable with the exception of the years 1990-1992 when there was a decline in turnover due to the recession. The sector's activities include retail sales of goods in stores and the provision of related services such as installing and servicing equipment purchased.

A breakdown of the industry into subsectors – automotive, food, hardware and furnishings, clothing and accessories, other durable and semi-durable goods, pharmaceuticals and cosmetics, and other outlets – shows that the automotive sector

Table 5.1. **The retail trade in Canada: employment and sales, 1981-92**

	Employment (thousands)	Sales	
		Billion C$ [a]	Percentage of GDP
1981	1 388	103.4	29.1
1982	1 363	107.1	28.6
1983	1 367	116.6	28.7
1984	1 431	127.4	28.6
1985	1 476	142.2	29.8
1986	1 507	153.8	30.4
1987	1 552	168.9	30.6
1988	1 602	181.7	30.0
1989	1 623	189.3	29.1
1990	1 659	192.6	28.8
1991	1 607	181.2	26.9
1992	1 603	185.0	26.9

a) Estimates for retail sales do not include the Goods and Services Tax (GST). The figures for sales prior to January 1991 include the Federal Sales Tax (FST) and are thus overstated by about 4 per cent.
Source: Statistique Canada (1991), (1993a).

posted the highest volume of sales, followed by the food trade. In 1992 these two industries together accounted for no less than 60.2 per cent of Canada's total retail sales (Table 5.2).

In terms of the size of stores, most of these are small (90 per cent of retailers had a turnover of less than C$2 million) although the largest stores account for the bulk of sales. In the food sector, for example, according to the latest statistics, sales by supermar-

Table 5.2. **The retail trade in Canada: sales by subsector, 1992**

	Billion C$	Percentage
Automotive	62 957	34.0
Food	48 557	26.2
Hardware and furnishings	9 833	5.3
Clothing and accessories	10 748	5.8
Other durable and semi-durable goods	32 211	17.4
Pharmaceuticals and cosmetics	10 722	5.8
Other types of outlet	10 022	5.4
Total	185 050	100.0

Source: Statistics Canada (1993a).

kets and grocery stores accounted for 91.5 per cent of total retail sales in the food industry, compared with only 8.5 per cent for other food stores (bakeries, fruit stores, butchers, specialised stores, etc.) [Statistics Canada (1989)].

A geographical breakdown (by province) of retail sales in Canada shows that Ontario accounts for the lion's share of these (38 per cent), followed by Quebec (25 per cent); these two provinces, home to more than 60 per cent of the country's total population, account for over 60 per cent of retail sales [Bureau de la Statistique Quebec (1989)].

In order to satisfy the ever growing needs of consumers in terms of products and services, superstore chains (US-style hypermarkets) have been gaining ground. This trend is particularly marked in the food, home renovation and consumer electronics sectors [Allaire and Firsirotu (1990)]. Retailers are opening these large warehouse-type stores selling a wide range of products and offering substantial discounts as a means of boosting sales and expanding their market share [Government of Canada (1991)]. However, recent statistics indicate that independent retailers account for a far larger proportion of sales than chainstores, close to two-thirds [Statistics Canada (1992)].

C. EMPLOYMENT STANDARDS IN CANADIAN LEGISLATION

The retail trade is governed by both federal and provincial legislation on employment standards. Under the terms of the constitution both the Canadian parliament and the provincial legislatures can introduce labour legislation.

The provinces' powers in this respect stem from the provisions in the constitution concerning "property and civil rights" – *i.e.* the right to enter into contracts – and, given that labour legislation imposes certain restrictions on contracts between parties, the terms of such contracts are therefore a matter for the provincial authority. The right to pass laws governing "work and undertakings of a local nature" is also vested in the provincial authorities. The federal government has jurisdiction over national, international and interprovincial matters. There are relatively few firms that come within the jurisdiction of the federal authorities – no more than about 10 per cent of all Canadian businesses.

The government set minimum employment standards to prevent unfair competition between employers and ensure acceptable working conditions. This legislation, often based on the minimum terms and working conditions set out in collective agreements, has both economic and social repercussions. Minimum standards protect employees but can also restrict or enhance the employer's flexibility. It is therefore important to see which of these are likely to affect their flexibility as regards working time arrangements. The standards cover hours of work, overtime rates, days off, paid statutory holidays, paid vacation and parental leave.

Hours of work and overtime rates

Table 5.3 shows that standards differ widely across the country with regard to working hours and overtime. In some provinces the legislation is very flexible. Prince Edward Island and Nova Scotia set a normal workweek of 48 hours without, however,

Table 5.3. **Standards regarding working hours**

Jurisdiction	Normal hours per day/week	Maximum hours per day/week	Overtime rate
Federal	8/40	/48	NT 1/2
British Colombia	8/40		NT 1/2
Alberta	8/44	12/	NT 1/2
Saskatchewan	8/40	/44	NT 1/2
Manitoba	8/40 [a]		NT 1/2
Ontario	/44	8/48	NT 1/2
Quebec	/44 [b]		NT 1/2
New Brunswick	/44		MW 1/2
Nova Scotia	/48		MW 1/2
Prince Edward Island	/48		NT 1/2
Newfoundland	8/44 [c]	16/	MW 1/2
Northwest Territories	8/40	10/60	NT 1/2
Yukon	8/40		NT 1/2

NT 1/2: Normal time and a half.
MW 1/2: Minimum wage and a half.
a) Employees can refuse to work beyond these hours.
b) Under the terms of the Order on the food retail trade, the normal work week is 40 hours (Act respecting labour standards, L.Q., 1979, c. 45; after revision: L.R.Q., c. N-1.1).
c) The normal work week is 40 hours for store employees.
Source: Travail Canada (1991).

prescribing a maximum number of hours. Other provinces are more restrictive: for example, Saskatchewan sets a normal work period of 8 hours a day and 40 hours a week with a maximum of 44 hours a week.

Concerning retail trade, Quebec's legislation, the Act respecting labour standards, is more flexible than the Canadian Labour Code. Quebec sets a normal workweek of 40 hours, while the federal legislation prescribes eight hours a day and 40 hours a week, with a maximum of 48 hours for a normal work week. In Quebec, firms can exceed the 40 hours, provided they pay time-and-a-half for overtime.

Days off

Two types of legislation govern days off: legislation on labour standards limiting the number of working hours per week and legislation on Sunday work. The former is provincial (but also federal in certain cases) since it comes under property and civil rights, while the latter is federal, since it falls under criminal law. However, this federal law recognises provincial legislation allowing Sunday trading,[1] and this is why we shall be focusing in particular on labour standards legislation, that is to say legislation coming under the jurisdiction of the provinces.

Provincial legislation in Canada tends to recognise Sunday as a day of rest without, however, insisting on this, in view of the differing customs and religions. Generally, this legislation prescribes one full day off per week.

In Quebec, under the terms of Act 59 on hours of opening and days of admission to commercial establishments, stores are allowed to trade on Sunday only under certain conditions.[2] This is an issue we shall be discussing in more detail later given the current fierce debate on this subject.

Paid statutory holidays

The number of statutory holidays differs from one province to another. Alberta, British Columbia, Saskatchewan, the Northwest Territories, the Yukon Territory and the federal government itself accord the largest number of paid statutory holidays (nine days a year). Manitoba, Ontario and Quebec have eight; New Brunswick and Nova Scotia, six; and Prince Edward Island and Newfoundland, five.

As a general rule, in order to be entitled to pay for a statutory holiday, employees have to have been with their employer for a set period of time (usually 90 days), have worked the day before or after, and been available to work on the day itself. Employers are bound by law to give their employees the day off or to pay them at a higher rate if they are required to work.

Paid vacation

While all employed persons in Canada are entitled to paid vacation, the conditions, number of weeks and scale of pay vary. All employees after one full year's uninterrupted employment with the same employer are entitled to a minimum of two weeks' vacation paid at the rate of 4 per cent of their annual earnings or gross salary, except in Saskatchewan where the legislation provides for three weeks of paid vacation. Vacation entitlement can be longer depending on the number of years of uninterrupted service. For example, after six years of continuous employment (under federal legislation)[3] or ten years (under Quebec law)[4] employees are entitled to three weeks of vacation paid at the rate of 6 per cent of earnings.

Parental leave

Canadian legislation contains special provisions for parental leave, which is classified as either maternity leave or parental leave. The former entitles women to take time off work to have a child; the latter allows either parent to take time off work temporarily to look after a newborn baby or adopted child.

In the case of maternity leave, the Canadian Labour Code allows women to take 17 weeks unpaid leave to have a child and guarantees their jobs when they return, provided they have been working for their employer for at least six months. Some provinces and territories are more generous, allowing 20 weeks of maternity leave

(Northwest Territories) or 18 weeks (Alberta, British Columbia, Quebec, Saskatchewan). In British Columbia, New Brunswick and Quebec, women are entitled to maternity leave whatever their length of service with an employer.

In the case of parental leave, the Canadian Labour Code provides for 24 weeks of unpaid leave to look after a newborn baby or adopted child, over and above the 17 weeks of maternity leave; Quebec law allows 34 weeks' parental leave that can be split between the parents; Ontario allows 18 weeks, provided that the parent has been working for the employer for at least 13 weeks; in Manitoba, parents are entitled to 17 weeks of parental leave but, in this case, they must have been working for the same employer for at least 12 months.

D. SHOP OPENING HOURS

Legislation on Sunday closing is a product of the Judeo-Christian tradition. Canada's first Lord's Day Act was passed in 1907. Until recently, working on Sunday was prohibited altogether, with the exception of a few so-called "essential services".

Social pressure from retailers and consumer groups, however, gradually forced governments to liberalise opening hours and grant more and more exemptions (*e.g.* during the weeks leading up to Christmas and for certain types of stores such as drugstores, convenience stores, etc.). Then as now, retailers were primarily concerned with preventing unfair competition and increasing turnover by means of longer opening hours. To take Quebec as an example, prior to 1969 the municipal authorities were responsible for regulating opening hours. In 1969, due to the unfair competition that was being created by allowing each municipality to set its own rules, the provincial government of Quebec introduced Act 89 which transferred these powers to the provincial level.

However, several amendments to Act 89 in 1977, 1984 and 1990 allowed exemptions in the case of Quebec's tourist areas and border zones. Despite the fact that Sunday trading is now regulated by the province, Quebec's retailers are still unhappy. They claim that there is still unfair competition. For one thing, some types of outlet are exempted from the restrictions on Sunday trading imposed by the Act respecting hours and days of admission to commercial establishments: for example, furniture can be bought from second-hand or antique dealers outside the hours set by law, but not from dealers selling new furniture. Secondly, there have been several cases of stores opening on Sundays in defiance of the law, thereby creating unfair competition and giving retailers cause for complaint.

It is the medium sized and large stores that are lobbying for a relaxation of the law, because of what they see as the substantial financial advantages this offers, particularly in the case of food outlets. Their main argument is that they have to be able to satisfy the consumer's need for more flexible shopping hours, a need that has been accentuated by the substantial increase in the numbers of working women and single-parent families [Dutrisac (1989)].

Smaller retailers, however, are opposed to more liberal opening hours. This is understandable in view of the fact that they have fewer resources and less margin for manœuvre (in terms of their costs, number of employees and training) and would be

108

unable to compete on an equal footing in the event of extended opening hours. They feel that permitted opening hours (70 a week) are sufficient for consumers to do their shopping;[5] they cite the additional costs that would be generated by any extension of hours and which would have to be included in the price of the goods. They also maintain that longer opening hours are not socially acceptable and would adversely affect the family life of both storeowners and their employees.

Small retailers also fear that their market share will be eroded as a result of more flexible opening hours and that it will be the supermarkets, superstores and chain stores which will be the ones to benefit. Many expect a higher degree of concentration within the retail sector in the event of further liberalisation. Medium-sized and large stores, particularly in the food sector, want flexible working hours because they hope to take over the market share that smaller retailers have acquired over the years (Table 5.4). Supermarket sales have declined since 1982. In Quebec's case, their share of food sales dropped from 69 per cent in 1978 to 61 per cent in 1989. What they are demanding, therefore, is fairer competition. A 1990 amendment to the Act respecting hours and days of admission to commercial establishments came to the aid of food retailers by allowing them to open on Sundays between 8.00 a.m. and 5.00 p.m., provided that no more than four employees are on duty in each store.[6]

International competition is also contributing to this process and customers are being lost to US competitors, with the loss in retail sales being estimated at an annual total of over C$250 million, representing about 2 per cent in 1990 of the total volume of purchases by Canadian consumers according to the Retail Council of Canada [Des Roberts (1991), (1992)]. In an effort to counter this trend, the governments of Quebec and Ontario have introduced a law allowing border-zone stores and tourist areas to adopt more flexible opening hours.[7] In Quebec, for instance, the government will authorise the municipal authorities concerned to decide on opening hours; however, the risk here is that this could mean a return to unfair competition between traders in different towns.

Table 5.4. **The retail food trade in Quebec: market share by type of outlet**

Percentages

	1978	1982	1986	1989
Supermarkets	69	69	65	61
Convenience stores	24	21	25	28
Other	7	9	10	11
Total	100	100	100	100

Source: Allaire and Firsirotu (1990).

For the last 10 years or so, municipalities in most provinces have been allowed some flexibility with regard to Sunday opening [Labour Canada (1991)]. In Ontario, Act 113 of 1980 allowed municipalities in tourist areas to waive the regulations on Sunday opening. Alberta, British Columbia, Prince Edward Island, New Brunswick and Newfoundland have adopted similar legislation allowing municipal authorities to set opening hours.

Quebec passed a law in 1993 giving more freedom to stores as regards opening hours. All stores are now able to open on Sunday, but only between the hours of 8.00 a.m. and 5.00 p.m. There is no longer any distinction made between new and second-hand goods. Some protection will be provided for workers already on the payroll in that their employers will not be able to require them to work on Sundays. Quebec has thereby amended the Act respecting hours and days of admission to commercial establishments so as to bring its opening hours into line with those of its neighbours, the United States, Ontario and Manitoba.

It is obvious that these changes in the law are likely to alter substantially the structure of the retail sector. Some economists expect sales volume to jump by C$30 million and the number of employees by 8 000, of whom it is reckoned about 25 per cent will be part-timers. Others think that the resultant higher costs could be reflected in prices, thereby reducing sales.

E.   PART-TIME EMPLOYMENT

Part-time employment has been an issue for a number of years, since it has been gaining ground rapidly in some sectors at the expense of full time employment. The number of part-time jobs in the retail sector in Canada rose from 313 000 in 1976 to 491 000 in 1991. The percentage of part-time employees has also risen, from 26 per cent in 1976 to 30.5 per cent in 1991 [Statistics Canada (1991)]. Among the factors contributing to this trend have been the growing participation of women in the labour force, the series of recessions that has encouraged a shift from full-time to part-time employment and, no doubt, the somewhat more flexible opening hours.

A survey carried out in Quebec in 1987/88 by the Centre de recherche et de statistiques sur le marché du travail assessed the scale of the trend towards part-time employment in the retail trade and described its main characteristics. The survey was based on a sample of some 178 employers and 418 employees in the sectors of retailing and non-government services.[8]

According to this survey, employers hire part-timers for two main reasons: 1) "Part-time employees are essential on weekends and during especially busy or peak periods" and 2) "Part-time employees are needed to replace full-time employees who are sick or on vacation". Employers, therefore, consider that part-time staff give them the flexibility they need to adapt their workforce to the pattern of retail activity and to replace full-time staff.

The findings highlight the importance of part-time employment in the retail sector, given that in about one-quarter of the retail firms surveyed part-timers represented between 60 and 100 per cent of the total workforce; the average proportion of part-time employees, however, was 44.7 per cent. Retail stores with between 40 and 125 staff employed the most part-timers. In particular, checkout and sales assistant positions were more often than not filled by part-timers.

Two of the main problems with part-time work in Canada are, on the one hand, the lack of security in some of these jobs and, on the other, the terms and conditions of work as regards pay and social benefits, which are not prorated to the hours worked by full-time employees.

Relative stability

The survey revealed that 43.2 per cent of part-time positions in the sectors of retailing and non-government services are filled by regular employees working at least 15 hours a week; the smallest category was that of casual assistants (6.2 per cent). Regular part-time employees with indefinite contracts represented the largest category, about 73 per cent (Table 5.5).

Prorating

The survey indicated that the terms and conditions of work of part-timers are not necessarily prorated to those of full-time employees. This was particularly marked in cases not covered by the Act respecting labour standards. In 1991, Quebec amended this Act's provisions regarding prorating (Section 41.1), with the result that employees working in stores whose main activity is food retailing are no longer covered by these prorating requirements.[9] Employers in food retailing can therefore apply lower wage scales for part-timers than for other employees who perform the same tasks, which means they have more flexibility as regards pay-scales than employers in other sectors. Part-time employees covered by Section 41.1 of the Act have to be paid the same wage rates as full-time employees, provided that they do not earn more than twice the minimum wage.

Table 5.5. **Part-time employment by category**[a]

Category	Type of contract	Percentage
Regular, working at least 15 h/week	indefinite	43.2
Regular, working fewer than 15 h/week	indefinite	29.7
Seasonal, all categories	fixed term	11.7
Replacements, normal hours of work	fixed term	9.1
Casual	fixed term	6.2

a) Based on employers' replies to a survey in retailing and private services.
Source: Travail Québec (1991), p. 9.

However, in the case of all regular part-timers working at least 15 hours a week, 75 per cent of employers prorated seniority, base wage, raises, overtime rates, paid vacation, paid statutory holidays and paid breaks. Employers were less likely to apply prorating for regular part-timers working fewer than 15 hours a week.

The number of hours worked seems to have a positive effect as regards pay-scales: whereas over two-thirds of employees working fewer than 15 hours a week were paid less than C$7.00 an hour, only 43 per cent of those working 15 hours or more were paid less than C$7.00. Roughly 13 per cent of part-time employees working fewer than 15 hours a week earned C$9.00 an hour, while the figure ranged from 35 to 38 per cent for employees working 15 or more hours a week. The minimum wage at the time of the survey was C$4.55 an hour.

F.   FLEXIBILITY PRACTICES FROM EMPLOYER AND TRADE UNION PERSPECTIVES

Unionisation in the retail trade

Two concepts are used in measuring the scale of unionisation: the unionisation rate and the rate of union presence. The unionisation rate is the ratio of unionised employees to the total number of employees. The rate of union presence is the ratio of employees covered by a collective agreement to total employees.

Recent statistics show that the retail sector is poorly unionised throughout the country, although the situation varies from province to province. In 1991, 12.1 per cent of employees in the retail sector in Canada were unionised, compared with a figure of

Table 5.6.   **Unionisation rate by province for the retail and services sectors and for all sectors combined, 1991** [a]

	Retail trade	Services sector	All sectors combined
British Columbia	11.2	34.5	38.7
Alberta	13.6	28.5	26.4
Saskatchewan	11.8	35.6	32.9
Manitoba	12.4	37.9	37.1
Ontario	12.2	29.4	31.9
Quebec	13.8	39.4	40.6
New Brunswick	5.7	33.6	36.8
Nova Scotia	6.4	29.2	31.0
Prince Edward Island	0.2	38.9	33.2
Newfoundland	7.1	39.9	53.3
Canada	12.1	33.5	35.1

a)   Unionisation rate calculated on the basis of the number of paid workers.
Source: Statistics Canada (1993b) and unpublished data.

Table 5.7. **Union penetration in the retail trade in Quebec[a], 1986-92**

	Employees covered by a collective agreement	Total employees	Union penetration
1986	46 614	294 732	15.8
1988	51 225	327 055	15.7
1990	57 803	319 132	18.1
1991	57 686	300 387	19.2
1992	65 847	349 830	18.8

a) Proportion of employees covered by a collective agreement.
Source: Travail Québec, Le marché du travail, various years.

33.5 per cent for the service sector as a whole and 35.1 for all sectors combined. Quebec and Alberta had the highest unionisation rates for the retail sector with figures of 13.8 and 13.6 per cent respectively, while New Brunswick and Nova Scotia, among others, had particularly low rates (Table 5.6). Unionisation in the retail trade is therefore relatively low, partly owing to the small size of businesses in this sector, most of which are owner-operated.

In Quebec, the number of retail employees covered by a collective agreement has increased: between 1986 and 1992 the rate of union presence rose from 15.8 to 18.8 per cent (Table 5.7). Virtually two-thirds of unionised employees and those covered by a collective agreement were represented by the Quebec Federation of Labour (QFL), followed by the independent unions and the Confederation of National Trade Unions (CNTU).

The low level of retail employee unionisation in Canada and in Quebec would seem to indicate that store owners are on the whole operating from a position of strength whereby they are able to manage their businesses without much opposition from employees, particularly in terms of flexible management of their workforce.

Interviews of employer and union representatives

The authors considered that it would be pertinent to interview some retailers and a union president in order to identify the main flexible working time practices and the key reasons for these.

Interviewees were selected on the basis of their representativeness and proximity. The retailers interviewed were chosen from the most representative subsectors, i.e. the automotive and, in particular, the automotive parts business, and the food trade. The companies that dominate the market in both cases are national in scope, Canadian Tire Ltd. (automobile parts) and Loblaw Ltd. (food). However, given the distance involved, Loblaw was ruled out and, instead, Provigo (Distribution) Inc. was chosen. The union interviewed was the United Food and Commercial Workers (UFCW) union which, despite being very independent, is affiliated to the Quebec Federation of Labour.

113

The owners of three "Canadian Tire" stores were interviewed as well as the owners of two "Supermarchés Provigo Inc.", one of which is unionised, and the UFCW's president.

Union standpoint

Unions accept flexibility because of their relative weakness

The President of the UFCW indicated that the union accepted flexible working time practices when these were dictated by contextual and structural factors such as amendments to regulations, fluctuations in demand leading to an uneven pattern of trade throughout the week, market pressures, efforts to increase market share or to keep operating costs down. However, because unions were not in a position to exert pressure on employers, it was by means of lobbying that they endeavoured to make both the government and the opposition aware of the adverse effects of the liberalising of opening hours on the social fabric and on the quality of life of employees, small shopkeepers and people in general.

Unions are trying to extend the duration of collective agreements to protect themselves against anticipated changes

UFCW Local 500, which represents food sector employees, has negotiated the renewal of the collective agreement for a longer period – three years – in order to safeguard what has been gained so far at a time when change is the order of the day, both in the legislation and in the structure of the industry. What is more, the duration of the most recent collective agreement negotiated at Zellers and Zellers Inc. (Montreal North) in May 1992 has been set at 5 years [Travail Québec (1992)]. This trend is particularly marked in the case of the employees of supermarkets, whose future is less bright than that of discount stores ("hypermarkets" and "warehouse outlets"). Discount stores have recently expanded at the expense of conventional supermarkets because of their lower costs and higher return. According to the UFCW, these two types of food store are cutting each other's throats, because the hypermarkets are draining customers away from the supermarkets – as in the case of the Supermarchés Provigo and the Maxi or Héritage hypermarkets owned by Provigo Inc.

The spread of superstores is encouraging part-time employment, a trend unions are trying to curb

Although unions are being co-operative, they are nonetheless trying to curb the growing trend towards part-time employment in superstores. Again according to the President of the UFCW, whereas some 50 per cent of his members were working part-time in 1982, by 1992 the figure had risen to 68 per cent, which is far higher than the average for the sector as a whole. The recent success of hypermarkets, such as Club Price is accentuating this trend: for example, the five Club Price retail sales outlets in metropolitan Montreal employ 2 000 people, 90 per cent of whom are part-timers, many of them students.

Employer standpoint

Part-time employment and flexibility

The employers' responses to the interviews were remarkably consistent. Flexibility practices consisted of extensive use of part-time employees, mostly with indefinite contracts. Most peak-period employees are part-timers. In addition, part-time workers are used to replace full-time employees who are temporarily absent. These practices are explained by the need to adjust to fluctuations in the pattern of business, and particularly the very busy or peak periods, *i.e.* Thursday and Friday evenings and the whole of Saturday.

Employer/employee co-operation as regards the allocation of working hours, especially in the smaller stores

Flexibility practices are established in consultation with the employees, although this is more likely to be the case for smaller stores. Employers claimed that there is no opposition to flexible working time arrangements because the climate is one of trust. In smaller stores in particular, the drawing up of weekly work schedules is a bilateral process, with employees indicating on a timesheet when they are available and the employer scheduling them accordingly. If there are any extra hours that need to be worked, employers give first preference to their permanent staff.

Concentration of part-time work on weekends

Employers were anticipating that hours of work would be readjusted during 1993 because of an amendment to the Quebec Law on opening hours. They were forecasting a greater concentration of working hours on weekends because of the shift in the pattern of trading. The retailers interviewed said that they would start by rearranging working hours, allocating any necessary additional hours among their part-time employees and concentrating working hours more on weekends. Depending on the increase in the volume of work, they would hire further part-time employees in order to retain their flexibility. They expected that the numbers of part-time employees would grow over the long term in step with a steady increase in sales as the result of the relaxing of opening hours.

Flexibility practices

In order to highlight some of the differences between employers, the following section will analyse certain of the more specific aspects of flexible working time practices such as hiring, the employment relationship and the duration of the normal workweek.

Hiring and the employment relationship

The main flexibility practices take the form of extensive reliance on part-time employees with indefinite contracts, where the employment relationship is a stable one. The individual stores hire their own staff and new employees begin as part-timers.

However, in-house mobility is encouraged through access to full-time positions for part-time workers, provided that they have the requisite skills and experience. In addition, any extra hours of work required can be shared among the part-time workers. Employers want to create an internal market in order to motivate their employees and increase their loyalty to the company. However, they have to compromise between this aim and ensuring maximum flexibility. Retailers want to maintain this extensive use of part-time employees, since this is an efficient and cost-effective way of dealing with a situation where much of their activity is concentrated within a short period of time. The UFCW representative understands this argument, but is opposed to excessive use of part-time staff, who tend to be looked upon as "objects" rather than people.

Normal workweek

The workweek varies. It is 40 hours at Canadian Tire, while in the collective agreement at one of the Provigo supermarkets it is set at 38 hours. It is 44 hours at the other, non-unionised, Provigo supermarket; the employer in this case applies the minimum terms and conditions of work required by the Act respecting labour standards because his store is located in an area that is exempted from the Order relating to the retail trade which prescribes a 40-hour week.

Looking at the number of hours constituting a normal workweek, it is apparent that there has been a trend towards longer hours for full-time employees in the food trade. In 1983, collective agreements set the normal workweek at 37 hours, with this rising to 38 hours in 1988-89 and to 39 and 40 hours in 1992.[10] This has not been accompanied by an equivalent increase in wages, so that real wages have effectively declined. From the employer's standpoint, this has meant a cut in labour costs. The UFCW, because of its weak bargaining position, has been unable to arrest this trend.

Characteristics of part-time employment in the retail trade

According to the retailers interviewed, the proportion of part-time employees ranged from 25 to 80 per cent. Part-timers accounted for 60 per cent of all workers at the Supermarchés Provigo and 25, 45 and 80 per cent at the three Canadian Tire stores. These variations are mainly due to geographic location, the supply of available labour and the cyclical or non-cyclical nature of the business. For example, in a small rural town like Shawville labour is scarce and workers are not very interested in part-time employment. The only form of flexibility available to the store in this case is in the scheduling of days off.

The reason for the relatively low proportion of part-time workers – 45 per cent – at one of the Montreal stores is the fact that it has only recently opened and needs experienced employees, at least to start with. However, it is expected that the store will require even more full-time employees in the medium and longer term because of its more even flow of customers during the week and more regular volume of work. The Canadian Tire store employing the most part-timers is located in Saint-Hubert, a Montreal suburb and dormitory town. It has sharp fluctuations in customer flow during the week and has more need of part-timers to cope with peak periods.

The employers interviewed said that most of their part-timers were regular employees, with temporary replacements and casual workers making up a very small minority. Unlike other outlets which employed shift workers for their stock handling and processing operations, they seemed to use this system very little, preferring to have their sales staff perform these tasks.

Reasons for using part-timers

According to these retailers, the prime reason for using part-time employees is the fluctuating pattern of business. Secondly, part-time labour is less expensive than full-time labour. The employers interviewed did not usually prorate wages, with the exception of the unionised supermarket where this is stipulated in the collective agreement. However, not even all of the unionised stores apply prorating, although the UFCW is currently endeavouring to obtain this for all its members. A third reason is the cost effectiveness achieved through flexible use of part-time employees. Fourthly, according to the owners of the Canadian Tire stores, taking on part-time employees is a good way of finding high calibre staff. At a time when there is an abundant supply of labour, this is an excellent way of picking out the most suitable applicants. Finally, retailers are having to increase their flexibility in preparation for a possible further liberalisation of opening hours.

For employers such as Supermarchés Provigo, Sunday opening without preconditions, as provided for in the new 1993 Quebec legislation, will mean either switching some of the hours usually worked on Monday and Tuesday to the weekend, or allocating additional hours to their part-time employees but not creating new jobs. For stores such as Canadian Tire, which could not open on Sunday until 1993, the change in the legislation will increase their customer traffic, which in turn should boost their turnover by 10 to 15 per cent. Accordingly, they are planning to increase the number of part-time employees, with more of them working weekends because of the change in shopping patterns. Days off will be moved to the beginning of the week, *i.e.* Mondays and Tuesdays.

The UFCW representative felt that the relaxing of opening hours will affect both part-time and full-time employees. He considered that more experienced and more highly skilled workers would be needed to cope with the Sunday trade. Both unions and employers agreed that willingness to work weekends would become a prerequisite for those seeking employment in the retail sector.

The impact of relaxing opening hours on the quality of life in the retail sector

The retailers interviewed have mixed feelings about Sunday opening. On the one hand, they realise that this will adversely affect the quality of life of an important part of the population: employees, retailers, families, etc. On the other hand, there is no question that they will have to open on Sundays; they will be forced to do so by the pressure of competition; otherwise, they will risk losing customers and market share. In addition, they are convinced that competition from cross-border trade is inevitable and that they have to win back the market share lost to neighbouring businesses in the United States, Ontario and New Brunswick.

The UFCW's president condemns the attitude of employers. He believes that they have no qualms about damaging the social fabric of a society ill-equipped to cope with these changes. Both the employers and the union are in agreement as regards the repercussions that the change in the law will have on the structure of the industry. The result will be that a considerable number of small stores will disappear, whatever the subsector concerned, to the benefit of the larger retailers, thus causing further concentration in the industry.

One would imagine that this trend would help to increase the level of unionisation in the sector, given that it is easier for unions to organise within larger companies. But increasing its membership is not the UFCW's sole aim. Its lobbying of the government has resulted in the incorporation into the recent Act respecting hours and days of admission to commercial establishments of a clause preventing employers from requiring their employees to work on Sundays. However, this rule will be difficult to apply because of the number of non-unionised businesses – around 85 per cent of all retail outlets in Quebec – and because employers have the upper hand owing to the chronically high level of unemployment.

G. CONCLUSIONS

As we have already seen, in Canada, with its low level of unionisation in the retail trade, collective bargaining is able to exert only a slight influence over the regulation of worktime in this sector. As in other countries, employers' practices in this respect are governed by the legislation regarding working hours. For the most part this is provincial legislation and, in particular, that regarding shop opening hours and that regarding working hours.

In recent years this legislation has come under fire as the result of the increase in competition, the development of superstores and the demands of consumers. As a consequence of the recession, the introduction of new technologies and cross-border trade, this increased competition in the retail sector has meant that businesses have sought to improve the rate of return on their facilities by using them more intensively, whence the pressure in favour of changes in the regulations governing opening hours. The advent of superstores has also led to increased pressure in favour of a relaxing of opening hours. In addition, the rise in the level of female participation in the labour market has led to stores opening at hours that are more convenient for families where both partners work.

As regards working hours in the province of Québec, deregulation has come about through an amendment to the Act on shop opening hours, allowing greater flexibility in this respect and notably Sunday opening, which previously was permitted only in special cases. This has contributed to an increase in non-standard employment, particularly part-time employees who previously were hired in order to cope with peak shopping hours but who now provide the bulk of the staff who work in stores outside normal hours. The companies surveyed for this chapter use part-time employees to ensure flexibility, especially on weekends; the reasons cited include fluctuations in the weekly pattern of business and the lower cost per hour of part-timers. Unions acquiesce because of their relative weakness; however, they are attempting to extend the duration of collective agreements to protect themselves against any changes. While trade unions can be considered "co-operative", they are trying to curb the growing trend toward part-time employment in the big supermarkets and department stores.

Notes

1. *Lord's Day Act,* Revised Statutes of Canada, R.S.C. 1970.
2. *Act respecting hours and days of admission to commercial establishments,* Sections 2 and 3.
3. *Canadian Labour Code* (C.L.C.), Part III, Section 40.
4. *Act respecting Labour Standards,* Sections 68 and 69.
5. Section 2 of the *Act respecting hours and days of admission to commercial establishments* stipulates that stores can be open to the public at the following times:
   - 8.00 a.m. to 7.00 p.m. on Mondays and Tuesdays;
   - 8.00 a.m. to 9.00 p.m. on Wednesdays, Thursdays and Fridays;
   - 8.00 a.m. to 5.00 p.m. on Saturdays;
   - 8.00 a.m. to 9.00 p.m. on Mondays and Tuesdays in December prior to December 25th;
   - 8.00 a.m. to 5.00 p.m. on Sundays in December prior to December 25th;
   - 8.00 a.m. to 5.00 p.m. on December 24th and 31st when they fall on any day other than Sunday;
   - 1.00 p.m. to 7.00 p.m. on December 26th when it falls on a Monday or Tuesday, 1.00 p.m. to 9.00 p.m. when it falls on a Wednesday, Thursday or Friday, and 1.00 p.m. to 5.00 p.m. when it falls on a Saturday.
6. Revised Statutes of Québec, 1990, *Act respecting hours and days of admission to commercial establishments,* Section 6.
7. *Act respecting hours and days of admission to commercial establishments,* Sections 12 and 13.
8. These are the two sectors with the highest concentration of part-time employees. The non-government services sector includes finance, insurance, real estate and business services, and other services of a commercial or personal and social nature.
9. Regulation respecting the suspension of the application to certain employees of Section 41.1 of the *Act respecting Labour Standards,* Gazette Officielle du Québec, 24 December 1991.
10. Based on collective agreements in Québec that came up for renewal in 1983, 1989, 1990, 1991 and 1992; see Travail Québec, *Le marché du travail,* various years.

Bibliography

ALLAIRE, Y, and FIRSIROTU, M. (1990), *L'entreprise stratégique: les stratégies de marché*, mimeographed document.

BUREAU DE LA STATISTIQUE QUÉBEC (1989), *Annuaire du Québec, Le Québec statistique*, Les publications du Québec, 59th Edition.

DES ROBERTS, G. (1991), ''Commerce transfrontalier: Ottawa se porte au secours des marchands'', in *Les Affaires,* Vol. 63, No. 9.

DES ROBERTS, G. (1992), ''Le Commerce outre-frontière n'a pas fini de prendre de l'ampleur'', in *Les Affaires,* Vol. 64, No. 4.

DION, G. (1986), *Dictionnaire canadien des relations du travail,* Les presses de l'Université Laval.

DUTRISAC, B. (1989), ''Les heures d'ouverture des commerces de détail'', in *PME*, Vol. 4, No. 10, January.

GOVERNMENT OF CANADA (1991), *Industry Profile: Retail Trade, 1990-1991*, Department of Industry, Science and Technology.

STATISTICS CANADA (1989), *Retail Commodities Survey*, Cat. 63-541, special issue.

STATISTICS CANADA (1991), *Labour Force Annual Averages*, Ottawa, Cat. 71-220.

STATISTICS CANADA (1992), *Canada Yearbook*, 125th Anniversary.

STATISTICS CANADA (1993a), *Canadian Economic Observer* 1992/1993, Cat. 11-210.

STATISTICS CANADA (1993b), *Calura: Unions*, Cat. 71-202.

TRAVAIL QUÉBEC (1991), *Le marché du travail*, November.

TRAVAIL QUÉBEC (1992), *Le marché du travail*, August.

LABOUR CANADA (1991), *Employment Standards Legislation in Canada.*

Chapter 6

FRANCE: THE CASE OF RETAIL TRADE

by

Michel Lallement

A. INTRODUCTION

Since the early 1980s, labour flexibility has undoubtedly been one of the major elements which has led to changes in the industrialised countries' productive systems. Working hours, one of a number of factors which firms have sought to control, have been subject to significant changes in France, in terms of both legislation and collective agreements. Retailing had in fact long seen the benefits to be gained from flexibility in this area, sometimes at the risk of breaking the law. Yet it is symptomatic of the last decade that the trend seems to have accentuated considerably. It has also been legitimised by legislation and collective agreements which have in part ratified the principle of the flexible management of working time. The recent debate on working time and negotiations on part-time working demonstrate the determination of certain unions to produce clearer guidelines for management practices in a sector which is extremely heterogeneous, increasingly open to competition and marked by the absence of a strong trade union tradition.

This contribution sets out to assess contemporary changes in the employment situation and new practices with regard to flexible working in the French retail sector. As will be seen, two main aspects will be considered. The first is the issue of industrial relations in retailing. Given an increasing international emphasis on the decentralisation of negotiations, coupled with the more specific context of a French society which has never really shaken off its Jacobin traditions, the relevance of an analysis of contractual relationships will be readily apparent. The second main aspect will be food retailing. While the non-food sector will certainly not be ignored, the discussion will focus on the area of retailing – food – where the most significant changes in the management of working hours have taken place.

This work is based on previous research, which the author has substantially added to and updated on the basis of documentary material available in France and a series of meetings with trade union officials from this sector. Supplementary information which should further clarify the situation regarding French retailing has been included in the annex. The first part of the report offers a brief description of the retail sector.

B. CHARACTERISTICS OF FRENCH RETAILING

Definition of the sector

In the French system of classifying activities and products, commerce is defined in terms of the resale in an unaltered state, without processing, of products purchased from third parties. The activity may include certain associated operations such as packaging and presentation. This area of activity therefore excludes bakers and pastry shops and trading services such as cafes, hotels, restaurants, car repairs and dealers, hairdressers and laundries and dry cleaners. It is also useful to distinguish between food and non-food retailing.

Historical development

In France, alternatives to traditional small retail shops date from the nineteenth century. Increasing urbanisation, higher living standards and new techniques which made it possible to rationalise operations were the principal forces for change. The first shops selling made-up men's clothes appeared in Paris in the 1770s. Low-price stores first appeared in 1929. However, the major revolution was associated with food retailing and came much later, dating from the 1960s.

Up to the 1960s, the organisation of the retail sector was easy to describe. A distinction could be drawn between:

- Low-price and department stores run by enterprises and groups which specialised in this one activity. This was, and still is, the case with such outlets as Printemps, Prisunic, Galeries Lafayette, Monoprix and BHV.
- Mini-supermarkets organised as chains or cooperatives. These shops operate regionally, so that in the North one finds Ruche Picarde, in the West, les coopérateurs de Normandie and in Lorraine, Codec and Gro-Est.

Most innovation at the start of the 1960s was in the food sector. The first French supermarket opened in 1957 and the first hypermarket in 1963. The break with traditional management practices at that time – the widespread adoption of self-service, reduced handling and storage costs, low-cost installations, such as large shed-like buildings erected in the countryside and simple interior fittings – was undoubtedly the key to their success.

Until 1974, it was relatively easy to open supermarkets; chains and cooperatives did so, seeing them as a means of diversifying their activities and of benefiting from significant economies of scale – centralised purchasing, means of transport and supply, increased leverage over suppliers and so on. However, independents also entered the market by developing their own super- and hypermarkets.

After 1974, the previous pace of development was interrupted by the Royer Act of 27 December 1973. The Act imposed stricter conditions on the opening of new supermarkets in order to protect small retailers. The opening of shops with a surface area exceeding 1 000 sq. m was made subject to the prior approval of a regional commercial development committee. The effects were far from negligible: the new legislation slowed down the growth in supermarkets of more than 1 000 sq. m, their turnover and the number of jobs created.

In the early 1980s, a new trend emerged. Henceforth it was the independents, that is supermarkets formally managed by independent traders, who made the running. Their operating principle is a simple one. As early as the 1960s, independents had united to form centralised purchasing groups. Today, based on the principle of discount selling, several purchasing groups have continued this tradition and sell their trade name to independents. There are few obligations; independent outlets have the opportunity to stock up from the central purchasing organisation without any interference in the other aspects of their operations. To judge from the growth in the 1980s of supermarkets organised in this way, the discount + independence formula is a profitable one. However, there is another side to the coin: the growing number of independents has led to increased competition and pressure on prices, margins and labour costs.

The scope of retailing

In France, the retail sector consists of two branches: food and non-food. The former covers the sale of general food products, of meats and of other specialist foods. Excluding small independent shops, general food outlets comprise:[1]

- *i)* branches and other shops with a surface area of less than 400 sq. m;
- *ii)* supermarkets: establishments in which general foods account for more than two-thirds of the turnover and which have a sales area of between 400 and 2 500 sq. m; the range of items on offer varies between 3 and 5 000;
- *iii)* hypermarkets: establishments in which general foods account for more than two-thirds of the turnover and which have a sales area of more than 2 500 sq. m; the range of items on offer varies between 25 and 50 000.[2] Hypermarkets may be classified according to the types of company which operate them.

A number of important distinctions should be drawn within this sector. The first is between integrated groups and independents. The former combine, at least to a certain extent, the retail and wholesale functions and comprise a number of trading groups based on financial links and majority and minority share holdings. The latter benefit from the concentration of resources but are not financially integrated into a single organisation. Independent traders retain the ownership of their business and responsibility for its management. They are particularly characterised by retail cooperatives – the most important being Leclerc and Intermarché – in which the different enterprises form groups for the purposes of joint purchasing and the provision of common services.

The second distinction to be noted is between chains and hypermarkets.[3] The former involve enterprises with a very centralised structure which focus on the quality end of the market; their headquarters centralise purchasing, impose uniform standards for branch management, favour internal growth and, finally, rely on an internal labour market, with the emphasis on progression based on seniority and internal promotion and training.

In contrast, hypermarkets, which rapidly adopted a policy of discounting to keep down their prices, have a much more decentralised structure, with no generalised rules of management. This has led to:

- the extremely important role played by department or section managers, who have total responsibility for innovation and who organise the self-service staff; the result is a very short hierarchy and a somewhat authoritarian management style;
- more recourse to the external labour market, with an organised internal market restricted to a minority of employees; the recruitment of staff is made possible under this approach by higher than average wages for this sector and, above all, the fact that the jobs concerned are often suitable for female labour and offer an alternative to factory employment.

Among non-food retailers, department stores (grands magasins) constitute the most interesting group. Since 1987, the national committee for traders' accounts has applied the following three criteria to distinguish department stores: the ownership of at least one shop with a sales area of 2 500 sq. m or more; the ownership of at least 10 shops; and the employment of at least 100 staff.

In considering the food and non-food sectors as a whole, it is necessary to identify a number of differences in legal status, which are important because to a considerable extent they reflect differences in strategy. Thus, a distinction should be drawn between:

- chains which initially managed networks of small stores run by managers; these chains have diversified their activities on the basis of larger outlets (Uniprix, Casino, Mammouth, etc);
- co-operative enterprises, which developed on the same organisational lines but with a more centralised structure (a national federation, central purchasing organisation and a co-operative bank); in recent years, these undertakings have experienced grave financial problems which have led to a series of major reorganisations;
- large supermarket and hypermarket chains (Auchan, Carrefour, Continent, Cora, Euromarché and Rallye);
- chains running department stores and popular or low-price stores, which initially operated a single form of outlet: low-price stores in the case of Monoprix and Prisunic; department stores in the case of Printemps, Galeries Lafayette and Au Bon Marché;
- independents linked in various ways, in particular through common purchasing organisations (Leclerc, Intermarché, Unico, etc.).

Description of the Sector

Growth of the sector and the circumstances of this growth

The number of outlets

Relatively stable since the early 1970s, the number of retail food outlets has fallen slightly in the last few years, from 130 800 on 1 January 1987 to 118 000 on

1 January 1991. Within these overall figures, there was a significant decline in specialist shops (91 600 in 1987, 83 000 in 1991) and in small independent grocers (from 35 800 to 30 100), whereas large supermarkets and hypermarkets showed the opposite trend, increasing over the same period from 3 400 to 4 900. On 1 January 1991, there were:

- 854 hypermarkets, with a total surface area of 4.6 million sq. m; these were divided into 313 independents and 541 belonging to hypermarket chains;
- 6 550 supermarkets, with a total area of 6.3 million sq. m.

In 1970, hypermarkets and supermarkets accounted for 6 per cent of retail sales; by 1990 this had risen to 28 per cent (16.7 per cent for hypermarkets, 11.6 per cent for supermarkets). The main impetus for the development of supermarkets has undoubtedly come from the extension of self-service, the search for economies of scale through mass distribution and the increased size of outlets[4] and the rationalisation of logistical operations, particularly purchasing and supplies [CEREQ 1990)]. Moreover, during the 1980s, increased competition led to a more pronounced trend towards restructuring and the creation of alliances. As a result, just four central purchasing organisations now account for 60 per cent of the goods sold in hypermarkets.

As in the food retailing sector, the number of non-food, non-specialist retail enterprises shows a downward trend, with 2 500 recorded in 1987 and 2 100 in 1991. Notwithstanding this greater concentration, non-food sales have continued to expand. Between 1985 and 1988, the sector benefited greatly from this trend, which has since been less marked. The main reason for the slow-down has been a fall in sales of household equipment, though this has been compensated for in part by increased demand for personal equipment and, above all, for products in the health-culture-leisure-sports area. Paradoxically, this ''second wind'' is largely attributable to firms in the food retailing sector which have developed specialist outlets in fields such as do-it-yourself and gardening. These firms have also expanded into such diverse areas as travel, health foods, textiles, sports goods, insurance, financial services and even medical care.

The forms of competition

With the rise of the independents in the food sector, the forms of competition which have developed over the last ten years have essentially been price-based. These independents, which are not affiliated to employers' organisations, have not been bound by the requirements of existing collective agreements.[5] As a result, they have pursued an essentially regressive employment and wages policy, aimed at reducing costs.

As Le Corre (1991) has noted, the reduced level of mark-ups, which typifies such a strategy, has mainly involved food products and other non-durable goods, which were already subject to low margins. This has helped to swell the volume of sales made at a loss and has placed increased pressure on suppliers. Another sign of this trend has been the emergence since 1976 of distributors' own brands. The logical culmination of this type of strategy has been the relative decline of food *vis-à-vis* non-food products.

Two other factors help to maintain this price-based competition. Firstly, there is the German competition from firms such as Aldi, Lidl and Norma. In the last few years, the Germans have introduced heavy discount outlets in northern and eastern France and the

Paris region which pose a serious threat to independents like Leclerc which have themselves specialised in this area. Adopting an approach based on bulk purchasing, a limited range of goods on offer and low operating costs, these German companies have increased competitive pressures. Thus, in 1991, Leclerc was forced to establish a range of products for low-income consumers. These are sold at a price at least 20 per cent below that of other goods.

The recent reform of methods of paying suppliers may also – to a lesser extent – favour the continuation of price competition. Until now, French supermarkets have benefited greatly from the period allowed for settlements with suppliers – between 30 and 110 days, compared with 21 in Germany and 30 in Great Britain. Under legislation adopted by the National Assembly in May 1992, this period was reduced to 15 days for perishable products. The result has been a fall in the level of inter-firm credit, thus jeopardising firms which lack an adequate line of bank-based credit, and even more importantly, making it no longer possible to pursue the normal negotiations with suppliers designed to secure the maximum possible delay in payments. Price has therefore become an even more determining factor in the choice of a supplier.

Currently, the situation is such that the extremely competitive environment could lead to two quite contrasting strategies:

- attempts to secure ever greater price and cost reductions, through the integration of logistical support services, increased centralisation of purchases, automated scanning at check-outs (which reduces inventory and labelling costs) and so on;
- a greater emphasis on quality, such as a better trained staff and the development of customer services (child care facilities, long-distance ordering, credit and banking facilities, etc.).

Of the two possible approaches, the independents appear to have opted clearly for the former while the others are still reluctant to come down unambiguously for the latter.

The employment structure

The composition of the workforce employed in the retail sector gives a good indication of the changes that have taken place in this area: in 1968, there were 467 120 self-employed and employers, 148 040 employed members of families and 860 460 other employees. The equivalent figures for 1990 were 362 299, 80 308 and 1 205 577.

This rather small increase in the number of people employed in the retail sector (an average of 8 000 new jobs each year) itself conceals:

- variations reflecting the state of the economy, with an absolute fall in employment between 1983 and 1985, followed by a recovery;
- a steady and significant increase in employment in large food outlets, largely balanced by a fall in other outlets, particularly small independents;
- a growth in part-time work, which accounts for much of the increase in total employment: part-time employment is more established in hypermarkets than in supermarkets (see below).

A breakdown of trends since 1980 into food and non-food sectors shows a rising level of employment in food outlets (particularly in large supermarkets and hypermarkets) and a U-shaped curve in the non-food sector, with a low-point in 1986. In the food sector, the large chains and cooperatives accounted for most of the employment creation in the 1970s and the independents in the 1980s. This is clearly linked to the general growth of the independents: between 1980 and 1987, the total sales area of the Leclerc stores increased by a factor of 2.3 and that of Intermarché by 4.9, whereas the chains only increased their sales area by a factor of 1.6.

As CEREQ (Centre d'Études et de Recherches sur l'Éducation) has observed, the main features of the labour force in the food distribution sector today are:

- its youth: 24.5 per cent are aged under 25 (compared with 10.7 per cent in the economy as a whole, thus placing it in second place in the overall ranking of sectors);
- the high level of female employment: 60 per cent (48.3 per cent in the economy);
- its mobility: 23.5 per cent turnover (14.5 per cent);
- the level of part-time employment: 22 per cent (12 per cent);
- the low levels of pay: 69 967 francs per annum in 1987 for the food retailing sector as a whole (93 037 francs average for the economy; second lowest by sector).

The level of training undoubtedly compounds the problem of the relatively poor quality of the jobs on offer. In the case of jobs in self-service departments and on the till, various surveys undertaken by CEREQ and studies carried out by Bertrand highlight the contrast between the situations in France and Germany, which is often held up as a model. Firstly, the French CAP/BEP vocational training programme, which is more theoretical and less geared towards a knowledge of the actual field, involves a smaller number of people (fewer than 10 000 per year group); secondly, according to CEREQ (1990), ''such jobs (sales assistant or other employee in a large supermarket) are more likely to be filled by those who have failed the examination in the particular option they have chosen or who have completed a commercial option. The greater the difficulty in finding employment on the completion of education or training, the more likely it is that such jobs will be seen as one of the few available opportunities''.

This explains the low level of initial qualifications of new recruits and of those entering the apprenticeship training stream for the profession of sales assistant. It seems very likely that the low esteem in which this occupation is held is linked to certain conditions of employment, including working hours, wages, career prospects and so on.[6]

In the case of management staff, the larger outlets have long benefited from a regular supply of former managers with experience on the ground. This transfer has been made possible by the increase and decline in employment which have accompanied, respectively, the growth of large supermarkets and the concurrent decline in traditional small retail outlets. Now that the supply of managers from the traditional sector has dried up, the major outlets have for several years been turning to graduates of higher education (universities and the grandes écoles). The large supermarkets continue therefore to recruit senior managers (approximately 2 500 per year), but there are considerable difficulties attached, with turnover at about 20 per cent. The continuing influence of traditional values, the workload and the hierarchical relationships are all factors militating against this sector [Baret (1991)].

The social consequences of recent reorganisations

To recap, the French retail trade is now characterised by a high degree of concentration which, spurred on by European competition, has become more marked in the last few years. One significant consequence of these recent reorganisations is that company agreements and practices from which employees benefit are constantly being reassessed. The recent take-over of Euromarché by Carrefour provides a perfect illustration. Euromarché had a justifiable reputation for good industrial relations and staff conditions, but the recent reorganisation has put a number of its previous management practices into question. One concrete example is the decision to end the practice of closing branches at 8 pm, in order to extend opening hours.

C. THE FRENCH MODEL OF FLEXIBLE WORKING TIME IN THE RETAIL SECTOR

The formal working hours of full-time employees in the retail sector are the same as for all categories of employee: thirty-nine hours. Naturally, the inclusion of part-time work would reduce this figure. The actual working hours of management staff are significantly higher than those laid down in agreements. Thus, in 1988, supervisory staff worked an average of 60 hours per week (including Saturdays). The situation regarding management is particularly linked to the high incidence of part-time employment, with managers needing to be almost permanently on the spot to ensure that staff working hours are properly co-ordinated and to allocate and organise the work. Such working hours have particularly undesirable effects, since they not only make it difficult for women to advance and lead to a high turnover of staff but also contribute more generally to the negative image of this sector, particularly among young graduates.

This section will focus on the particular case of the food retail sector – especially super- and hypermarkets – for two reasons:

- French research has hitherto concentrated on this sector, which has undoubtedly developed and expanded in a very spectacular fashion.
- The ways in which working time has been made more flexible raise problems similar to those in the non-food sector, but in an even more socially acute form.

Ways of managing flexible working time

Although the issue of flexibility has not arisen out of the blue for those concerned, in France it took on a new and special dimension with the onset of the economic crisis. Between 1963 and the mid-1970s, it was easy to run supermarkets and achieve a high turnover on the basis of permanent contracts of employment. Since the mid-1970s, supermarkets have had to cut their costs in response to the difficulties associated with the Royer Act and increased competition. One aspect of this strategy has been the increasing use of part-time employment and overtime working to reflect peaks and troughs in daily and weekly activity, and of fixed-term contracts to meet seasonal demands (summer and Christmas/New Year).

It has to be borne in mind that fluctuations in the number of customers are the key factor underlying the issue of flexibility in the contemporary retail sector. Customers can only visit shops outside their working hours, thus leading to a very cyclical pattern of activity. However, the problem is even more complex, with fluctuations varying according to:

- months: April, September and December are the busiest months, with January, February, July and August the least busy;
- weeks: the second and third weeks represent the slack periods of the month;
- days: Friday and Saturday are the busiest; and
- hours: the busiest periods are between 10 and 11.30 am and 5 and 8 pm.

Despite this range of fluctuations, shops in both the food and non-food sectors tend to have very detailed – in some cases, half-hour by half-hour – information on customer flows. Those responsible for staff management therefore have to choose between flexible scheduling of existing employees and a type of employment flexibility based on the external market. Given the opening hours and days currently in operation in France, existing methods of organising working time, whether these be based on the traditional approach or those used abroad (such as team working), are not sufficient. Today, in the majority of French shops part-time work is the main means of making the adjustment.

Flexibility of working hours

As Guélaud (1991) has shown in the case of mainly food-based supermarkets, there are two ways of ensuring this flexibility: by adjusting the hours worked and/or by the use of short-time contracts. The methods used vary according to the types of work concerned.

In the case of work which involves no direct customer contact (storage and the stacking of shelves), the principal constraint governing flexibility is the level of custom on the day concerned. A high turnover requires more restacking of shelves. Above all, shelves must be stacked in the morning and possibly restacked during the day. This constraint influences the hours worked by staff in the different sections but it does not prevent their schedules from being fairly regular and planned in advance. The most normal hours worked in this case are from 6 or 7 o'clock in the morning until noon or 1 o'clock, with a possible extension into the afternoon to restack the shelves. Flexibility is more likely to be achieved by adjusting the hours worked than by the use of short-term contracts (these jobs are mainly filled by men, relatively few on a part-time basis).

Where activities involving customer contact are concerned, flexibility becomes much more important. In order to minimise costs, employers try to make sure that checkout operators are never unoccupied. The first way of achieving this is to vary the number of hours which part-timers are required to work. In practice, contracts vary greatly, ranging from eight to thirty-six hours! It is not unusual to find three, four, five or

129

even six different contracts within the same shop. Not surprisingly, Guélaud has also identified a correlation between the length of time a shop has been established and the proportion of checkout operators with full-time contracts. But while the extent to which part-time staff are used depends on the particular chain concerned, the higher the proportion of full-time staff the more short-term contracts (8, 16, or 22 hours per week) are required to fine-tune the response to fluctuations in the number of customers.

The growth in the number of supermarkets has led to a rapid increase in part-time employment, which is still continuing. The two main causes are their relatively extended opening hours and the high proportion of female employees.[7] In 1988, of non-qualified staff in the food distribution sector (checkout, self-service and reception staff), 80 per cent of women and 37 per cent of all categories of staff worked part-time.[8] Out of 27 firms responding to a CEREQ survey in 1989, 66 per cent predicted an increase in part-time employment, 30 per cent no change and only 4 per cent a decline.

Behind these figures lies a wide range of differences between employees. The age groups most affected by part-time employment are the young (under 25) and workers aged 50-54, while the most important category of staff is manual employees, particularly checkout operators: 43 per cent according to the employment survey. Finally, more women than men are affected. The over-intensive use of part-time, which is often not the employee's preferred option [Maruani and Nicole (1989)], leads to a high turnover of female staff, particularly where the local labour market offers alternative employment opportunities (as in the Paris region).

In addition to part-time contracts, considerable use is made of overtime, to cover emergencies (absences from work or unexpected changes in customer demand) and, above all, to adjust hours worked according to the day or week concerned. The number of overtime hours worked often exceeds 10 or even 20 per cent of total part-time contracted hours. These extra hours worked, and the individual and often arbitrary way in which they are allocated, tend to lead to an explicit policy of keeping staff heavily dependent.

The organisation of normal working hours shows the same pattern. In large French supermarkets, checkout supervisors draw up forecasts of manning requirements on a half-hourly basis. The result is a wide range of working hours which are practically on an individual basis. Collective agreements do stipulate that at the time of their recruitment, staff must be informed of the length of their contracts and of the allocation and timing of the hours worked. The hours must be regular over a period of one or several weeks. In fact, very often, checkout operators do not know more than eight to ten days in advance what hours they will be working. Although in the majority of outlets, these variable hours only affect a limited number of checkout staff (often the most recently recruited and those on the shortest contracts), field surveys have revealed the existence of shops where all the checkout staff are working variable hours. In any case, it is difficult to avoid flexibility, since the practice of overtime working effectively implies some variability in hours worked (including for those who have regular hours) and inevitably has a certain impact on family life.

One final method of achieving flexibility, which is much less common, is the self-management of working hours. This involves the establishment of self-managed teams of ten to fifteen checkout operators who plan their own workload over a three week period.

The system – based on a credit-debit system which takes account of additional hours worked or those still to be worked – is a simple one: the checkout operators enter their names on the timetable according to their preferences. An organiser then adjusts the staffing levels, records the credits and debits, makes sure that the legal working time is not exceeded and organises overtime if this is required. A still more sophisticated version involves a combination of self-management of hours worked with mobility between shelves and checkouts (which encourages the use of scanners) [Guélaud (1991)]. Although desirable, in that it makes it possible to offer all the staff a more or less full-time (35 hour) contract, this approach is still very much at the experimental stage.

Flexibility of employment

The second method of organising the flexibility of working time, recourse to the external labour market, involves the use of fixed-term contracts, short-term replacements and seasonal employment. The use of replacements is practically unknown in French retailing but greater use is made of fixed-term contracts. As provided for in legislation, such employment arrangements – which may involve any function, including checkout and aisle staff – are used to respond to regular variations in demand: in summer (particularly in tourist areas), over the Christmas-New Year period and for special promotions. They are also used to cover permanent staff for annual holidays, maternity leave and so on. It has been recorded that in large food-based supermarkets, fixed-term contracts account for 78 per cent of hirings and 12 per cent of staff employed [Bertrand (1990)].

To these continuing arrangements, the following should be added:

• in the retail sector: staff made available to shops by suppliers to ensure the organisation and stocking of certain departments (large consumer electrical goods, hardware, cooked meats, etc.);

• in the non-food sector: staff paid according to turnover, pupils and students on placement, qualification-related contracts and all the other forms of state-sub-sidised employment.

The economic impact of flexibility

At present, as far as the author is aware, there are no studies or reports offering a precise assessment of the economic impact of flexibility. It is clear, however, that certain developments have had limited effects, both economically and socially. One example is the Sunday opening of certain categories of shop. A recent study by French researchers has shown that:

   i) at the micro level, an extension of opening hours may lead, not to an increase in turnover but to a staggering and rescheduling of purchases over the course of the week;

   ii) at the macro level, the impact on employment is extremely limited [Cette et al. (1992); see Table 6.7. at the end of the chapter].

This is not, of course, to cast doubts on the potential effectiveness of other ways of organising working time in order to match staff resources to customer demands. Nevertheless, here again, the use of a particular approach by chains and individual outlets cannot be judged simply by the yardstick of strict economic rationality. Thus, Guélaud considers that there is no direct relationship between the amount of overtime offered to employees on part-time contracts and absenteeism, unforeseen circumstances and so on. Short contracts coupled with overtime appear to have become a form of staff management which places the employment relationship on an individual basis rather than simply a way of adapting to specific circumstances. Above all, it is a policy which increases the power of checkout supervisors, who can offer a greater or lesser number of overtime hours at their own discretion to whomever they choose.

The relationship between opening hours and employees' working time

Opening hours: the current situation and trends

There is no legislation in France governing shops' opening hours. In this regard, France, like Spain and Sweden, differs from numerous other European countries which have legislation governing closing times. Attention therefore has to be focused on what happens in practice. Shop opening hours in France often range between 8.30 a.m. and 10 p.m., some 78 hours per week. More precisely, French retail outlets are open for an average of 56 hours per week, though there are wide variations since 18 per cent exceed 66 hours. By way of comparison, the average number of opening hours in the European Community as a whole is 53 hours per week.

Another feature of the situation in France is the substantial difference – nearly 18 hours – between the average number of hours laid down in collective agreements for a full-time employee and the hours of opening. For the Community as a whole, the average difference is only 14 hours (53 compared with 39 hours). This significant gap is also a feature of French industry (30 hours).

As to future trends, in France the next few years will undoubtedly see an extension of opening hours, night-time opening and Sunday morning and weekend opening in tourist areas. The movement originated with the emergence of super and hypermarkets in the early 1960s. The principles of competition and of the market economy which prevailed in the 1980s did much to legitimise the notion that responding to customers' needs – even if this means offering potential services such as late opening which are far from fully used – takes precedence over retail employees' working conditions.

A supporting argument for the trade is that this gradual extension of opening hours and days also corresponds to new ways in which individuals organise their time [Cette *et al.* (1992)]:

- a desire to save time by concentrating purchases in the same location and within a short period of time. The pleasurable aspect of shopping is another reality which certain shops have attempted to exploit (for example, by the creation of "life-style centres");

132

- an increased tendency for the economically active (particularly employed couples with children) to postpone their shopping to the weekend: the 1975 budget-time survey showed that the economically active spent 40 per cent of their shopping time at weekends (mainly Saturdays), compared with 25 per cent for the inactive population;
- the high proportion of time spent on shopping compared with other leisure activities: in 1986, French adults reportedly averaged 25 minutes per day on shopping, compared with 27 on reading, 9 on entertainments and trips out, 17 on walks and 8 on sport.

A 1989 survey carried out by the EC also suggests that retail outlets' opening hours have increased in recent years, since 38 per cent of traders questioned said they had extended still further their opening hours. This figure corresponds exactly with the Community average (with 9 per cent claiming a decline and 52 per cent no change).

Working hours in commerce

According to Guélaud (1991), "in the 1970s, the majority of till staff worked full-time and had relatively long working days (often with breaks in the middle of the day when trade was relatively slack). The hours were fixed at the time of recruitment, which left shops little scope for responding to fluctuations in demand". Competition intensified in the mid-1970s, leading to an ever increasing search for flexibility in working hours to reduce wage costs. The result was the development of part-time contracts coupled with overtime – a sensible step since overtime only costs more once 39 hours has been exceeded!

The particular feature of the French model in this almost frenetic search for flexibility is its response to the problem of how to relate shop opening hours (which are tending to become longer) with the timing of certain operations such as deliveries and the hours worked by staff. In France, the long hours of opening and the organisation of work around a single team have helped to encourage the use of part-time employment and a division of labour into checkout operators and other self-service staff. In the United Kingdom and the United States, in contrast, the system of rotating shifts is, as in industry, much more fully developed.

This method of organisation is nevertheless not without its problems. Thus, management has to cope with complex timetabling arrangements to deal with breaks, meal times and absences, while staff face two disadvantages: part-time work, which is rarely what they would choose, and work schedules which do not necessarily fit in with their private lives.

D. STATUTORY CONTROLS AND COLLECTIVE AGREEMENTS GOVERNING FLEXIBLE WORKING TIME

The law governing working time

The legislative framework and recent developments

Until 1848, there were no significant statutory restrictions on working hours. The key date in this respect is 9 September 1848, when a decree laid down a maximum twelve hour working day in factories (but not workshops). This was followed over the next 130 or so years by a series of mainly government inspired regulations, covering such areas as the reduction of working hours and the right to paid holidays. Lastly, in response to the economic crisis and the difficulties which the two sides of industry were experiencing in finding a lasting agreement, the French Government established new legal restrictions under an order dated 16 January 1982. This reduced the statutory working week to 39 hours from 1 February 1982, extended universal paid holidays to five weeks, limited overtime to an annual total of 130 hours and reduced the average working week for employees doing continuous shift work to 35 hours from 31 December 1983.

The order also increased the scope for new regulations governing working hours: thus, following negotiations, sector agreements could be signed waiving any of the provisions relating to the organisation and reduction of working time. Under certain circumstances, firms could be exempted from the Sunday closing requirement, schedule the total hours worked on an annual basis, adjust the hours in which female night work was prohibited and establish individual working hours. This trend was reinforced by the Auroux acts, which made it a statutory requirement for firms to enter into annual negotiations on working hours.

After the failure of the all-sector negotiations on flexibility initiated in 1984, the Delebarre Act of 28 February 1986 on the organisation of working time, repealed the 1982 order and placed negotiations on an individual sector basis. Under sector agreements, it became possible for firms to adjust working hours from week to week, subject to an upper limit of 42 hours per week (on condition that the average weekly total did not exceed 39 hours). The second stated aim was to encourage agreements which offered employees social benefits in return: a reduction in working time, stability of income and the option of substituting compensatory time off for overtime payments.

In a liberalising move, the Séguin Act (19 June 1987) made working hours more flexible. The Act made it possible to waive the prohibition on night-work for women (by an extended sector agreement, supplemented by a company agreement), repealed certain provisions relating specifically to women (breaks, shift work and public holidays) and, above all, allowed firms and individual establishments to contract flexible scheduling agreements directly. In addition, it authorised the abandonment of the obligation to reduce working time in exchange for annual flexible scheduling. By adopting a "type II" form of scheduling, the two sides to the negotiation could decide on alternative forms of compensation, such as pay, training or a different length of working day.

Finally, the Séguin Act introduced numerous other changes to the existing regulations, such as an extension of the circumstances when it is permitted to make up for overall hours lost; authorisation to calculate overtime hours over a period of several weeks; the right to substitute time off in lieu for the payment of overtime; and the establishment of intermittent work contracts, on the basis of sector or enterprise-based agreements.

The 1993 five-year Labour, Employment and Vocational Training Act merely confirmed the shift towards ever more flexible working hours. First, the Act explicitly institutionalised the principle of "an apportionment of working time over the entire year or a portion thereof, involving in particular a collective reduction of that time, by convention or labour agreement" (Article L 212-2-1). Second, insofar as it would give rise to new hiring or avoid redundancies, the Act encourages the conversion of full-time jobs into part-time positions through a system of allowances for employees willing to accept such a conversion. Similarly, the relief on contributions for social security, accident insurance and family grants that is accorded employers who hire part-time workers or convert full-time jobs to part-time ones was extended. The relief is now applicable to contracts calling for weekly working time of between 16 hours (excluding additional hours and overtime) and 32 hours (including additional hours and overtime).

Regulations governing Sunday working

In recent years, the different types of retail outlet have been faced with a particularly difficult problem – that of Sunday working. It is a significant problem since one employee in five in France is now affected by Sunday working. Reflecting a general trend in the French economy, there has been a marked growth in Sunday working in supermarkets: in 1984, 9.3 per cent of employees were affected; the figure for 1991 was 26.1 per cent. Approximately a quarter of all supermarkets open on Sundays and the smaller they are, the more prevalent the practice.

Sunday opening is governed by legislation dating from 1906, which granted a weekly day off to all employees, according to two principles:

- that there should be a rest day, which meant that employers were prohibited from requiring their employees to work more than six days per week. The rest period had to last at least twenty-four consecutive hours. Exemptions were permitted in the case of emergencies to prevent accidents or repair the resulting damage, in industries processing perishable materials and in establishments working for the state or for the country's defence;
- the weekly day off had to be on a Sunday.

The grounds for this legislation are that individuals should have an opportunity to spend time with their family, exercise their civic and religious rights and take part in social activities. There are numerous exemptions. Because economic and social activities cannot cease on a Sunday, there are full exemptions – *i.e.* for which authorisation need not be sought – for firms which cannot stop operating for technical reasons, those which meet ongoing client needs (food products, hotels, restaurants and cafes), health care institutions, transport and heating undertakings and leisure/entertainment activities, such as newspapers, cinemas, etc. Exemptions may also be sought from the prefect by employers not on the previous list. Statutory provision exists for alternative arrangements: a weekly day off other than Sunday, a twenty-four hour break from midday Sunday to midday Monday, Sunday afternoon off plus a compensatory rest day on a rotating basis once a fortnight or, finally, the rotation of Sunday working among some or all of the staff. Exemptions may be granted by local authorities to commercial retail outlets on an exceptional basis for a maximum of three Sundays per year.

The Sunday opening of shops has been the subject of animated debate in French society. The 1906 Act had to be updated since economic developments and new social patterns had rendered it obsolete. The growth in the transport, energy distribution and foodstuffs industries has meant that an increasing number of employees are covered by exceptions to the 1906 legislation and are thus allowed to work on Sundays. The re-emergence of local shops, such as bakers and pastry shops, the increase in purchasing power and, above all, the appearance of new cultural facilities have also helped to encourage Sunday working. In 1989, all these factors, coupled with innumerable breaches of the existing legislation (with the IKEA case being given extensive media coverage), led the Government to ask Mr. Y. Chaigneau to examine the subject.

His report proposed in particular to expand the system of exemptions in order, without renouncing the 1906 Act, to make the options for work on Sunday considerably more flexible. The controversy led to new proposals, in the form of draft legislation, from the Minister for Trade, Mr. Doublin, in 1991. The proposals would have involved slightly more flexibility in the scope for Sunday opening, greater regional harmonization and the exemption of cultural facilities, but were not adopted. The 1906 Act, and thus the Sunday closing of shops, remains in force. In May 1992, the Government decided to reinforce the sanctions against those breaking the law and added nineteen new activities to the hundred or so already legally exempt. Moreover, since then, in deciding on exemptions in the case of activities which are not in the list of sectors covered by the legislation, prefects have had to take into account:

- the views of important bodies such as chambers of commerce and trade unions;[9]
- the importance of tourism in the area;
- the reciprocal concessions to staff offered by the firm seeking authorisation for Sunday opening.

This stance was confirmed in 1993 by the provisions of the Labour, Employment and Vocational Training Act. The principle that the weekly day off is Sunday still stands, but possibilities for exemptions are increasing. Opening conditions were redefined for stores that sell leisure goods or services, as well as for recreation specialists in areas where tourism is prominent. Lastly, the number of exemptions that the authorities can deliver to enable Sunday opening was increased from three to five.

Regulations governing overtime

With regard to overtime, the retail trade operates in accordance with French labour legislation and with standards laid down in the different agreements covering the food and non-food sectors.

In the food sector, under the terms of the collective agreement and article L 212.6 of the Labour Code, overtime hours are subject to a maximum quota of 120 per employee per year. The first 80 must be reported, if possible in advance, to the works council or, failing that, to the staff representatives at their regular monthly meeting. The next 40 hours must be subject to prior consultation with these bodies, who may formulate recommendations on the subject. Any overtime hours in excess of this maximum may only be worked with the approval of the labour inspectorate. Flexible scheduling hours are not included in the overtime total.

Similar principles apply to the non-food sector – an annual quota of 130 hours and a required average of 65 hours for all full-time staff in every establishment of each enterprise.

Collective bargaining

The participants and their positions

The heterogeneity of the firms involved, the relative immaturity of a sector in a state of continuing change and, as a corollary, the absence of a general branch tradition make retailing an area where the structure of industrial relations is fragile and unstable.

The trade union organisations

In those parts of the retail sector which employ staff, the structure of industrial relations reflects, and even accentuates, the characteristics traditionally attributed to French trade unionism. Although contractual arrangements are agreed at the level of the sector's two branches, the disarray in social relations, negotiations and practices is symptomatic of the situation. On the union side, division and weakness appear to be inherent: depending on the organisation concerned, the estimated rate of union membership varies between two and ten per cent! Nevertheless, in elections for representative bodies, votes are divided between the different unions in more or less the same proportions as the national averages for other sectors of the economy.

An overview of the trade union position reveals a general condemnation by all organisations of the employers' failure in both branches to plan their employment requirements properly, which above all leads to the breakdown of the notion of standard working hours. The (Communist led) CGT portrays the retail sector as a leading example of deregulation and vigorously condemns part-time work as forced on those concerned, rather than as being a form of employment deliberately chosen by the women involved. The CFDT and FO take a similar position. More specifically, the FO would like the use of part-time work to be subject to a quota at the sector level. All the unions are united in condemning abuses of Sunday working (also the recent extension of the 1906 Act) and want its use to be restricted. All recognise the need for forms of flexibility (such as fixed-term contracts) to be applied on a case by case basis. However, there is not full consensus here: whereas the CFDT favours the practice of autonomous work teams for cashiers (in so far as this can offer employees more autonomy), the CGT is more sceptical, arguing that the first experiments have quickly revealed various shortcomings and contradictions.

Finally, all the trade unions so far appear to have succeeded in harmonizing the positions of the national federations with local agreements. Thus officials of the retail sectors of the three unions have said that they normally undertake preparations for enterprise-based negotiations and agreements in conjunction with the employees who represent them at the local level. In fact, agreements which have been repudiated by the national organisations are very much the exception.

Employers' associations

In the food retailing sector, diversity is also the rule on the employers' side. With regard to large distributors, several employers' organisations have emerged: the *Syndicat des maisons à succursales multiples* (MAS – the multiple chain stores' organisation), the *Groupement national des hypermarchés* (GNH), the *Fédération nationale des coopératives de consommateurs* (FNCC – the consumer co-operatives' federation) and the *Fédération nationale des entreprises à commerce multiple* (the national federation of multiple stores, FE. NA. COM. MULT.), which organises the large department stores and low-cost stores.

In July 1988, the MAS, the FE. DI. PAC. (the wholesalers' organisation) and the GNH merged to form the FE. DI. MAS. and the *Association pour le Commerce Moderne*, an organisation which centralises and rationalises the administrative, financial and commercial resources of these bodies. Today, the FE. DI. MAS. – within which the MAS plays the leading role – covers 75 per cent of the hypermarkets (the others are in the GNH) and is the major player in regulating social conditions in the industry, signing agreements on employment, new technology, personnel planning, etc.

Despite this formal machinery, a major problem remains: that of the continued progress of the independents who refuse to participate in sector negotiations. The independent operators are not signatory organisations to the national collective agreement, yet they represent – super- and hypermarkets combined – 40 per cent of the large food distribution market. The result, as has been seen, is a tendency to force down employment conditions since the independents resort heavily to defensive flexibility (special forms of employment, maximum use of overtime and so on).

In non-food retailing, there is still greater fragmentation. Organisations include the national federation of multiple stores, the French do-it-yourself federation, three employers' federations in the furniture sector, seven or eight for household electrical appliances and many covering personal goods. The collective agreements covering hardware are regional.

The state of negotiations on working time

Shops selling food and general provisions (the major food distributors) and the big multiples (city centre department stores and mainly non-food low-cost outlets) are each covered by a different collective agreement, though the 1982 agreement on part-time work is common to both branches.

In the retail food sector, the first global agreement was in 1968. Before then, there were only regional agreements signed by the multiples. In 1968, two national agreements (signed by the MAS, GNH and FE. DI. PAC.) were ratified, covering shops and warehouses. Also in 1968, the collective agreement for general food outlets (signed by the MAS) was extended to cover all shops, including those operated by independents.

One of the main characteristics of formal negotiations in the retail food sector is that agreements often ratify individual enterprise practices and agreements. Thus, the part-time working practices which had operated since the mid 1960s were not made subject to an MAS agreement until 1974 and to an FNCC one until 1972. The same applies to fixed-term contracts, which were in use well before they were covered by an MAS agreement in 1976 and an FNCC one in 1980. Nor is flexible scheduling an exception to this: the 1988 collective agreement was largely based on the enterprise-based agreements already in existence (Carrefour's 1986 agreement; SASM's 1988 agreement).

The most recent discussions in the food part of the sector concern annual part-time and intermittent work (a form of employment designed to help limit the unregulated use of fixed-term contracts). There was a considerable gap between sectoral agreements and individual companies' practice; thus, the first agreement dated June 1987 sectoral did not bring about any expansion of intermittent work. Nevertheless, discussions on the two themes of part-time and intermittent work resumed in late 1989, leading to the renewal of the 1987 agreements. Finally, on 19 February 1993, parties in the sector ratified a new accord by which they acknowledge that intermittent work (which may be authorised by enterprised-based agreements) is a minor phenomenon and that it is important to improve the regulation of part-time employment. It was for this reason that the minimum weekly working time for part-timers was raised from 16 to 22 hours.

The conditions under which flexibility in shops has been achieved

The particular circumstances of the sector mean that the question of whether greater flexibility has been secured by a countervailing reduction in hours elicits a paradoxical reply:

- when flexibility is introduced in exchange for some system of compensation it is often taken as an opportunity not to reduce work time but to increase pay;
- employees themselves often seek an extension of work hours. The reason is straightforward: since flexibility in French retailing is mainly achieved through part-time working, the great majority of employees wish to achieve employment conditions more akin to full-time work, thus ensuring greater financial security and more stable hours worked, since part-time employment is often combined with fairly unpredictable overtime hours. This is shown by the recent experience of a Paris suburban hypermarket. The employees agreed to Sunday working at the end of the year on condition that all the hours released by employees leaving the firm (starting with those taking retirement) were allocated in the form of an upgrading of part-time employees' contracts.

The weakness of the trade unions and the precarious nature of the employment conditions means that industrial relations in these undertakings are often tilted in favour of the employer and the law is not always respected. However, this statement has to be qualified in view of the great differences esixting between companies; outlets which form part of chains have always been run on a centralised and paternalistic basis whereas hypermarkets have always favoured decentralisation. According to Le Corre, the current trend is towards even greater localisation from the firm to the establishment (which is understandable, given the increasing success of the independents). It is also necessary to draw attention to the weakness of branch negotiations, which gives enterprise-based negotiations a crucial role. Indeed, one of the characteristics of French retailing is the high degree of homogeneity within firms – strategies for achieving flexibility of work time may vary from one enterprise to another, but within shops with the same name the methods are often very similar.

Enterprise-based negotiations and the establishment of new flexible working time arrangements in shops

As with firms in other sectors of the French economy, employers always retain the prerogative with regard to organisational change. Moreover, under French legislation as it currently stands, firms are required to enter into annual negotiations with trade unions (and not with other representative bodies) on working time. In practice, the French situation has two particular features:

- When the negotiations are not purely formal, employee representatives in shops do negotiate on the content of proposed new working time arrangements, but any compromise reached focuses much more on the compensatory benefits to be provided in exchange for flexibility. The repeated absence of genuine counter-proposals from the union side largely reflects their limited presence in a sector where the personnel policy of each individual chain has a key impact on local contractual arrangements.
- Changes in the organisation of working time are not always laid down in formal agreements. Nevertheless, it is possible to sketch out the changes which have been negotiated within firms in the last few years.

In the food sector, following the multi-sector agreement of March 1989, an assessment was carried out on the basis of a questionnaire produced by the chamber of commerce and industry, to which few firms replied. Of those that did, the results were as follows:

- Negotiations had taken place on the provision of two consecutive days off and the organisation by staff of their own hours. These experiments were very much the exception and were in no way typical of underlying trend.
- The review showed that six firms had concluded annual agreements on part-time work and only one on intermittent employment arrangements.
- In contrast, there was a significant trend towards agreements on flexible scheduling, which have been adopted by numerous firms, such as SASM, Carrefour and Auchan.

Since then, a range of approaches to achieving greater flexibility have been adopted in enterprise-based agreements. Experiments have been tried with flexible scheduling (as provided for in the legislation), the organisation by staff of their own hours and autonomous work teams, different opening hours (earlier opening and closing times), the continuous use of part-time working – accompanied by a policy of upgrading contracts – and Sunday and public holiday working.[10] Almost no success has been achieved with intermittent contracts, with very few agreements concluded by shops.

Although a number of innovative enterprise-based agreements have also been concluded in the non-food sector (Printemps, BHV), there is very little innovation in this sector; part-time is the principal option chosen, with very little flexible scheduling.

The reorganisation of working time and its negotiation in a department store

"I". is a Paris department store employing 2 000 staff (including 150 on fixed-term contracts). In addition, there are 1 000 demonstrators who have employment contracts with their employers – the suppliers of particular products – and whose job is to demonstrate and sell these products within the store. I.'s own employees cover a range of tasks from sales and handling operations to management. The basic grade of employee is a sales assistant with an average wage of 6 500 to 7 000 francs per month. Eighty per cent of the sales staff are women.

The normal practice among the company's administrative staff is full-time work with a variable timetable. Manual staff have a 39 hour week with a fixed set of hours for each day. The situation is different for shop staff since the level of activity varies according to the number of customers. The store is open continuously from 9.35 am to 7 pm. This enables it to serve all the employees from surrounding establishments during the lunch period and in the last half-hour of the day. It operates two teams, one working from Monday morning to Friday evening and the other from Tuesday morning to Saturday evening. There is also a dual system to cover the hours of opening: the first team works from 9.30 am to 6.30 pm and the second from 10 am to 7 pm. The working week is 39 hours. For those working to 7 pm, the actual working hours are 38¼, which are paid as 39. However, this system does not suffice to deal with variations in the number of customers.

The management is well aware of the seasonal nature of its sales. Over the year, December (with 15 per cent of annual turnover) is the equivalent of two months of February. In addition there are the traditional promotion periods: linen goods in January, toys in November-December and the new school year in September. During the week, Saturday is the busiest day, followed by Wednesday. Friday is the day on which the "best" sales are made. The sales profile is also known for each individual day. Sales start slowly, then peak at lunchtime, after which they fall before rising again in the final hour. On Saturdays, there is a mid-afternoon peak followed by a late afternoon fall. There are also variations according to department, with the children's department particularly busy on a Wednesday.

These fluctuations create two problems. Firstly, the shop opens six days a week whereas staff work five and the collective agreement requires the day off to be adjoined to the Sunday. In fact, 40 per cent of the staff have a day off on Saturday (a busy day for customers) and 60 per cent on Monday. The second problem is a permanent one: the shop remains open all day but staff need time off for their lunch. Yet sales activity reaches a peak between 12.30 and 2.30 pm, while staff meals are scheduled between 11.30 am and

3 pm. To cope with these two problems, the store makes use of two forms of part-time employee. Firstly, there are those who work two, three or four days per week and who, apart from other days, cover Saturdays and Mondays. Secondly, there are those who work from 11 am to 3 pm (*i.e.* four hours per day) to cover the lunch period.

Part-time staff constitute 30 per cent of the workforce and account for 17 per cent of the hours worked. Almost no men work part-time. The trade unions are opposed to part-time work, which they consider to be a form of disguised unemployment; they also have great difficulty in recruiting from outside the ranks of full-time employees. Nevertheless, the use of part-time labour has increased over the last ten years, from the time when the shop decided to open six days a week. Fixed-term contracts are used during promotions and in the summer (40 per cent of the employed staff go on holiday in July and 50 per cent in August); this involves the recruitment of students aged 18 to 22. Use is also made of retired people (2 000 in November and December) to provide end of year reinforcements.

To enable them to organise total working hours, the personnel department uses a system which provides information, on the basis of forecast turnover per hour, on the theoretical staffing requirements of each department. Under this system, each department's sales can be monitored on almost a half-hourly basis and compared with previous years, outside factors – such as the weather, holiday dates and promotions – can be taken into account and manpower requirements can then be adjusted accordingly. Despite the fact that this technical system has already been fully developed for several years, the complexity of the situation and staff resistance have led to some tempering of the use of part-time employment to achieve flexibility. Two enterprise-based agreements signed in 1986 and 1987 in response to this have had a limited effects. Under the first, the hours of staff aged over 50 were to be reduced to 32, though paid as 35.5; this has been a failure, with only a hundred or so individuals across France affected. The second created the option of four day working (with an eight hour day), excluding Saturday. The results varied widely between shops. A new formula was then adopted: four days of nine hours per day, *i.e.* 36 hours paid as 37.5.

At present, by a unilateral decision of the management after fruitless negotiations, external flexibility continues to be the rule. The following approaches are used:
- the continuation of four hour part-time working during the day to cover meal times;
- the continued use of three day part-time working to cover Mondays and Saturdays and its extension to a fourth day to make this form of employment more attractive. In 1990 a new system was established: which involved working four days, including Saturday and Monday, from 9.30 am to 7.00 pm with one hour for lunch, making a total of 34 working hours, which are paid as 37.5. Eighty recently recruited staff work this system;
- other earlier systems remain in force, even though they were not ratified by a new enterprise-based agreement:
  - extension of the formula, established under the March 1986 agreement, of 32 hours worked, paid as 35.5 (four 8 hour days or five 6.5 hour days, with Saturday and Monday obligatory). This formula is available to volunteers aged 50 and over on permanent contracts;

– extension of the formula, established under the 1987 agreement, of 36 hours worked, paid as 37.5 (four 9 hour days worked, with Saturday and Monday obligatory).

E. CONCLUSIONS

Like many other sectors of the economy, retail trade provides a particularly clear illustration of the possible interface between labour relations and ways of managing employment. As we have seen, the organisational weakness and fragmentation of both employers and employees, is a major obstacle to long-lasting compromise on terms of employment that are not too detrimental to workers' personal and professional lives. The direct result was that the flexibility of working time increased throughout the 1980s. In this regard, the formula "part-time work + overtime" sums up the sector's dominant practice. On the other hand, the categories of workers involved (essentially women), the widespread precariousness of employment and working conditions, and the absence of any strong professional identity are all factors undermining the social achievements of a powerful, cohesive trade union force. As it turns out, the recent debate over the flexibility of the French economy has only confirmed the determination of those employers who would compete on the basis of prices and wages rather than striving for quality and customer service.

The conflicts and controversies surrounding working on Sunday are especially revealing of the strains in French labour relations, as well as of the choices – but also the reluctance to make them – in the management of work time. The upholding of a basic principle (the prohibition of work on Sunday) while granting an increasing number of exceptions to meet consumer demand or bow to pressure from certain employers, gives a perfect illustration of how an employment norm can gradually be called into question. Its gradual undoing inevitably poses serious social questions (which workers are going to work on Sunday, and to benefit what part of the population?), but it also mirrors one of the fundamental movements in the French model of working time: the shift, under newly mounting State pressure, from "Taylorist" scheduling (regular hours set on a weekly basis, with time off conforming to traditional patterns) towards more flexible arrangements. There can be no doubt that in this movement the retail trade is one of the sectors in which experimentation with flexibility remains most robust.

Table 6.1. Hypermarkets: changing trends in the 1980s

Type of store	Number of shops (units, %)			Sales area (%)		
	1978	1986	1991	1978	1986	1991
Specialist supermarket companies	135 (36.5)	260 (44.8)	349 (41.0)	49.1	56.9	55.1
Other chains	121 (32.7)	164 (28.3)	145 (17.0)	29.6	25.1	16.6
Independents	65 (17.6)	108 (18.6)	307 (36.1)	11	11.2	23.4
Department/low price stores	16 (4.3)	23 (4.0)	27 (3.2)	3.8	3.1	2.4
Co-operatives	33 (8.9)	25 (4.3)	23 (2.7)	6.5	3.7	2.5
Total	370 (100.0)	580 (100.0)	851 (100.0)	100.0	100.0	100.0

Source: Le Corre   (1991).

Table 6.2. The principal distributors in France, 1991

Group	Turnover[a]	No. of hypermarkets
Leclerc	93 600	256
Intermarché	90 000	42
Carrefour	67 900	145
Casino/Rallye	53 500	101
Promodes[b]	41 200	83
Auchan	36 000	47

a) Including taxes other than fuel. In millions of francs.
b) 27 billion francs additional turnover from franchises.
Source: Sales outlets.

Table 6.3. Numbers employed in retailing
Annual average in thousands

	1986	1987	1988	1989	1990
Food retailing: total	669.8	680.0	683.3	686.0	692.9
paid employees	506.6	516.9	521.2	526.9	536.4
Non-food retailing: total	926.1	944.2	956.6	967.6	975.9
paid employees	616.7	630.0	340.3	653.9	664.5

Source: INSEE.

Table 6.4. **Percentage breakdown of persons employed in retailing (31.12.1988)**

	Employees	Self-employed	Total workforce
Large food outlets	26.9	0.2	20.4
Hypermarkets	*14.7*	–	*11.1*
Supermarkets	*12.2*	*0.2*	*9.3*
Low-cost stores	2.0	–	1.5
Small grocery supermarkets; chains and co-operatives	0.6	0.4	0.5
Non-specialist non food outlets	4.9	–	3.8
Department stores only	*2.7*	–	*2.1*
Large specialist non-food outlets	8.9	–	6.7
Others (small and medium-sized shops)	56.7	99.4	67.1
Total	100.0	100.0	100.0

Source: INSEE.

Table 6.5. **Part time employees in retailing**

As a percentage of all employees in each sector, in December

	1985	1986	1987	1988	1989
General food outlets:	20.9	22.2	23.2	25.7	27.7
Hypermarkets	23.6	25.1	25.9	28.7	32.2
Supermarkets	17.9	18.7	18.1	22.5	23.2
Low-cost stores	13.5	16.8	22.4	20.7	23.2
Small independents	28.2	28.7	29.9	31.1	28.9
Specialist food outlets	33.0	30.9	31.4	34.3	32.5
Non-specialist non-food outlets	19.1	21.2	20.7	21.3	23.9
Specialist non-food outlets	30.9	29.0	28.5	28.7	27.3
All retail outlets	26.0	26.5	26.7	27.9	28.2

Source: INSEE, Annual surveys of retail enterprises.

Table 6.6. **Summary of trade union strength in French retailing**

Percentage of votes cast for each trade union confederation in the works council elections of 1988 and 1991

	CGT	CFDT	CFTC	FO	CGC
Food retailing					
1988	17.2	9.2	2.6	23.9	4.2
1991	12.8	9.2	9.3	23.0	2.9
Non food retailing					
1988	15.2	8.9	7.7	9.8	3.9
1991	17.0	16.5	4.6	12.0	4.6

Source: Ministry of Labour.

Table 6.7. **The possible effects of Sunday opening of shops**

Summary of the effects compared with non-Sunday opening

	Year 1	Year 2	Year 3	Year 4	Year 5
GDP (% change)	0	−0.05	0	0	0
Total employment (thousands)	10.0	−3.0	−3.0	−2.0	0
Trading balance (billions of francs 1989)	− 0.5	1.5	−1.0	−2.5	−4.0

Source: Cette *et al.* (1992).

Notes

1. The definitions which follow are taken from CEREQ (1990).

2. The notion of a large hypermarket selling a very wide range of food and non-food products seems to be largely confined to France and has no real equivalents outside of Southern Europe.

3. The following description is taken from Le Corre (1991).

4. In practice, most of the development in recent years has tended to involve smaller hypermarkets (less than 4 000 sq. m).

5. Or at least of those which have not been the subject of an extension procedure.

6. According to the Ministry of Labour's labour force survey, in 1988, the level of qualifications of the working population employed in the distribution of food products was as follows: none: 40%; BEPC: 12%; CAP/BEP: 35%; Baccalauréat or above: 13%.

7. Twice as many women, proportionately, are employed in retailing as in wholesaling, for example.

8. That is, all jobs involving fewer than 39 hours, and not 32 hours as in the legislation.

9. Anecdotal evidence is supplied by the Champs Elysées branch of Virgin-Megastore (mainly records and discs), which received authorisation from the prefect in July 1992 to open on Sunday, even though all those involved on the industrial relations side had expressed their opposition. A few months before, the store had been the subject of considerable media attention when it opened illegally on Sundays. Since the law does allow enterprises offering cultural goods and services to operate on Sundays, a national debate had ensued on the extent to which records, CDs, etc. were cultural in nature.

10. In practice, more or less all shops take advantage of the opportunities for exceptional opening which the law offers; in the case of non-food outlets, regular illegal opening is now the rule.

Bibliography

BARET, C. (1991), "Quelle place pour les cadres diplômés dans la grande distribution?", Mimeograph, LEST.

BERTRAND, O. (1990), "La grande distribution à prédominance alimentaire", CEREQ Bref, March.

BOSCH, G. and LALLEMENT, M. (1991), "Emploi et temps de travail dans la grande distribution alimentaire allemande", *Formation-Emploi, No. 36.*

CEREQ (Centre d'Études et de Recherches sur les Qualifications) (1990), *Emploi, travail, formation dans la grande distribution à dominante alimentaire,* La Documentation Française.

CETTE, G., CUNEO, P., HERBAY, J.P. and PREEL, B., (1992), "Ouverture dominicale: Impact macro-économique", *Futuribles*, No. 164, April.

CLÉMENT R. *et al.* (1990), "La dynamique des rapports salariaux: lieux, règles, sens", research report for MIRE, GREE-Nancy, Mimeograph, November.

ECONOMIE ET STATISTIQUE (1987), "Le commerce en mouvement", No. 196, February.

GUÉLAUD, F. (1991), "Les diverses formes de gestion de la flexibilité dans les hypermarchés", *Formation-Emploi, No. 35.*

GUÉLAUD, F., *et al.* (1989), "La flexibilité du travail dans les hypermarchés", LEST research report, Aix-en-Provence, Mimeograph.

INSEE (1990), *Enquête annuelle d'entreprises du commerce,* collections de l'INSEE, série E.

INSTITUT FRANÇAIS DU LIBRE SERVICE (1986), "La distribution en France, évolution et tendances lourdes", L.S.A., No. 1022, April.

LALLEMENT, M., with BOSCH, G. (1990), "La flexibilisation du temps de travail en France et en Allemagne", MIRE research report SET-Paris I, Mimeograph, December.

LE CORRE, S. (1991), "Modèles d'entreprises et formes de gestion sociale dans les hypermarchés: diagnostic et évolution", *Formation-Emploi*, No. 35.

MARUANI, M. and NICOLE, C. (1989), *La flexibilité à temps partiel*, La Documentation Française.

WORKING TIME UNDER THE FOOD RETAILING COLLECTIVE AGREEMENT

(Retail shops selling food and general provisions; National agreement of 29 May 1969, updated on 1 January 1988; agreement of 11 February 1982 on working time; and agreement of 19 February 1993 on part-time work)

Paid holidays: there are six public holidays per year, in addition to 1 May.

Statutory working hours:

- 39 hours per week,
- over any 12 week period, the average number of weekly hours worked may not exceed 44.

Division of weekly hours:

- working time does not take account of break periods,
- the uninterrupted period of time off between two days worked may not be less than 12 hours,
- in addition to Sundays and public holidays, employees receive one day or two half days off per week; in services open on Sundays, non-working Sundays are to be organised on a rota basis.

Overtime:

- quota of 120 hours,
- overtime hours are paid according to the regulations, but may be compensated for by time off in lieu.

Scheduling of hours worked:

- the work of individuals or teams may be organised on the basis of a shorter period (4 days), on condition that those so employed are not required to work over a period exceeding 12 hours in any one day for a full day or 6 hours for a half day and that the period actually worked in a day by any individual does not exceed 10 hours.

Methods of scheduling:

- anyone working 5 hours continuously is entitled to a fifteen minute break,

- the scheduling of work to deal with increased levels of activity is permitted on condition that, over the year, the average weekly hours worked do not exceed the statutory working week,
- hours worked, their allocation and the use of equipment must be the subject of annual programmes and reports. Other than in exceptional circumstances, enterprises must post up working hours one week in advance,
- the practice of smoothing out fluctuations in wages is recognised.

Part-time and intermittent work:
- part-time work may not be less than 22 hours per week or an average of 95.7 hours per month,
- overtime cannot be required by the enterprise. When it is provided for contractually, it may not exceed one third of the weekly or monthly work time stipulated in the said contract,
- the periods of the year to be covered, the intervals at which adjustments can be made and the periods when the employee declares him or herself to be available must be fixed in advance,
- payment for intermittent work is based on the number of hours worked each month, but regulations governing payment should be established.

WORKING TIME UNDER THE DEPARTMENT STORE COLLECTIVE AGREEMENT

(National agreement of 22 March 1982 extended by an official order of 29 June 1982; agreement of 6 April 1982 on part-time work)

Paid holidays: leave based on seniority or working below floor level.

Statutory working hours: 39 hours per week.

Division of weekly hours: prohibition of Sunday opening other than for mainly food shops. The latter may open six days per week. The second day off must be Monday or Saturday, though exemptions are possible. Working hours may be distributed unevenly over the different days of the week.

Overtime: quota of 130 hours. Overtime may not exceed an average of 65 hours per week for all full-time employees in each enterprise and in each establishment.

Scheduling of hours worked: in the absence of an agreement, scheduling is subject to three limitations:

- 1 hour more or less per week over the year,
- 2 hours more or less per week for a maximum of twelve weeks, not necessarily consecutive
- 3 hours more or less per week for a maximum period of eight weeks, not necessarily consecutive (this does not apply to individualised working hours).

Methods of scheduling:

Where there is an agreement: the number of hours worked weekly may vary, subject to them not exceeding the statutory weekly total when averaged over the year; there must also be an annual programme setting out the flexibility arrangements.

In the absence of an agreement: if fewer than 39 hours are worked there must be no reduction in wages; if more than 39 hours are worked, the excess must be reckoned as overtime.

Part-time:

For food product divisions and specialist non-food outlets in department stores:

- part-time work may not be less than 16 hours per week or 200 hours per quarter, other than at the express request of the individual concerned,
- those concerned may not be required to work overtime,

- part-time employees must be given two weeks' notice before agreeing to any changes to their regular hours of work,
- unless the individual concerned agrees, the enterprise may not require him or her to work less than three hours continuously,
- any overtime worked may not be such as to bring the number of hours actually worked in a week above the statutory or contractual working week.

Chapter 7

ITALY: THE CASE OF RETAIL TRADE

by

Giovanni Gasparini

A. INTRODUCTION

Labour market flexibility became one of the major problems facing industrialised countries in the late 1970s. Ever since, it has had a continuing impact at several levels, and specifically in industrial relations.

Several studies on economic, sociological and legal aspects have been conducted in different countries, discussing various forms of flexibility – numerical, quantitative, functional, etc. – and identifying a number of general trends and processes common to all western countries which have tended to encourage flexibility in the use of manpower [see, *inter alia*, Boyer (1987); Blyton (1991)].

Some of these trends reflect industry's turbulent, not to say volatile, economic and institutional environment, the globalisation of economic and financial markets, the new computer, data transmission and robotics technologies through which work can be made flexible in previously unimaginable ways, and new attitudes on the part of workers towards flexible working time.

Although such processes are exerting a widespread and unifying influence, the fact remains that every country and national system has its own legal, political, economic and sociological approach to labour flexibility [see, for example, Brunhes (1989); Rojot (1989)]. Here, industrial relations are especially relevant, since every industrialised country retains a "social culture", gradually built up over decades, which can change only slowly, even though the constraints on it may be similar or, indeed, identical from one country to another.

B. ITALY'S SYSTEM OF INDUSTRIAL RELATIONS

Before presenting the case of Italy's retail sector, a few words need to be said about certain aspects of the country's industrial relations system. Above all, a general feature of

Italy's system is the importance attached to collective bargaining and agreements (at the three levels of the national economy, individual industries and individual firms), rather than direct government intervention via legislation.

Italian trade unions have always relied primarily on the method of collective bargaining between social partners rather than on legally established regulations. This is illustrated by the fact that the legislation on working hours, which dates from 1923, has been totally superceded by the progress made in the industry-wide collective bargaining agreements of recent decades.

The proportion of unionised workers is still relatively high, twenty years after the end of the wave of industrial disputes during the late 1960s and early 1970s, out of which the three leading unions, CGIL, CISL and UIL, emerged more powerful than ever. The most recent data [Squarzon (1992)] show that the proportion of employees who were members of the three main unions was approximately 39 per cent in 1990 and had remained virtually stable over the five preceding years; it was higher in 1980, when 49 per cent of employees were union members.

The authorities (central government and, in a number of negotiations and disputes at local level, regional authorities as well) play an active part in mediation, in suggesting and determining certain economic constraints in the more important pay rounds. Government is now a fully committed third party in industrial relations.

During the early 1980s, as the economic crisis deepened and unemployment became worse, there was a tendency in Italy to centralise collective bargaining, in which political and institutional considerations came increasingly to the fore (cost of labour, wage escalator mechanism, maximum salary increases, curbing unemployment, etc.). This resulted in very close government involvement. Significant examples were the tripartite "Scotti" agreement of January 1983, the protocol agreement of February 1984 (although the Communist-oriented CGIL, Italy's largest union, did not ratify it) and the "IRI-Sindacati" protocol of 1984 which was a watershed for industrial relations in IRI, the State holding company.

In recent years, there has been a new trend towards "institutionalising" industrial relations. This has resulted in a certain "normalisation" of relations between unions and employers and has sharply reduced industrial disputes, with all sides inclined to take a more co-operative approach, dealing with practical, "qualitative" issues such as labour market flexibility and firms' policies at several levels [see Baglioni and Milani (1990)].

From the second half of the 1980s until the present time, bargaining has resumed with marked intensity at the decentralised level of the firm or establishment. But that does not conflict with national industrial agreements, which continue to represent the general framework in which more specific and detailed bargaining occurs (in individual firms and even in individual local units, which is often the case with major retail chains).

The bargaining covers topics such as wages and productivity bonuses, mobility, skills and professional status, and also working hours. This last topic is especially prominent. It often crops up in enterprise agreements, various aspects being discussed, such as the general organisation and pattern of working hours, flexible scheduling, overtime and part-time work [see Olini (1990)].

Throughout the serious political crisis which Italy has been undergoing since 1992, in which a number of parties and certain institutions have been discredited, the unions have maintained their influence over workers and still exercise considerable power in the economic and social sphere. This is borne out by, among other things, the recent general agreement of 3 July 1993 on "labour costs", which was signed after much discussion and hesitation by the three social partners, employers, unions and the government. This agreement, which covers incomes policy, collective bargaining guidelines, and labour and employment policies, was considered by the government to be a crucial factor in the context of developing policies to promote employment and to combat the economic crisis. This agreement, which is a watershed in the system of industrial relations, directly addresses the problem of effectively supporting the Italian production system in a European framework.

C. WORKING HOURS IN RETAILING[1]

Bargaining over, and experiments in, flexible working time in Italy's retailing sector are a remarkable phenomenon, as we shall be seeing. However, this is a recent phenomenon, particularly bearing in mind the socio-economic structure of retailing, which was characterised until the early 1980s by very rigid working hours and still largely consists of small, family-run stores employing on average fewer than two workers each [see Negrelli (1989)].

Available statistics [see Piccoli (1991); Ministero Industria e Commercio (1992)] show that the concentration process is slowing down in food retailing but is still growing in other sectors. At the beginning of 1992, Italy had some 298 000 food outlets, down from over 600 000 ten years earlier (compared with 136 000 in France, 124 000 in Germany and 157 000 in Great Britain) and about 582 000 non-food outlets (290 000 in France, 279 000 in Germany, 187 000 in Great Britain). Italy has some 4 500 "modern" outlets in the form of supermarkets, hypermarkets and department stores. Despite political and administrative obstacles, and the somewhat negative attitude of small retailers, large-scale retailing surged ahead during the 1980s (averaging more than 5 per cent growth per year) and this is undoubtedly the sector where flexible working hours have formed the main subject of bargaining between social partners.

Table 7.1 shows the trend for large-scale retailers between 1971 and 1990 in terms of outlets, surface area and staff employed by supermarkets and department stores. Most striking is the spectacular development of supermarkets, which expanded from barely 600 in 1971 to nearly 3 400 in 1990. The growth of department stores was slower, but was still remarkable in terms of the number of outlets (from 550 in 1971 to 942 in 1990) and surface area (from 205 000 to 1 573 000 square metres), while the number of staff employed remained nearly the same (approximately 28 000). What should also be noted is the emergence of hypermarkets, which appeared somewhat later in Italy than in France and some other countries. There are currently (1991) 182 such outlets.

Some 2.4 million work in the retail sector, though only 40 per cent of them are dependent workers. Large-scale retailing, the most important and influential sector in terms of industrial relations and collective bargaining agreements, employs some

Table 7.1. Department stores and supermarkets in Italy, 1971-90[a]

Years	Number				Size (square meters)				Total employed
	North	Centre	South	Italy	North	Centre	South	Italy	Italy
Department stores									
1971	278	125	147	550	469 039	195 723	204 872	869 634	28 751
1975	339	162	191	692	653 493	266 502	302 302	1 222 297	33 902
1980	367	177	241	785	727 866	288 610	358 127	1 374 603	31 384
1985	371	179	251	801	723 062	291 278	348 402	1 362 742	28 699
1988	369	212	249	830	656 888	324 625	348 545	1 330 058	25 336
1989	410	212	267	889	726 853	321 937	373 912	1 422 702	26 925
1990	449	220	273	942	840 613	353 134	379 421	1 573 168	28 318
Supermarkets									
1971	444	140	65	609	283 121	95 129	44 597	422 847	13 378
1975	630	190	125	945	473 302	135 001	83 625	691 928	21 866
1980	862	274	260	1 396	691 324	206 384	183 681	1 081 389	29 229
1985	1 296	460	442	2 198	1 084 708	359 644	304 278	1 748 630	45 439
1988	1 629	564	625	2 818	1 361 090	464 880	450 425	2 276 395	59 010
1989	1 798	619	759	3 176	1 535 281	517 104	558 610	2 610 995	64 687
1990	1 912	679	808	3 399	1 689 883	575 797	600 207	2 865 887	70 531

a) Up to 1985, data include the non-food products section in supermarkets.
Source: Ministero Industria e Commercio (1992).

115 000 dependent workers [Negrelli (1989); Pannozzo (1991); Ministero Industria e Commercio (1992)], of whom approximately 70 000 work in supermarkets, 23 000 in hypermarkets and 28 000 in department stores. According to trade union statistics, unionisation rates for these workers are rather low at around 20 per cent. As regards legal and administrative measures covering the retail trade, it has to be borne in mind that in Italy, opening any kind of store (from a small local outlet to a hypermarket) requires a licence from the local authority (governed nowadays by regional legislation). Working hours prior to the Marcora Act 887 of 1982 were very rigid, matching the requirements of smaller retailers. Act 558 of 1971 established a maximum opening time (or "trading" time) of 44 hours over 5½ days (closure on Sunday and one other half-day) which exactly matched the weekly working hours of retail workers at that time; the only exceptions were for Italy's numerous tourist areas, and then solely during the "high season".

Subsequently, the move towards a more modern approach imposed by the supermarkets was given legal backing in the 1980s by a new legislative framework (the Marcora Act of 1982 and Act 121 of 1987) under which opening hours could be extended and could vary across the country. Responsibility for determining opening hours was devolved to the regions, which are now empowered to promulgate laws and approve trials, in particular experiments with working hours.

Taking Lombardy as an example, Regional Act No. 32 of 21 June 1988 authorises Sunday opening during a limited number of weeks (the month of December, particular holidays) and changes in opening hours for up to 110 days in the year. That measure has mainly been used to extend opening times in hypermarkets and large retail centres until 9 or 10 p.m. on two days a week.

The foregoing suggests that the 1982 change in the legislative framework has provided a basis (or a necessary pre-condition) both for dealing with the issue of flexible working hours today confronting the large-scale retail firms, and for incorporating new working time arrangements into collective bargaining agreements. The new legislative framework, accompanied by trends in collective bargaining to be illustrated below, has widened the gap between the weekly working time (between 38 and 40 hours maximum) and the "trading" or opening time which can now amount to some 70 hours or, perhaps more accurately, "disconnected" working hours from opening times altogether. This has become a widespread and common practice in recent years, in manufacturing industry as well as the tertiary sector, reflecting industry's need to use equipment ever more intensively (even continuously, *i.e.* 24 hours a day, seven days a week) in order to cope with stiff competition.

One consequence has been the introduction or extension of shift work and of other arrangements such as part-time work, which can be regarded to some extent as a form of shift work. As was said in the Taddei report (1986), this means recognising that machine time no longer necessarily corresponds to human time (*i.e.* employee working hours) and drawing the consequences of this, by strongly promoting shift work under certain conditions, one condition being to avoid work on Sundays and at night so far as possible.

The recent surge in part-time working in large-scale retail outlets is especially interesting and relevant in this connection, particularly bearing in mind that in Italy part-time work accounts for a very small proportion of total employment (between 5 and 6 per cent). The spread of part-time work today represents one of the key approaches to flexible working that large-scale retailing has adopted, as shown by, *inter alia*, the findings of some recent research into non-typical working hours [see Gasparini (1991)]. These revealed figures of up to 50 per cent for the proportion of part-time workers in certain stores. Retail firms have to cope with a fairly complex pattern of customer flows, which varies according to the time of day (peaking in late afternoon), the day of the week (Monday, Friday and Saturday being the busiest selling days), and the month and season of the year (Christmas makes December the most important month, especially for department stores).

By introducing a combination of different part-time work arrangements, such as "horizontal part-time" (*i.e.* a fixed number of hours every day, *e.g.* four hours a day from Monday to Saturday), "vertical part-time" (work on certain days only, *e.g.* eight hours on Monday and eight hours on Saturday) and "annualised part-time" (a number of hours per year concentrated in certain seasons, especially December and the summer holiday period), firms can react satisfactorily to fluctuating customer flows, increasing the number of staff on hand as necessary. For example, one department store quoted a ratio of 1 to 7 for staff present at a slack time on a certain day of the week at a particular time of year, and at a peak time on another day.

This system of adjusting staffing via part-time work, which certainly represents a significant aspect of flexible working time in retailing, usually means that employers can avoid having to resort to flexible staffing practices, such as hiring temporary agency staff or recruiting employees on fixed-term contracts, which are moreover discouraged or restricted by legislation and collective agreements.[2] It also directly or indirectly activates internal labour market forces. Moving on from some shorter part-time working arrangement to a longer arrangement, and more particularly from a part-time contract to a full-time contract, works to the advantage of both the worker and the employer.

D. COLLECTIVE BARGAINING AND THE POSITIONS OF THE SOCIAL PARTNERS

In Italy's industrial relations system, industry-wide collective agreements always have been and still are highly important, even when important matters are left to be settled in enterprise or establishment agreements and incorporated as amendments or additions to the national agreement, as is the case for retail trade.

The national collective agreement at present covering the retail and tertiary sector was concluded on 14 December 1990, replacing its predecessor of 28 March 1987. It contains a number of provisions on working hours and flexibility which to some extent clarify the positions of employers and unions on these matters [see Contratto Colletivo Nazionale di Lavoro (1990)]. The national collective agreement also expressly provides that working time arrangements, forms of flexibility and part-time working should be matters for enterprise bargaining.

The national agreement stipulates that the normal working week shall be 40 hours (Article 29) but should be reduced to 39 or even to 38 hours when a firm is adjusting working hours to customer needs for the purpose of "improving service to the consumer'' (Article 30). In this case the adjusted working hours, which will be valid for a year, are to be notified to trade unions at the annual meetings provided for by the agreement (Article 17 ''Rights to information'') and at latest in the month of November to the employees concerned. To a large extent working hours will be adjusted by means of ''paid hours off'' in groups of four hours or eight hours, as expressly provided for by Article 64 of the agreement.

Article 33 on ''Flexible hours'' directly addresses this subject. It lays down the principle that hours may be adjusted for up to 16 weeks each year and to a maximum of 44 hours per week. No salary increase is specified but the agreement does establish both that an employer is obliged to notify workers concerned of the annual programme for implementing flexibility and that workers should so far as possible benefit from having the number of compensatory hours off to which they are entitled taken together in the form of half days during slacker periods.

Consequently, the firm is in theory required to make known well in advance, that is, at the beginning of the year, its scheduling of flexible hours. Nevertheless, the same article does allow for changes during the year, in which case the firm is required to give employees ''adequate notice''. In practice, changes in working hours may be made through monthly or even weekly schedules. However, it should be noted that, under the terms of the collective agreement, employers cannot ask their staff to work more than 200 hours of overtime per year.

Under these provisions of industry-wide collective bargaining, it is consequently for the employer to take the initiative in matters of flexible hours, though agreements often refer to customer flow patterns and ''consumer interests''. Moreover the trade unions state they are now ready to accept forms of flexibility (often justifying these in their literature in terms of ''modernising'' the retail sector). They have succeeded in obtaining a number of benefits in return, about which judgements may however differ, namely:

- advance notification of how working hours are to be arranged;
- the right to take compensatory time off in the form of half days or full days;
- a slight overall reduction in the number of hours, in return for certain patterns of working hour arrangement, although no trade-off is openly acknowledged and the reduction stems more from an underlying trend throughout industry;
- a move away from the non-continuous day to the continuous day as regards the scheduling of working hours, to the benefit of workers, and of women in particular.

Considering what the unions have achieved, special attention must be drawn to Act 426 of 1971 on ''Retail trade regulations'' under which special committees were set up to regulate retailing at regional and commune level. These committees are responsible for drawing up retail trade development plans at local level and for issuing licences. Every such committee includes three or four union representatives alongside employers' representatives and independent experts. This gives the unions some indirect bargaining power in awarding licences and granting permission for new larger-scale retailing outlets.

Another very important contributor to the process of making working hours flexible in retailing is part-time work, already covered to some extent in the paragraphs above. Article 39, the first of a whole chapter on part-time work, makes a number of relevant general statements. Part-time work is seen as an appropriate means of matching supply and demand for labour, while also allowing "flexibility of the labour force so that it can be adapted to patterns of activity during the day, the week, the month and the year". It also states that this flexibility accords with the individual preferences of workers.

Other provisions (Article 42) emphasize the voluntary nature of part-time work and of changes in the arrangement of working hours.[3] The "reversible" nature of the part-time contract (in the sense that it can be transformed into a full-time contract if both partners so wish), and the priority that an employer should give to existing workers (rather than new employees) in converting a full-time contract into a part-time contract or vice versa are also provided for in Article 42.

The statements of principle on national collective bargaining in the retailing sector seem to suggest two especially relevant considerations. Firstly, the full, unreserved acceptance of part-time working by the unions represents a considerable change of outlook from the unions' position of only a few years ago. Secondly, the employers' preference for flexibility is matched by individual workers' preferences. This latter aspect is indeed important and it partly reflects the structure of the retail labour force (young women, women with young children). However, part-time work is today mainly used for reasons of flexibility on the employer's side and dictated by the particular requirements of the work process. On recruitment, workers very often have no choice but to agree to a part-time contract even when that is not what they really want or would prefer.

To complete the review of flexible working time patterns at the level of collective industry-wide bargaining, mention should be made of the provisions for fixed-term contracts and for overtime. For fixed-term contracts, the collective agreement specifies those cases in which firms may offer fixed-term contracts (to replace employees on holiday, for exceptional kinds of work, etc.), while Article 19 sets a 7 per cent limit for the number of fixed-term workers in all. In other words, the legal and contractual limitations on the number of fixed-term contracts mean that they cannot be considered a particularly significant means of making work time more flexible.

As regards overtime, the 200 hours maximum laid down in the national agreement (Article 56) is rather high compared with other industries and allows retailers a fairly substantial margin of flexibility, especially as the bonus rates are not very high: an extra 15 per cent up to 48 hours per week, 20 per cent beyond 48 hours, 30 per cent for public holidays, 50 per cent for night work (Article 57).

Finally, employers in retailing, as in other industries, have for some years been employing young workers (under 29) to take advantage of the special concessions offered by the "training and work" contracts which the government successfully introduced during the 1980s. These contracts carry lower social security charges. They are fixed-term contracts of 12 or 24 months, and the general experience has been that almost all these hirings are subsequently converted to permanent contracts.

E. COLLECTIVE BARGAINING AT ENTERPRISE LEVEL

As already mentioned, aspects concerning flexibility and working hours are among the first topics which national collective agreements devolve to the level of firms and individual local units. To judge from the Articles of the latest collective agreement of December 1990, the division of powers between trade unions at national and local level seems not to cause any problems, this kind of division being a traditional feature of mainstream industrial relations in Italy.

Large-scale retailing has many patterns of work organisation which mainly reflect fluctuations in the pattern of sales activity and have been made possible both by a relaxing of the legislation on working hours and by collective bargaining developments.

One influence has been the kind of regional legislation already referred to for Lombardy, exempting stores from the limit on evening opening on 110 days per year. In practice, this has meant that twice a week (generally on Thursdays and Fridays) hypermarkets and other large retailing outlets can stay open until 9 or 10 p.m. Local authorities can grant other exemptions: for example, in the centre of large cities like Milan and Rome a very limited number of specialist outlets (books, records) have been authorised to open on Sundays. Italian legislation does not allow stores to remain open 24 hours a day; the possibility of opening all-night drugstores in major cities has been under discussion for years, but this has yet to happen.

It must be borne in mind that on top of all this, because of the role of tourism in Italy, local authorities allow stores in tourist areas (seaside, mountain, lake, etc.) to open on Sundays during the season, which may extend over several months of the year. Exemptions from Sunday closing are also granted during the Christmas period and for various local holidays.

So the pattern of hours worked by employees in larger retail outlets will usually be quite varied and complex, since it will include:

- full-time workers with permanent contracts;
- workers with fixed-term contracts;
- workers on horizontal part-time;
- workers on vertical part-time;
- workers on annualised part-time;
- workers employed under a training and work contract (full time or part time).

The pattern of working hours at company or even store level is further complicated by variations in opening hours, which can vary from one day to the next (especially for hypermarkets, which usually close on Monday morning and stay open for late-night shopping twice a week) and which will differ from one worker to another not only according to type of contract but also according to the team or department concerned.

Enterprise agreements do not necessarily establish any link between flexibility and lower hours, but generally set the number of hours well below 40, usually between 37 and 38½. That usually includes contractual paid rest periods, between 15 and 20 minutes per day, which reduce the number of hours actually worked per week.

However, some firms have established a direct, very detailed link between the rise in the number of hours for which facilities are used and the reduction in working hours. This particularly applies to the Rinascente group, which pioneered part-time working and flexible hours in large-scale retailing in Italy, and certainly affords an example of successful bargaining. In the Rinascente group, the first collective agreement at enterprise level dates back to April 1974 and was very advanced for its time. The latest agreement, concluded in 1989, contains a preamble which acknowledges that all collective bargaining agreements have three simultaneous aims: to promote the development of the firm, to protect and if possible increase jobs, and to improve employees' working conditions. One of the features of this agreement is that it explicitly spells out the principle of reducing the number of hours worked as the counterpart of more intensive "utilisation of plant" (the expression used has been directly borrowed from manufacturing industry). It contains a correspondence table for the number of hours' utilisation of plant (from 11 hours and 30 minutes to 16 hours and 59 minutes) on a certain number of days over the year, for a reduction in work time of between 4 hours and 24 hours per year.

In other cases, unions have obtained trade-offs in the form of modest pay increases for hours worked in the evening (this applies to the Euromercato Agreement of February 1989, giving a 15 per cent increase for hours worked after 9 p.m. and before 7 a.m. on top of the increases provided for by collective agreements on night-time working, *i.e.* between 10 p.m. and 6 a.m.).[4] Another has been a rise in the number of contractual hours for part-time workers. This was also an aspect in the negotiations at Euromercato in Lombardy, with respect to part-time workers employed for late-night opening, whose contractual hours have been increased from 20 hours a week to 24.

Another interesting case is the Esselunga group, whose latest enterprise agreement introduces flexitime for full-time workers. Under the December 1991 agreement, 37½ hours are worked over 6 days, but the number of hours worked each day can vary from 5½ hours to 7 hours, while the 7-hour limit can be exceeded by no more than 30 minutes per week. This agreement reflects the fact that, for historical reasons, Esselunga has a higher proportion of full-time workers than other large-scale retailers. This is an instance where flexible hours and flexitime apply directly to full-time workers, with flexibility extending not only to work over the year, but also over the week and over the day.

F. CONCLUSIONS

This analysis of retailing in Italy clearly indicates that it is an ideal field for experiments in flexible working time, especially in the case of the larger-scale retailers. This is because of the interaction of collective bargaining, legal provisions at national and regional level and local authority regulations. As we have seen, the overall legislative framework has radically changed since the 1980s, encouraging the transition from a rigid pattern of uniform working hours throughout the country to today's flexible working hours, the considerable extension of opening hours, the diversification of hours at local level from one town or region to another and between city centre and outskirts, etc. This process has coincided with the expansion of large-scale retailing over the past two decades at the expense of small stores, even though the latter remain remarkably widespread because of the system of granting licences by communes mentioned earlier.

While certain features, such as Sunday closing, are still the rule, here too, in addition to long-standing exemptions for tourism areas, new exemptions are being granted (albeit only a few so far) in cities and for highly specialised non-food outlets. In this regard, the Roman Catholic Church, which recently opposed allowing Sunday work in industry, does not object to the opening of stores in tourist areas or during certain holidays.

Larger-scale retailers have undoubtedly taken the lead in promoting and guiding the flexibility process. This has been brought about by a number of different means (part-time work, flexible hours on an annual basis, weekly flexitime for full-time workers, overtime, etc.) and, on the whole, without recourse to insecure forms of employment. There is no temporary agency work and very little fixed-term working.

Meanwhile the trade unions have been recommending modernisation for the retailing industry for the past ten years and have agreed, in principle and even more often in practice, to the employers' constraints as regards flexible working arrangements. It must be stressed however that the unions, following Italy's tradition in industrial relations, have maintained a typically contractual approach and have succeeded, through co-ordinated bargaining at various levels, in achieving direct and indirect trade-offs, especially in terms of pay and, to some extent, the reduction of hours worked. Furthermore, as already mentioned, the unions have benefited from the influence and power that the 1971 Act conferred on them by stipulating that unions should be represented in the regional and municipal trade committees.

In short, it would be fair to say that industrial relations in the retail trade and especially in large-scale retailing, play a substantial role in the determination of flexible working hours, both at the level of general industry-wide agreements and at the level of individual enterprises.

Notes

1. I would like to thank I. Piccoli for his help in collecting certain statistics used in this section.
2. Italian legislation does not allow temporary work organised by agencies "leasing" workers to firms for limited periods. Furthermore, use of fixed-term contracts is closely regulated and limited.
3. It should be borne in mind that all part-time work contracts are covered by the general provisions in Act 863 of 19 December 1984, under which such contracts must be in writing and must show, *inter alia*, exactly how each worker's hours are to be scheduled.
4. It should be mentioned, however, that the problem of night work is virtually non-existent in the retail trade.

Bibliography

AMBROSINI, M. (1991), "La flessibilità temporale nelle relazioni industriali", *Studi di sociologia*, Vol. 29, No. 4.

BAGLIONI, G. and MILANI, R. eds., (1990), *La contrattazioni collettiva nelle aziende industriali in Italia*, Milan: F. Angeli.

BLYTON, R. (1991), "Temporal flexibility: some recent developments and some unanswered questions", *The Work Flexibility Review*, Vol. 1, No. 2.

BOYER, R. (ed.) (1987), *La flexibilité du travail en Europe*, Paris: La Découverte.

BRUNHES, B. (1989), "Labour Flexility in Enterprises: A Comparison of Firms in Four European Countries", in *Labour Market Flexibility – Trends in Enterprises*, Paris: OECD.

Contratto collettivo nazionale di lavoro per i dipendenti da aziende del terziario della distribuzione e dei servizi, Rome, 14 December 1990.

Contratto integrativo aziendale Euromercato Spa, Varedo (Milan), 16 February 1989.

Contratto integrativo aziendale Gruppo La Rinascente, Rome, March 1989.

GASPARINI, G. (1991), Introduzione a "Gli orari atipici in Italia e in Francia – Materiali di ricerca", *Studi di sociologia*, Vol. 29, No. 4.

Ipotesi di accordo Esselunga Spa, Milan, 19 December 1991.

MINISTERO INDUSTRIA E COMMERCIO (1992), *Caratteri strutturali del sistema distributivo in Italia*, Rome.

NEGRELLI, S. (ed.) (1989), *Le relazioni sindacali nel commercio*, Milan: F. Angeli.

OLINI, G. (1990), *L'orario di lavoro*, in G. Baglioni and R. Milani (eds.).

PANNOZZO, G. (1991), Contribution in *Il commercio in Europa*, Rome: Ediesse.

PICCOLI, I. (1991), "Grande distribuzione e flessibilità temporale in Italia", *Studi di sociologia*, Vol. 29, No. 4.

ROJOT, J. (1989), "National Experiences in labour market flexibility", in *Labour Market Flexibility – Trends in Enterprises*, Paris: OECD.

SQUARZON, C. (1992), "La sindacalizzazione", in CESOS, *Le relazioni sindacali in Italia – Rapporto 1990/91*, Rome: Ed. Lavoro.

TADDEI, D. (1986), *Des machines et des hommes*, Paris: La Documentation française.

Bibliography

Chapter 8

THE NETHERLANDS: THE CASE OF HEALTH CARE

by

W.A.M. de Lange and D.H.C. van Maanen

A. INTRODUCTION

Until about 1970 there were few noteworthy developments in working time arrangements in the Netherlands. Working time had been decreasing gradually and there were some atypical contracts such as shift work and home-based employment, but overall there was little variation in working patterns.

In the 1970s, however, and increasingly over the following decade, new patterns emerged and many more workers came under some form of atypical contract or were using flexible working time arrangements. Between 1982 and 1985 the main issue in collective bargaining was a reduction in working time; after 1985 the accent shifted towards achieving a greater flexibility in labour utilisation. Employers considered work organisation and labour/management relations to be too rigid and insufficiently responsive to a changing economic environment.

These changes in Dutch labour relations were not without impact on health care, and much has changed in this field over the past twenty years. This chapter gives an overview of recent developments. It is composed of three main sections. Section B below discusses the general issue of flexible working time arrangements in the Netherlands. This is followed in Section C by a presentation of the Industrial Relations system in the Netherlands, and in Section D by an analysis of the specific problems relating to flexible working time arrangements in the Dutch system of health care.

B. FLEXIBLE WORKING TIME ARRANGEMENTS

Flexible working time arrangements

Management needs a degree of flexibility in order to adjust the organisation to its environment. This adjustment process may, among other things, concern operating hours and working time patterns. This chapter focuses upon the character of the employment relationship: has it changed as a result of management's need for flexibility?

The present section discusses three important issues: the extent of flexible working time arrangements in the Netherlands, the different forms these arrangements may take, and the reasons why employers and employees favour flexible working time patterns.

Only 25 years ago, differentiated working time patterns were seldom encountered. While shift work and seasonal work, for example, were not unusual, neither part-time employment nor other atypical contracts were widespread. Since 1980, however, there has been an enormous growth in the proportions and diversity of atypical work. Part-time work has become very popular, especially in the commercial services and in health care, with the Netherlands now having a higher share of part-time employment than any other European country.

A survey of more than 700 firms has shown that 30 per cent of all employees have some kind of atypical working time contract [OSA (1990)]. They may be subdivided as shown in Table 8.1.

In the Netherlands, part-time work is usually considered as atypical, but not as flexible employment. Such arrangements as on-call contracts, temporary work, staggered hours, home-based employment, overtime, functional flexibility, annual hours contracts and seasonal work are, under certain conditions, believed to achieve more flexibility in labour relations. Of course, this overview is not complete. Within a short space of time new forms have been introduced while others have become much less widespread. The field is clearly a very dynamic one.

At the end of the 1970s, the Netherlands was confronted with a severe economic recession. This resulted in a reduction of personnel and a dramatic rise in the unemployment rate to 17 per cent of the labour force. After the introduction of general working time reduction in 1982, the expected growth of employment proved to be disappointing.

Table 8.1. **Share of employees under atypical working time arrangements, 1990**

Percentages

Indefinite part-time contracts	20
Temporary full-time contracts	3
Temporary part-time contracts	1
Other atypical arrangements	6
Temporary employment by agencies	1.5
On-call contracts	2.5
Home-based employment	0.5
Freelance contracts	0.5
Seasonal work	1.0

Source: OSA (Organisation for Strategic Labour Market Research). (1990).

Instead, the workload of employees tended to increase. In addition, the twin goals of reducing labour costs and achieving greater flexibility made employers less inclined to create new "normal" jobs (*i.e.* full-time jobs of unlimited duration).

Employers tend to consider Dutch labour law as being too comprehensive and too rigid. It is, for example, quite difficult to dismiss an employee working under an indefinite contract, and the procedure is felt to be too time-consuming. In principle, every dismissal has to be approved by the district employment office. However, in 1991 only five percent of requests for dismissal submitted to labour offices were refused (whereas eleven percent of requests were withdrawn, so that in 84 per cent of all cases employees were dismissed as requested). In 75 per cent of all cases there was a judgement on the request within a period of six weeks.

Under the minimum wage law, employers have limited possibilities to vary wages. There are also strict rules concerning the duration of the probationary period. Employers claim that such regulations make it very difficult for them to run a company in an efficient and flexible way and in fact have a negative influence on employment. Hence, they try to get around over-rigid regulations, seeking to decrease their labour costs as much as possible. They may do this by handing out small part-time jobs and temporary contracts or by resorting to temporary employment via agencies to prolong the probationary period [Smitskam (1991)].

Productivity and cost impacts on firms of flexible working time practices

Data documenting the impact of atypical or flexible working time practices on productivity and cost are scarce. Part-time work can sometimes reduce the total illness rate of employees within a firm or sector, especially when the rate for full-time employees is high because of bad working conditions or monotonous work. Part-time workers sometimes have higher labour productivity than their full-time colleagues. The most important reason is that overcapacity can be avoided by scheduling part-time workers.

The OSA report mentioned earlier concludes that using more part-time work can have a positive effect on productivity. Increased use of other forms of flexible working patterns will, however, tend to have a somewhat negative effect on productivity because of the lower commitment, skills and experience of employees. This would tend to suggest that, apart from part-time work, atypical working time arrangements will not bring about significant economic advantages [OSA (1990)].

Working time reduction and company operating hours

Since World War II, working time has gradually been reduced. Two events require special attention: the introduction of the five-day working week around 1965 and the central agreement of 1982. The first event was the result of economic improvements following post-war reconstruction. With Saturday no longer a working day, the working week was reduced from 48 to 40 hours. This process took place quite smoothly; by contrast, with the crisis of the mid-1970s it became more difficult to make further reductions. Rising unemployment and unstable economic growth impaired the ability of employers' and employees' organisations to come to centrally negotiated agreements on conditions of employment.

However, there was general agreement on the necessity for drastic measures, as the Dutch economy was in a severe crisis and unemployment had reached unacceptable levels. The breakthrough came in November 1982. Employers and trade unions came to a historic agreement within the bipartite Foundation of Labour. This foundation, composed of representatives of employers' and employees' organisations, was set up to improve the relationship between these organisations and between government and the private sector, to give advice to the government and to negotiate wage developments. In the 1982 agreement both parties expressed the view that the reduction of working time constituted one way of achieving both profitable business conditions and lower unemployment. Between 1982 and 1986 the average reduction was about 5 per cent, *i.e.* two hours a week.

There has been little or no reduction in working time since 1986. Instead, employers have focused upon the goal of greater labour market flexibility. There is, however, a close interrelationship between working time reduction and increased flexibility. The introduction of part-time work had made way for general working time reduction; at the same time working time reduction facilitated flexibilisation. The demand by employers for increased labour market flexibility has arisen in direct response to trade union demands for general working time reduction. In fact, in a number of branches unions have been prepared to make concessions.

Originally, in most workplaces general working time reduction was organised in the same way for everyone. No distinction was made between different departments or jobs. The most common way of achieving working time reduction was the use of roster-free days, sometimes together with a reduction of the opening hours of the firm or of a department. This type of working time reduction often had a negative impact on flexibility.

In many cases the reduction of individual working hours also led to shorter company operating hours, resulting in higher costs because capital was not being used in an optimal way. However, a number of firms, by introducing a compressed work week, staggered hours or new shift work arrangements, showed that working time reductions can also lead to increased operating hours.

Differentiated working time reduction, combined with an extension of company operating hours, tends to increase the need for functional flexibility. Because of the extended operating hours, employees work at different times and, more importantly, they do not always work with the same group of colleagues because everyone has his own working schedule. Hence it is important that employees can replace each other and can perform several different tasks.

In the most recent agreement in the Foundation of Labour (November 1993), labour flexibility is the central issue, together with wage moderation. By contrast, there is no mention of working time reduction. The agreement notes that flexibility may be to the benefit of both employers (flexible operating hours and personnel utilisation) and employees (adjusting flexible working hours to personal needs, *e.g.* to take care of children).

Social protection of contingent workers

In comparison with core employees, social protection for contingent workers (*i.e.* employees under "atypical" or "flexible" contracts) is generally inferior. A few examples are given below. First it is important to know whether a worker has a labour contract and is therefore considered to be an employee. According to Dutch labour law, a labour contract is deemed to exist if there is a relationship of authority between the employer and the employee. Furthermore, there has to be an obligation for the employee to perform labour during a certain time.

Whether there is indeed a contractual relationship in the case of certain types of flexible labour, can therefore be questioned. Especially with regard to on-call contracts, there have been a number of law-suits between employers and workers. These have shown that employees often have more rights than the employer might think. If someone works regularly for an employer, *de facto* a contract of indefinite duration exists. Nevertheless, in practice, employees tend to be unaware of this and fail to assert their rights. An important problem with on-call contracts remains: the employer is not obliged to pay a wage if no work is available (at least if this is laid down in a contract).

Collective agreements or certain regulations within these agreements are not always extended to contingent workers. Sometimes regulations within collective agreements are valid only if an employee works more than a certain number of hours (for example, regulations dealing with overtime). Increasingly, however, trade unions are trying to regulate the terms and conditions of such workers by means of a collective agreement, and to harmonise them with those of regular employees.

C.   FEATURES OF THE INDUSTRIAL RELATIONS SYSTEM

There are three important union federations: the Confederation of Dutch Trade Unions, the result of a merger between a Socialist and a Roman Catholic Federation in 1982 (FNV); the Protestant National Trade Union Confederation (CNV); and a Federation for middle- and top-level white collar employees (MHP). Together these federations cover approximately 85 per cent of unionised workers. Both the FNV and CNV are made up of individual unions organised by industrial sector. While policy is framed primarily on the federation level, the individual unions do have some autonomy. There are also unions that do not belong to one of the federations. As a consequence, they are not, as are the FNV, CNV and MHP, represented in consultative bodies such as the Foundation of Labour and the Social Economic Board, the latter being the most important advisory body to the government on social and economic questions.

Decreasing economic growth and mass unemployment have had a negative impact on trade union density. Between 1980 and 1986 it fell from 39 per cent to 29 per cent of the workforce and is currently around 25 per cent.

There are two major employers' organisations which have representatives in the Foundation of Labour and the Social Economic Board: the Organisation of Dutch Enterprises (VNO) and the Organisation of Christian Employers (NCW). The VNO is strongly business-oriented and is geared primarily to its members' interests. The NCW is smaller and tends to concentrate more on societal and ethical issues [Reynaerts and Nagelkerke (1986)].

Works councils occupy an important position within firms. Obligatory in firms with 35 employees or more, they have two goals: to represent and protect the interests of the employees on the one hand, and to influence the social and economic policy of the company on the other. The works council and the management meet regularly. The council is given a number of participation rights, such as the right to advise the employer on important social and economic decisions that influence the position of the employees.

In certain cases works councils have the right to approve decisions. For example, they have to agree to any proposed changes in regulations concerning working time arrangements (Works Council Act, art. 27). Though no figures are available, case-studies have shown that works councils make use of this right when major changes are proposed in working time arrangements, such as the introduction of new shift work schemes or a compressed working week. Any changes put forward by the employer must be carefully prepared and justified. No new work pattern can be introduced without the works council's consent. Disputes are normally referred to an outside body for arbitration. There is hence a healthy balance of power between the employer and the works council, based on effective co-determination rights.

At present the Dutch industrial relations system may be characterised as follows:
- Negotiations on labour conditions tend to take place at an increasingly decentralised level.
- The national government interferes as little as possible in negotiations on the terms and conditions of employment.
- Despite the merger in 1982 of the two largest union federations, there is now a wider variation of employee representation, with the recent rise to prominence of the trade union federation for middle and top level staff.
- The decentralisation of bargaining, the internationalisation of enterprises, and the loss of membership have considerably diminished trade union power.
- The position of the unions at the enterprise level has not become stronger. While works councils exercise increasing influence on company policy, they function more or less autonomously, apart from the unions.
- In contrast to the situation in the 1960s and 1970s, there is a trend towards higher wage differentials (between branches, professions, etc.).
- In the legislation on working time, too, a shift in accent is apparent. Initially, the protection of the employee, who was thought to be the weaker party, was stressed by means of extended regulations. Nowadays, the emphasis is more on the freedom of agreement, although certain minimum norms relating to, for example, standard working hours and rest periods continue to apply.

Position of the actors concerning flexible working time arrangements

Trade union organisations tend to view most of the flexible labour contracts as a threat to the traditional employment relationship. While the FNV and CNV are afraid of labour market segmentation, part of this segmentation may itself be attributed to trade union policy towards flexible labour contracts. The rejection of flexible labour contracts by trade unions does not stimulate the employees concerned to become active trade union members. The fact that trade unions have hardly any members among categories of workers with a weak labour market position results in trade unions not bargaining for them. Moreover, in the bargaining rounds trade unions have traded working time reduction for flexibility. Various studies show that working time reduction has stimulated atypical employment [Delsen (1991)].

The FNV has a special committee of women members which has come forward with its own views on the issue of working time flexibility. The committee has asked unions to pay more attention to the interests of the members with a flexible labour contract. The unions, in their view, concentrate too much on full-time employees and trade working time for flexibility. In this way a vicious circle is created in which employees with flexible labour contracts are little represented and therefore poorly organised. Because many women who work (or are willing to work) do so under some type of flexible arrangement with their employer, women members would like to see the FNV strive for better regulations concerning flexible working time contracts.

The long-term objectives of the committee are the economic independence of women and a better re-allocation of paid and unpaid labour. Collective agreements should be applicable to all employees; there should be a legal maximum in the number of a company's flexible employment contracts; on-call contracts should be prohibited; provision for further education and training should be available for contingent employees as well as core personnel; everybody should be guaranteed a minimum wage and social security, etc. [FNV (1986)].

Just as in other European countries, the employers and their main representatives in the Netherlands are in favour of flexibilisation and deregulation. In their view, increased flexibility is necessary to remain competitive and will result in a better functioning labour market. A study by the Ministry of Social Affairs and Employment shows that two-thirds of 1 000 enterprises surveyed make use of some form of labour flexibility, such as overtime regulations, temporary employment, on-call contracts and labour pools [Loon-technische Dienst (1991)].

Since the end of the 1970s, the Dutch government has advocated a redistribution of jobs through the expansion of part-time employment in order to fight unemployment. Over the years, government policy has tended to adopt a more employer-oriented approach. It has been made easier to hire and dismiss personnel, and the restrictions on the use of agency workers and fixed-term contracts have been relaxed. Besides the changes in legislation, the Dutch government subsidises temporary jobs for unemployed youths and the long-term unemployed. Government and employers believe that flexibility and deregulation of the labour market are useful weapons in the fight against unemployment, and that a further loosening of labour regulations would have a positive employment effect. However, research on such employment effects has been limited and remains inconclusive [Delsen (1991)].

D. FLEXIBLE WORKING TIME ARRANGEMENTS IN HEALTH CARE

This section is subdivided into three parts. The first part presents an overview of the organisation of the Dutch health care sector, and the situation concerning atypical employment. The second and third parts present the views of the trade union and the employer association operating in the health care sector on flexible labour relations and flexible employment contracts.

The health care sector

Health care can be subdivided into hospitals, psychiatric hospitals, nursing homes and homes for those with a severe mental handicap. Furthermore, there are two types of institutions: private hospitals (owned by foundations, often religious in origin) and government hospitals. The total number of full-time equivalent employees is approximately 260 000 (210 000 in the private institutions and 50 000 in the government institutions). The total number of employees in the Dutch health care system is about 326 000. Seventy percent of them are female, and around 47 per cent of all employees have a part-time working contract [NZi (1992)].

Because of the general working time reduction, the number of working hours per year of full-time employees in health care decreased considerably during the 1980s. Since 1987 the number of hours worked has stabilized at 1 747 hours per year; this is three hours less than the average for all Dutch employees.

In a survey by the Ministry of Social Affairs and Employment involving more than 1 000 enterprises it was shown that health care (together with social work) has the highest share of atypical working time arrangements. In 86 per cent of the organisations in this sector one or more types of such arrangements can be found (see Chart 8.1).

Table 8.2 looks in more detail at the type of atypical arrangements used in health care, again in comparison with four other branches. When reading the figures it must be borne in mind that the survey asked whether these patterns were used to *increase flexibility* (not whether companies used these arrangements in general). We conclude that health care makes ample use of all the types referred to. On-call contracts and part-time employment especially are much more prevalent in this sector than in other branches.

In another survey [OSA (1990)], over 700 firms employing 100 employees or more were asked about their use of atypical contracts (see Table 8.1). A breakdown by industrial sector, given in Table 8.3, shows that the number of people working with an indefinite full-time contract is lowest in health care, while the extent of part-time employment and on-call contracts is highest in this sector. The share of workers with temporary contracts turned out to be low. In the past all student nurses had temporary contracts. Students obtained a special arrangement in the late 1980s and they are no longer considered to have a temporary contract.

174

Chart 8.1. **Organisations with atypical
working time patterns by industry**
Percentages

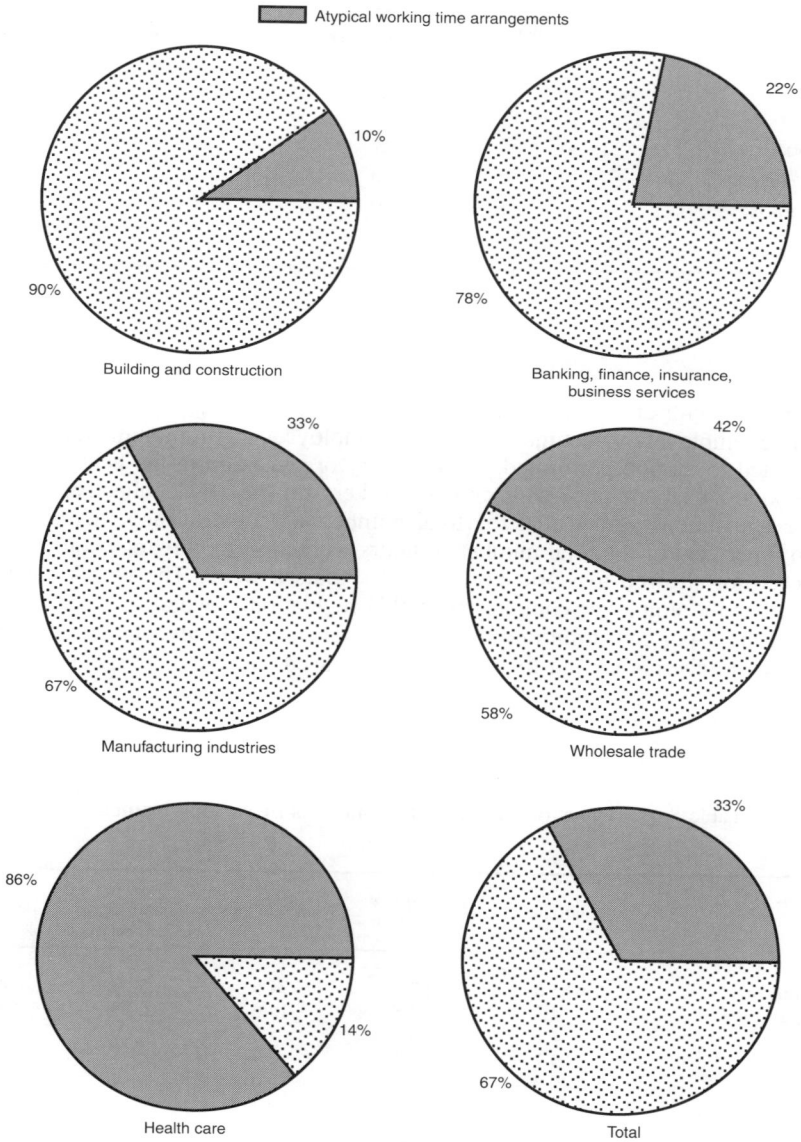

Atypical working time arrangements

10%

90%

Building and construction

22%

78%

Banking, finance, insurance,
business services

33%

67%

Manufacturing industries

42%

58%

Wholesale trade

86%

14%

Health care

33%

67%

Total

Source: Loontechnische Dienst (1991).

Table 8.2. **Use of atypical arrangements in various branches**

Percentages

	Manufacturing	Building and contruction	Wholesale trade	Banking, Insurance, Business Services	Health care
Part-time work	10	4	11	25	40
Agency work	53	17	45	40	39
Temporary contracts	16	20	11	11	23
On-call contracts	5	0	11	18	61

Source: Loontechnische Dienst (1991).

Employees with an on-call contract do not come within the collective agreement. For example, employers sometimes pay on-call employees the minimum wage instead of a wage related to the job performed. Nearly every organisation in the health care sector has some kind of labour pool with on-call workers. In the 1992 collective agreement, employers and unions agreed that the total number of on-call arrangements should be limited to 4 per cent of the total number of hours worked in the organisation. An on-call employee is not allowed to work more than 16 hours a week. The works council can check whether the employer complies with this regulation. Several organisations do in fact exceed the 4 per cent limit and there are no sanctions to prevent this. Management claims it has no alternative and that this pattern is used as little as possible.

Table 8.3. **Types of employment contracts in various branches**

Percentages

	Manufacturing	Building and construction	Wholesale trade	Banking, insurance, business services	Health care
Indefinite full-time	85.0	87.1	74.5	52.9	46.8
Indefinite part-time	4.3	3.5	14.0	29.8	42.5
Temporary contracts	4.1	6.1	5.0	7.9	3.1
Agency work	5.7	2.8	2.9	2.1	0.8
On-call contracts	0.3	0.0	3.0	6.4	6.7
Others	0.6	0.6	0.7	0.9	0.0
Total	100.0	100.0	100.0	100.0	100.0

Source: OSA (Organisation for Strategic Labour Market Research) (1990).

Table 8.4. **Employees in health care, 1991**

Percentages

	Regular duties	Irregular duties	Total number of jobs
Men	53	47	62 800
Women	38	62	198 500
Total	42	58	261 300

Source: CBS (Central Office for Statistics) (1992).

The above discussion has not included shift work. While shift workers have a regular contract, their working time pattern can be considered "irregular" and, to some extent, flexible. Table 8.4 shows the extent of irregular working time patterns in health care.

In health care more people are employed on some kind of irregular duty than in any other sector. Thus, while in the Netherlands 86 per cent of all workers have regular working hours, in health care the proportion is only 42 per cent (in manufacturing industries it is 80 per cent).

Although exact figures are not available, the incidence of sickness among part-time workers in health care appears to be lower than that of full-time workers. A possible explanation could be that part-time workers have more time to recover from pressure experienced during work. It is particularly those part-time employees with a small part-time contract (working less than 40 per cent of a full-time job) who have a lower sick-leave rate. No large difference in the rates between part-time and full-time employees appear when part-time employees work more than 40 per cent of a full-time job [see Windt (1990)].

Industrial relations in health care

Twenty-six percent of health care employees are represented by trade unions, two-thirds of these belonging to the "AbvaKabo" union, a member of the Confederation of Dutch Trade Unions (FNV).

The organisation of employees in the health care sector started only in the mid 1970s, while unionisation in industry began at the end of the nineteenth century. Health care has its origins in charity and therefore did not provide the "incentives" to organise employees. In time, the attitude towards health care changed and the sector became more professionalised. Collective agreements have now become common, and this has in turn encouraged employees to become union members. Of all members of works councils, 40 to 50 per cent are union members as well.

The NZf (Dutch Federation of Care) is the employer association in the health care sector. All of the 752 recognised private organisations are members of this association. Most of them are a contracting party in the sectoral collective agreement. However the 76 government organisations do not subscribe to the agreement.

The NZf not only negotiates with AbvaKabo on the terms of collective agreements, it also defends the financial interests of its member organisations *vis-à-vis* the Dutch government. Other tasks consist of providing support services for members, providing consultation services, etc. The NZf also runs its own research institute (NZi).

The employers find themselves in a difficult position when negotiating collective agreements. On the one hand, they are under the pressure of the trade unions to improve working conditions; on the other, their manoeuvrability is limited by budgetary considerations.

Normally collective agreements are concluded every two years. Before employers and unions start their negotiations, the government traditionally fixes the budget for labour costs in the sector. Against this background, the social partners negotiate the contents of the agreement. In 1991 the Social Economic Board advised the government to change this procedure. It is expected that within the next few years new procedures will be in place which will assign new roles to the major parties (the government, labour unions and the employer association). This procedure will provide for a new method of financing the health care sector, by giving a lump sum budget to the sector as a whole. As a result there will be more freedom for the organisations in spending their budgets, including wage determination.

In 1984 trade unions and the employer association agreed upon a 5 per cent reduction in working hours which resulted in a 38 hour working week. Unfortunately the goal of hiring new employees for 80 per cent of these hours was never realised, as the reduction in working hours coincided with a budget cut for the sector. This resulted in a spate of takeovers and reorganisations. One consequence for employees was a considerable increase in workload. The relatively low wages in the sector, together with the high workload, have had a negative effect on the image of the profession among recent graduates. This, in turn, has led to difficulties in recruiting nurses even in the western part of the country, where unemployment is high.

In January 1993 a new Working Hours Regulation for the health care sector came into force, replacing previous regulations dating back to 1957. Major changes have been made in mandatory rest periods and the limitation of maximum permitted services worked consecutively (ten for day shifts and seven for night shifts). It is forbidden to work more than nine hours a day or 48 hours a week. Some exceptions are possible; it is, for example, permissible to work an 11-hour day once every 14 days. The minimum daily rest period is ten hours. The minimum weekly rest period is 36 hours without interruption. All employees should have at least 17 Sundays off per year. These new limitations on working hours are expected to lead to 1 260 new jobs [Staatsblad (1992)].

Trade union attitudes towards flexible working arrangements in health care

This section reflects the view of the AbvaKabo trade union towards flexible working arrangements in the health care sector. AbvaKabo being the most important union in the sector, its positions may be taken as representative.

In defending the interests of full-time employees, Dutch trade unions have long opposed flexible labour contracts. Over the years their opinion has changed, at least concerning part-time work. Nowadays trade unions, in view of its beneficial impact on employment, tend to favour part-time work, especially contracts for 20 hours a week or more. In addition, it has become evident that more and more employees opt for part-time work because of the high workload prevalent in health care.

On the other hand, AbvaKabo strongly opposes on-call contracts because workers on such contracts do not enjoy the same rights as regular employees. Recently there has been an increase in the number of on-call contracts, and the union is trying to limit this development as far as possible.

The unionisation rate of temporary and on-call employees is not known. While the rate for part-time workers is also hard to document, it is lower than the unionisation rate of full-time employees. One of the reasons is that part-timers find membership too expensive. Although AbvaKabo has different contribution rates for full-time and part-time employees, this remains a problem.

In 1992 unions and employers agreed that on-call employees would have priority in applying for positions within the organisation where they were already working, if there was a suitable vacancy. AbvaKabo's goal is to bring these employees under the collective agreement. So far the union has not been successful because the employers do not want to give up the flexibility of the present situation.

AbvaKabo has, however, been successful in trying to improve employment conditions of part-time employees. Nowadays, there are hardly any differences between full-time and part-time contracts. The only difference that still remains concerns the payment of overtime. Employers pay part-time employees an overtime supplement only when they work more than 40 hours per week.

At present, the unions are not seeking a further reduction in general working time. In preparation for the latest collective agreement, AbvaKabo has organised 30 meetings with its members throughout the country. None of their 400 proposals calls for further working time reduction. Employees are more concerned about increases in workload. In addition, they do not wish to pay for working time reduction with a loss in income, as they had to do in the mid-1980s.

In contrast to the other industries, where more and more bargaining is taking place on a decentralised level, negotiations in health care are still centralised. Over the last few years, a growing interest in more decentralisation has been expressed by some of the organisations. In areas where it is harder to get qualified personnel, hospitals are in favour of regional labour agreements which would give them, among other things, the possibility to pay higher wages. The unions do not agree because they find that employees in the same profession should have the same terms and conditions of employment throughout the country. Nevertheless, the hospitals have succeeded in inserting a clause in the collective agreement which makes it possible for them to pay an employee a higher salary for a temporary period of time if the labour market is tight.

Over the last several years the unions have agreed that local works councils can negotiate about certain minor aspects of employment conditions. In this way local organisations are gaining more experience and can adjust provisions of the central agreement to their particular situation. AbvaKabo is prepared to give local organisations more authority if they have enough experience in negotiations to achieve satisfactory results for union members. The reimbursement of expenses for travelling between work and home, for example, is no longer part of the central negotiations. Overall, decentralisation of negotiations is seen as inevitable in the long run. However, the union is not willing to turn over all of its authority to the works councils which, as a rule, tend to be interested mainly in the employees in their own organisation.

Employer attitudes towards flexible working arrangements in health care

The main reason why employers favour flexibility in labour relations is that it helps them to cope with fluctuations in ''demand'' for health care. Health care is a labour-intensive sector. Since labour is the most precious production factor, the employers strive to utilise it in the most efficient and optimal way possible.

Among the available flexibility options, the employer association NZf tends to favour the so-called min-max contracts. This kind of part-time contract has a great potential for flexibility in reacting to fluctuations in ''demand'' and ''production''. In min-max contracts the employer is obliged to pay an employee for a certain minimum number of hours per week or per month. In turn, the employee is obliged to accept work for a certain maximum number of hours. In so called ''zero-hours'' contracts there are no such obligations on employer and employee. An advantage in comparison with employees working on a zero-hours contract is that employees with a min-max contract are much more integrated within the organisation. This has a positive effect on the quality of the health service.

As noted above, the unions are trying to regulate the extent of on-call contracts in collective agreements. So far the NZf has prevented this, but gradually more and more specific regulations are appearing in the agreement for the health sector. The 4 per cent quota is a clear example. As a result, the freedom of an organisation is increasingly limited.

The main reason why the NZf objects to on-call contracts falling under the collective agreement is the high cost of labour. Although some employers do pay the job-related wage agreed upon in the collective agreement to employees with an on-call contract, the payment of the minimum wage to such employees is also possible. Even if the normal wage is paid, on-call contracts are advantageous for the employer because overcapacity is avoided.

Like the unions, the NZf is not currently seeking any further reduction of working time. Reduced working hours would mean lower wages, which would cause still more problems in attracting new employees. At the moment, it is more important for employers to be able to pay higher wages to selected groups of employees.

In the past few years there have been some experiments in extending operating hours. This is especially important for the surgery rooms of hospitals. From an economic point of view, it is advantageous for employers to use expensive equipment for more hours per day and over the weekend. Another reason for this growing phenomenon is the demand of customers and the increased competition between public and private hospitals. Through the extension of service, employers can gain competitive advantage.

As mentioned earlier, part-time employees get an allowance for overtime only if they work more than 40 hours per week. Employers do not want to change this because labour costs would rise too much. A reduction in the number of part-time contracts would be the only way of coping with this potential financial strain.

Some employers are asking for more decentralised negotiations on employment conditions, especially the general hospitals who want their "own" solutions to their own specific problems. In the future a shift towards a stronger negotiating role for the works council and the local employer may be expected (although it is not clear to what extent). This would not only affect the relation between unions and works councils, but also the position and role of the employers' association. The NZf has its own local associations but, so far, the negotiation function has been kept on a central level – a position the federation does not want to give up.

The changing role of government is another important element in this process. It is generally thought that, in the past, the Dutch government has made too many special arrangements for the sector. For example, a few years ago the works councils in the health sector were extended with special patient representatives. Employers resisted this move, arguing that in the private sector customers and clients were not represented in the works councils either, and that as far as possible health care should be governed by the same regulations as private industry.

E. CONCLUSIONS

There are many atypical working time patterns in the Dutch health care sector. While the employment conditions of part-time employees equal – except for the payment of overtime – those of full-time workers, it is particularly employees with on-call contracts who are in an unfavourable position. Unions are attempting to reduce the importance of flexible work, while employers are trying to keep as much of it as possible, mainly because of restricted budgets. Neither the unions, nor the employers want further working time reduction.

Regarding labour relations, there is a marked trend towards decentralisation. In the future, more decisions concerning employment conditions are likely to be taken at a decentralised level, although it is hard to say how far this development will go. The employers' organisation in particular, whose members are pressing for more autonomy and manoeuvrability in negotiations, has problems with this trend because it implies that its own role as an umbrella organisation will become less important.

Over the past few years there has been some discord between employers and unions over the collective agreements, but at present the conflict is more between employers and employees on the one hand, and government on the other. At issue is the budget available for health services. Because of the difficulties they experience on the labour market, employers would particularly like more freedom in determining wage levels.

Bibliography

BOSCH, L. and LANGE, W. de (1987), "Shift work in health care", in *Ergonomics*, Vol. 20, No. 5.

CBS (Central Office for Statistics) (1992), *Werkgelegenheid en werkgelegenheidsstructuur: samenstelling van de uitkomsten over de structuur van de werkgelegenheid 1989, 1990 en 1991*, Voorburg.

DELSEN, L. (1991), *Atypical employment and industrial relations in the Netherlands*, Nijmegen: Nijmegen University.

DEURSEN, C. van (1992), *Arbeidssituatie en gezondheid van verpleegkundigen in dagdienst en ploegendienst*, Leiden: NIPG (Dutch Institute for Preventive Health Care), internal publication.

EMANCIPATIERAAD (1987), *Advies flexibilisering van arbeidsrelaties*, Den Haag.

FNV SECRETARIAAT VOOR VROUWELIJKE WERKNEMERS (1986), *Flexibele arbeid: onder de maat*, Amsterdam.

MINISTERIE VAN JUSTITIE (1990), *Wet op de Ondernemingsraden*, Den Haag.

MINISTERIE VAN SOCIALE ZAKEN EN WERKGELEGENHEID (1991), *Werktijden: arbeidstijd, bedrijfstijd, vrije tijd*, Den Haag.

LANGE, W. de (1989a), *Configuratie van arbeid*, Zutphen: Thieme.

LANGE, W. de (1989b), "Working and operating time in the eighties – the Dutch case", Paper for the International Symposium on Working Time, Vienna, 13-15 December.

LANGE, W. de (1992), "La configuración del trabajo en los Paises Bajos", in *Revista de Economia y Sociologia del Trabajo*, No. 15/16.

LOONTECHNISCHE DIENST (1991), *Veranderende arbeidstijdpatronen*, Den Haag.

NATIONAAL ZIEKENHUISINSTITUUT (NZi) (1992), *Sociaal economische kerncijfers ziekenhuiswezen*, Utrecht: NZi.

OSA (Organisatie voor Strategisch Arbeidsmarkten-onderzoek) (1990), *Flexibele arbeid: vormen, motieven en effecten*, OSA werkdocument W76, Rotterdam.

REYNAERTS, W. and NAGELKERKE, A. (1986), *Arbeidsverhoudingen, theorie en praktijk*, deel 1, Leiden/Antwerpen: Stenfert Kroese.

ROOD, M. (1987), "Over de toekomst van de medezeggenschap", in I. Asscher- Vonk *et al*. (ed.), *Schetsen voor Bakels*, Deventer: Kluwer.

SMITSKAM, C. (ed.) (1991), *Flexibele arbeidsrelaties*, Deventer: Kluwer.

STAATSBLAD (1992), *Werktijdenbesluit voor verplegings- of verzorgingsinrichtingen*, No. 167, Den Haag.

WINDT, W. van de (1990), *Ziekteverzuim in de gezondheidszorg*, Utrecht: NZi.

Chapter 9

SWEDEN: THE CASE OF HEALTH CARE

by

Casten von Otter and Birger Viklund

A. INTRODUCTION

Working time arrangements within the health sector in Sweden are currently being reappraised, primarily for two reasons. One is the demand for a more efficient provision of public health, the other a politically motivated pressure to deregulate and give market forces a freer rein in the regulation of the work process.

Following persistent economic and political pressures on its health system, Sweden is currently trying to improve both its efficiency and productivity. The administrative planning model, which has served fairly well for a generation, has proved to be less appropriate for managing the health care delivery process in times of economic stagnation, or to produce the resources to cope with the new needs resulting from technological development and changing demographic pressures.

In response to this dilemma, national and local institutions have begun to explore new methods based on freedom of choice and incentives by which to decentralise responsibility for management and economic decisions in the health sector. These methods have affected the labour/management relationship and the arrangements of the labour process in hospitals as well as ambulatory care in a number of ways. The county (*län*) administrations, which are responsible for the health care delivery system, have begun experimenting with new forms of work organisation. The development of more flexible working time arrangements is an important ingredient in this process [Saltman and von Otter (1992)].

Some rather impressive improvements in productive efficiency have been achieved. They may, however, be more indicative of slack in the old model than of persistent vigour in the new one. Stockholm county, one of the first to experiment with "planned markets" (competitive mechanisms within a public structure), was able to report increases in productivity of between 9 and 20 per cent in those departments taking part in the project; for many procedures, waiting lists have all but disappeared [Stockholms läns landsting (1992)]. While this achievement is based mainly on incentive-driven models of health care production, reorganisation of work on the basis of more flexible staffing and working time arrangements has been a key factor in achieving improvements in production, especially in areas such as elective surgery.

In organisational terms, the reform strategy has raised questions on how best to:

- create more task-focused units within hierarchically integrated local centres and hospitals;
- develop patterns of labour/management negotiation and consultation, as well as collective agreements which can meet the varying needs within decentralised, locally managed health care delivery sites;
- design a structure of work arrangements, including flexible working time, which can meet a broad set of professional and policy requirements.

A distinguishing characteristic of the health care system in Sweden is its specific combination of central planning within a decentralised structure. Responsibility for provision and finance of health care lies with the 26 counties. As well as operating the health care organisation they independently develop managerial and personnel policies, including working time scheduling, within a structure of national regulations. The essential parameters which determine the aims and structure of the system are decided among the three key national players, the Government, the National Board of Health and Welfare and the Federation of County Councils (Landstingsförbundet). In relevant cases the trade unions also contribute to decision-making.

B. STATUTORY REGULATION OF WORKING HOURS

Rules and regulations on working hours are the same for the health sector as for the rest of the labour market. They are found in the Working Hours Act which came into force on 1 January 1983, as well as in the 1975 Work Environment Act. Rules governing usual working hours, stand-by hours, overtime, etc., were transferred to the new Act from the General Working Hours Act of 1970. Paragraph 4 of the Work Environment Act comprised rules concerning the scheduling of working hours which were also transferred to the new Act.

The Working Hours Act is non-binding. This means that exceptions can be made, partially or wholly, as a result of agreements concluded or accepted by a national union. The Act, furthermore, permits local derogations from specific provisions. Nevertheless, the stipulations in the Working Hours Act are of great importance for collective agreements on working hours. For the health sector, provisions on working time are addressed in national agreements together with rules which pertain to salary scales and other aspects of the employment relationship.[1]

When discussing the possibilities of flexible working hours, it is important to bear in mind two specific aspects of Swedish labour legislation:

- The employer decides on the scheduling of working hours if no agreement has been concluded. This tends to give him the upper hand in local negotiations.

- The existence of personal contracts for part-time workers is a significant factor. As a rule, part-time employees sign individual agreements with the employer which may deviate from the collective agreement in force in the specific sector. There are no legal stipulations which entitle part-time employees to claim an increase in the number of working hours, or an extension to full-time employment. However, some collective agreements such as those applying to the health care sector, include recommendations of this kind.

Provisions in individual contracts determine to what extent employers may change the scheduling of working hours for health care workers. However, the employer has no general right to order shift work for any staff. This was the conclusion reached by the Labour Court in a precedent-setting case relating to a group of nurses in Nyköping.

Apart from the stipulations established in the Working Hours Act, and in the corresponding agreements, there are other laws and agreements that also affect the possibility of introducing flexible working hours. The following acts should be mentioned in this context:

- the Vacation Leave Act;
- the Act on Security of Employment which, among other things, regulates temporary posts and which is applicable should the employer wish to alter the number of working hours (8 per cent of all employees are under temporary work contracts);
- several Acts on leave of absence, among others the Educational Leave Act and the Child Care Leave Act (15 per cent of employees are on long-term leave);
- the Act on Part-Time Retirement.

According to the 1983 Working Hours Act, an ordinary working week must not exceed 40 hours. However, when needed, due to the nature of the job or the working conditions in general, working hours may exceed this amount if they average 40 hours a week over a period of up to four weeks.

The Act thus defines the upper limit of working hours permitted. On the other hand, an employer is completely free to permit fewer working hours than the stipulated upper limit. This means he cannot reject proposals for shorter working hours by making reference to the Working Hours Act. On the other hand, the Act also prevents those employees who might wish to work more than an average of 40 hours per week from doing so. By contrast, there is no limitation of daily working hours.

The question of whether the Working Hours Act prevents flexible scheduling requires a more detailed examination. Several provisions in the Act have to be taken into consideration. The required overall average of 40 hours over a period of up to four weeks in itself limits flexibility. It restricts the possibility of varying working hours (at least in the case of a full-time job) between summer and winter or over a period longer than four weeks.

Under the Working Hours Act, there is a general ban on night work between 12.00 midnight and 5.00 a.m. Exemptions from this ban are possible depending on the nature of the job concerned, the public need and other special conditions. They are made, for example, in the case of continuous process industries, nursing institutions, public transport, and data processing centres. Another stipulation affecting the possibilities of freely scheduling working hours is the one governing weekly rest. All employees are entitled to 36 hours continuous weekly rest for each period of seven days, irrespective of how the weekly rest is scheduled. It may be scheduled at the beginning of one period and at the end of another.

What are the practical consequences of the rules governing the scheduling of working hours? Certain conditions apply only to some categories of employees. Exemptions from the stipulations have wide-ranging consequences for the health sector. For example, those employed in hospitals and nursing, like those working in other sectors allowing no interruptions, are not covered by the ban on night work nor, in most cases, are they protected by the rule stipulating a pause after five hours of work. Theoretically, the Working Hours Act allows those employed in the above-mentioned sectors unlimited continuous working periods scheduled at any time throughout the 24-hour period. The only limitation is represented by the stipulation concerning the weekly rest.

During a four-week period, equal to 672 possible working hours ($4 \times 7 \times 24$), an employee may theoretically work as many as 428 hours taking into account the weekly rest, and the number of hours that fall under the ban on night work. Full-time workers, normally obliged to work a total of 160 hours during a four-week period, are given various opportunities to schedule their working hours. Furthermore, the Act does not express a strict ban on permanent scheduling of working hours on Saturdays and Sundays. The demands for weekly rest may be considered fulfilled by allowing time off during ordinary working days.

Proposed legal reforms

Working time regulations have been a much-debated topic for at least two decades. However, the focus has varied from a social concern about the possible difficulties of combining social and family responsibilities with full participation in working life, to a concern with the productivity and economic consequences of existing arrangements.

A commission report on working time was presented to the public in 1989 by a Committee led by Mona Sahlin, later to become Minister of Labour and currently deputy Prime Minister in the Carlsson cabinet [SOU (1989)]. The report suggested that working time should be approached from a life perspective, with ample paid time for education and sabbaticals. This perspective, borrowed from the well-known labour economist Gösta Rehn, can be seen as a reply to women's groups, including the Social Democratic Women's Federation, which for years have been advocating and campaigning for a reduction of the *daily* working time to six hours at full pay. This reform would make it possible, the women's organisations maintain, for both parents in a family to share equally the responsibility for bringing up the children and homemaking while holding a full-time job.

In support of the idea of working time flexibility, the Commission showed that, at least outside of manufacturing, actual working hours are very diverse and that people's preferences vary widely depending on age, family situation, geographic location and a number of other factors. The Commission report has had a considerable impact on changing the general attitude towards working hours. As a result, working hours are being viewed more from a yearly, if not from a life perspective, and the need for more flexibility, both in legislation and collective agreements, has become more apparent.

The only major criticism from the trade union side was that the Commission seemed to completely rule out daily or weekly working hour reductions. Many people in different functions still work overly long hours, for instance two-shift workers and workers on continuous night shifts. The unions maintained that there is no negative relationship between working hour reductions and productivity. In industry the opposite is often true – the shortening of working hours in the past has tended to increase productivity. However, most damaging to the Commission was the refusal at the time of the feminist movement to consider any alternatives but a shorter working day.

While representing a significant shift in the general attitude towards flexible working hours, the Commission report did not lead to any new legislation. However, a new Public Commission was appointed in February 1991, whose task was to suggest more flexible rules for working hours and paid holidays. In March 1992 the Commission submitted its report: *Annual Working Hours. New Law on Working Hours and Holidays* [SOU (1992)].

The report suggested that the legal 40-hour week be changed by law to an *annual* working time of 2 007 hours, and that the scheduling of these hours be decided in collective agreements. A proportion of this annual working time (216 hours) should be paid vacation. If collective agreements on the scheduling of working hours were not reached, the employer should be able to decide unilaterally within the framework provided by the new law, which includes rules on minimum nightly and weekly rest periods. A new Working Time Act was subsequently passed which, however, reduced the annual vacation period to 200 hours.

C.   TRADE UNION POSITIONS

The local government workers' union, SKAF, is the dominant union in health care, alongside the union of registered nurses, SHSTF, and the union of physicians. SKAF has discussed working hours in some detail at its recent conventions, as has the registered nurses' union. There is, however, a marked difference between the future-oriented attitude of the convention reports and resolutions on the one hand, and actual practice, on the other. Indeed, one can discern an integral split within the organisations which parallels divisions within the membership, reflecting branch of government, human vs. technical services, age and not least, gender.

The negotiators from the national trade unions continue to be influenced by ideas developed over the years in the male-dominated technical services that emphasize control over working hour arrangements. They insist that only the national union can sign agreements in the field. As a consequence, the practice of working time flexibility is not as established in health care and in other local government activities as in industry and private services, in spite of the fact that local government employees work much more often during uncomfortable hours and would thus stand to gain more from increased flexibility than industrial workers. In 1989, only 13 per cent of the SKAF members

187

reported that they had any flexibility in their working time schedules [SKAF (1989)]. This figure should be compared with that of 18 per cent among all members of the blue-collar workers' union federation, LO; 43 per cent among the members of the white-collar workers' federation, TCO; and 59 per cent in the federation of academic professions, SACO.

Women in local government report less flexible working time arrangements than men (11 per cent vs. 25 per cent). No other group in the labour market has so little flexibility in working hours as the women in local government. Most of them work in the health care field, including home care. Of the women in health care, 93 per cent say they have no possibility of influencing the time at which they start or leave their jobs. While this, to some extent, reflects the nature of the job, it is also a consequence of the traditionally rigid management policies in health care, especially *vis-à-vis* nurses and nursing assistants.

Other studies also show that women in health care suffer from a lack of personally adjusted or flexible work arrangements. This is a major disadvantage of their jobs and consequently a main reason for wanting to quit or being absent from work in order to meet other obligations. In fact a study by the employers' organisation in health care, the Federation of County Councils, showed that 82 per cent of women employees believe that it is very important to be able to have some say in the starting and ending time of the work day. Ninety two percent feel that it is very important to be able to decide on the scheduling of their vacation time [Landstingsförbundet (1992)].

The 1988 SKAF Convention did in fact decide that the union should help promote flexible working time arrangements. The union's 1989 report on working time makes it clear that the experience of flexible working time arrangements has so far been very favourable: "Flexible working hours have been shown to provide better adjustment of hospital routines to the needs of individual patients. Staff well-being and job satisfaction increase and stress is diminished. Overtime is reduced along with absenteeism. Employees can adjust their working hours to their own needs and the needs of their families. Shorter commuting times are a result of being able to avoid rush hours."

However, the report also notes a few possible negative effects or problems. While trade union officials in favour of more flexible working time arrangements understand that an automated (computerised) registration of actual working hours is necessary for flexible scheduling, they are also aware of the fact that existing registration systems are not designed to deal with the very complicated working hour systems in use in health care. Evaluations of existing flexitime systems also report constant criticism of unreliable time registration systems.

Concern has also been voiced about the possibility of understaffing during strategic hours of hospital activities if flexitime is introduced. The SKAF report refutes this allegation and states categorically that flexitime projects show that "health care personnel know best how working hours should be used to satisfy the patients' needs and the demands of production".

The number of union member working flexible hours may have increased somewhat since 1989, as is indeed suggested by the 1992 survey [Landstingsförbundet (1992)]. If this is the case, it occurred mainly through local arrangements outside the control of the central employer and union federations. There are a number of flexible working hours arrangements made locally without the consent or even knowledge of the official trade union or employer structure.

D.   WORKING TIME AND ORGANISATION IN HEALTH CARE

The labour market parties in the health sector have been debating policies regarding working time for at least a decade. The specific problems in health care, with more than two-thirds of all employees working irregular hours, and the fact that 84 per cent of all personnel are women (many of whom are faced with the double burden of work and family), make the issue a crucial one. During much of the 1980s, the health care sector suffered from severe recruitment problems. Working time arrangements were seen by the labour market parties as the main cause, next to lagging salaries. Issues which were keenly debated at the time include:

- the six-hour day on full pay;
- a reduction from one out of two to one out of three working weekends;
- and the abolition of "split shifts", with an extended break in the middle of the day.

The first of these issues has led to some experiments, but is still unresolved and likely to remain so while the present economic difficulties persist. The fact that 82 per cent of all clinics, according to the recent survey by the Federation of County Councils [Landstingsförbundet (1992)], have introduced some form of change in working time arrangements, mainly reflects the second issue. More than half of the new arrangements (53 per cent) concern a reduction in the number of weekends worked. Personal schedules (44 per cent) and flexitime (33 per cent) are other major directions of change (see Chart 9.1). The scheduling of physician's working hours, another issue which is seen as important in trying to improve the productivity and flexibility of the health system, has again been addressed in the negotiations for a national contract. Finally, the demand for unbroken shifts has led to a high frequency of part-time jobs (39 per cent of all employees).

These reforms have been "extremely expensive", as indicated by one spokesperson from the Landstingsförbund. They necessitated hiring more staff to fill weekend shifts. The amount of overlap between shifts, when abolishing the split shift, increased during the middle of the day, which is generally a slack period. Other problems, which caused recruitment difficulties or higher costs, concern scheduling during summer vacation periods when wards have sometimes had to be closed due to shortage of replacement personnel in key positions. With radically changing conditions in the labour market and rising unemployment, there is now increasing pressure to give priority to efficiency rather than employee preference.

Chart 9.1. **New working time arrangements in Swedish clinics**
Percentages

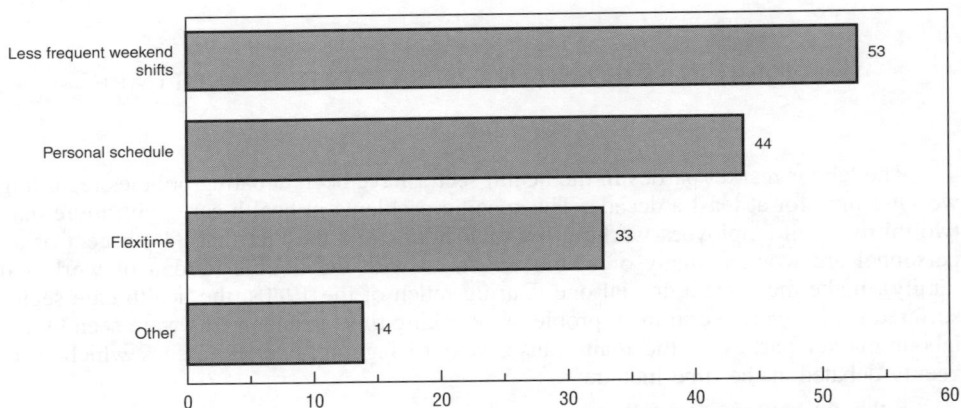

Category	Percentage
Less frequent weekend shifts	53
Personal schedule	44
Flexitime	33
Other	14

Source: Landstingsförbundet (1992).

Working time alternatives in practice

The departments in health care institutions that have introduced new forms of working time arrangements have tended to be nursing and home-help services catering to the needs of elderly and otherwise handicapped people. Alternatives which are being considered locally include the following (with some overlaps):

- **Flexibility schemes:**
  Flexitime
  Individual schedules
  Manning according to need
  Time bank
  Job rotation
- **Shift work arrangements:**
  Weekend shifts
  Bonus and reward systems
  Rolling three-shift schedules
  Combined day and night schedule
- **Long-term adjustment:**
  Summer and winter schedules
  Light holiday schedules
  Annual schedules

The first set of reforms relates mainly to achieving more individual flexibility and improving the match between workload and staffing levels. The second set refers to the problem of intermittent production, and the need in most hospitals to have year-round, day and night surveillance. The heavy burden placed on personnel, as well as the high shift-related costs, have led to a number of measures to spread shift work among the existing staff and thus make the share of the burden less for each individual.

It has become clear from the discussion of the legal framework and the handling of flexible working time policies at the national trade union level that initiatives are almost always taken at the local level. These initiatives are sometimes even outside the control of local representatives of the national unions, who usually negotiate local contracts in the name of the national union. As a result, most flexible working hours projects are started and run by local joint committees and personnel departments, without formal agreements.

Flexitime

A one-year flexitime project was introduced in four wards of a geriatric hospital. The initiative in this case came from the producer of time-recording technology. It was part of a larger programme which included at least one unit from all health districts in Stockholm county, the largest in the country. The scheme at this specific location was developed by a group representing employees, unions and management. Requirements for minimal staffing were established: for example, one nurse, as well as three nursing assistants, must always be on duty from 9.00 a.m. onwards. The number of hours worked was checked at the end of each month, and plus/minus 10 hours could be transferred to the next month.

The evaluation report showed that 37 per cent of the staff made regular use of the option, and the remaining 62 per cent made occasional use (1 per cent never). Most of the employees ''flexed'' only in the morning or in the evening. At the end of the period, 70 per cent wished to retain flexitime.

The general feeling was either that the work environment had improved or that it was not affected. The main disagreements with the project related to the flexitime frame. Some felt it should be extended to more than one hour (30 minutes for the night shift). Others were critical of the time-recording technology which was complicated and unreliable. In fact one of the main results to emerge from the project was that reliable technology is essential. Another problem was that most people could do little to organise their job to facilitate use of the flexitime arrangement.

Personal schedules are an even more common feature today. A radical example of this model has been developed in some clinics, where a blank paper, with only the minimum staffing indicated, is posted on a board. Everybody is invited to fill in his or her personal choice of hours for the coming week, and encouraged to talk with their workmates should they have some specific needs. Otherwise everything is on a ''first come, first served'' basis. Should major conflicts emerge, the head nurse will settle the issue. It is the general impression that this highly pragmatic arrangement works to the general satisfaction of those involved.

The Time Bank

This initiative is probably the best known experiment with new working time arrangements in Sweden in recent years. It was started in September 1989 in an intensive care unit in a country hospital (Ljungby), where jobs are demanding, but where the workload usually varies considerably. The project is led by a group with representatives from hospital management, the intensive care unit and the trade unions of nurses and nursing assistants. Before the new arrangements were set up, a secret ballot was taken which showed strong support for the project.

Three main components characterise the model: individual schedules; a time bank; and compensation funds. There is a standard schedule made up for each ward, covering days, nights and weekends for all employees except the physicians, who are not included in the project. In any departure from this schedule, each person makes the individual changes he/she wishes. Each team of employees is responsible for covering a minimum staffing level. Should the group be unable to agree on the arrangements, the head nurse will settle the discussion. Thus, for each employee a personal schedule is established to fit his/her needs.

Between 7.00 a.m. and 5.00 p.m. the value of each hour is equivalent to exactly that, 60 minutes. Work at all other times is worth 80 minutes per hour. The total sum should be 40 hours per week. No single shift should extend over more than 10 hours. Ordinary work can be exchanged for "on call duty" at an exchange ratio of 1:2.

As the workload is variable, an employee is allowed to take leave, for a few hours or the full day, if the head nurse agrees that this would not disturb the work process. A deposit is then made in the time bank: 60 minutes off puts 45 minutes in the bank, which the employer can reclaim when the work load is heavy. Depending on when and how time is reclaimed, the employee can be asked to work more – or even get a further discount if he/she is called in at very short notice. Each employee can deposit up to 24 hours on his/her own account, the rest goes into a "slush fund" which is shared by the whole ward. The latter gives an indication of the potential for staff reductions in the longer perspective.

There are three accounts for compensation: one for the group, one for the whole ward and one for the hospital administration. Each deposit in the time bank implies a corresponding money placement in the accounts, of which the balance is distributed to the three parties the following year.

Compared with conventional arrangements, the following observations may be made:

- There are no special provisions for holidays, preferences being expressed in one's personal schedule.
- Initially there were problems with information exchange between shifts when people tended to leave early or come in late. For this reason, it was decided that some shift changes should be scheduled more formally. Some oral reporting was found unnecessary and other reports concerning the patients had to be worked out within the permitted variations of schedules. In conclusion, it was observed that less time was required for reporting, compared to a conventional system.

Table 9.1. **Working time related cost – the Ljungby experiments**

In Skr

	1st period 15th Sept. 1988 14th Sept. 1989	2nd period 15th Sept. 1989 14th Sept. 1990	3rd period 15th Sept. 1990 14th Sept. 1991
Total "additional time"	697 342	341 515	150 431
Total cost ordinary work	4 312 116	4 264 436	4 468 702
Compensation for shift	407 500	400 300	383 300
Withdrawal from time bank		127 138	248 577
Deduction for illness	−280 182	−184 857	−160 813
Total	5 136 776	4 948 532	5 090 197

Source: *Västra Sjukvårdsdistriktet* (1992).

- The composition of work teams should be such as to allow as many employees as possible to meet their own preferences. Thus, it was found best to attempt a balanced share of full- and part-timers, of employees with young children and some other essential social characteristics. The size of the group can vary from five to as many as thirty employees.

The economic outcome has been analysed in several studies by the hospital's own specialists. The general trend is favourable in all studies, though different calculations and data bases account for slightly different figures. Staff turnover and absenteeism have been reduced compared to other clinics within the hospital. For three different periods, which cover the duration of the project, savings resulting from lower turnover were calculated at Skr 93 960, Skr 8 192 and Skr 4 096. The reduction of absenteeism by 40 per cent has saved an additional Skr 120 000. In all, over a three-year period, more than Skr 200 000 were saved on the personnel budget [Andersson, in Västra Sjukvård-sdistriktet (1992)]. Another study covering a shorter period and using a different model reports 8 per cent savings on all personnel costs out of a budget of Skr 1.5 million.

In Table 9.1, working time related costs are documented for three periods, the first prior to the experiment, and the second and third during the course of the project. The most dramatic differences are the reduction in costs associated with absenteeism and "additional time", *i.e.* irregular hours, overtime, etc. Overall, both senior managers and trade union officials speak favourably of the project.

Reduced working time

One set of projects, implemented in a number of hospitals, has focused on reducing working time in order to make jobs more attractive and to match the workforce more effectively to the actual needs of the delivery process. One case which has created much attention is the flexible working hours arrangement for home helpers in Kiruna, the mining town north of the Arctic Circle.

The Kiruna project is a result of efforts by the local government workers' union, SKAF, to deal with the problem of part-time unemployment among nursing personnel, who initially request part-time jobs and are then unable to obtain full-time employment when the family situation allows. In this situation, the union unemployment insurance fund has to pay unemployment compensation for the idle time.

A labour market survey undertaken by the employment exchange and the SKAF local branch found that 19 per cent of the SKAF members were registered as unemployed, of whom 30 per cent were part-time unemployed. The trade union attitude was that the number of part-time jobs should be reduced wherever possible in favour of full-time jobs, but the members revolted: "It is tough enough as it is. We cannot work eight-hour shifts!" This reaction from members is not limited to Kiruna. It was supported by the occupational safety and health administration which had recorded a large number of injuries among home helpers mainly as a result of strain and heavy loads.

One alternative was to introduce eight-hour shifts allowing time for physical exercise and physiotherapy, similar to arrangements in other local administrations, but the radical solution was to introduce six-hour shifts (a 30-hour week with wages for 40 hours). A formal agreement to that effect was signed in November 1988 between the town of Kiruna and the Kiruna branch of SKAF.

The Kiruna home helpers are organised in teams of eight or nine who, without supervision, are assigned some 35 patients. The group itself decides, in co-operation with the clients, how to schedule the work. Each home helper makes five or six visits a day. The number of home helpers involved in the reform was 224. The reform was carried out without lay-offs or new hirings. At the beginning of the project their average work day was 72 per cent of full-time work. At first glance the reform would seem quite costly: employment increased by 62 man years, corresponding to 28 per cent if measured in wages, or 2.9 per cent if measured in working hours.

An evaluation made three years after the introduction of the new system [Personalekonomiska Institutet (1991)] reported increased wage costs of about Skr 12 million, improved quality of care, and reduced costs for sick-leave, work injuries and turnover, amounting to savings of Skr 2.5 million. The costs involved in shortening working hours were Skr 2 113 000, i.e. there was a total gain of Skr 387 000. If the reduced costs to the health insurance and the municipality for relocation of injured home helpers were also taken into account, the reduction of working hours and the introduction of a new system of work organisation (with less supervision) turned out to be quite profitable for the community, both in economic terms and in terms of the quality of care.

Quality can be measured by the number of recipients of care per man year, which was reduced by 34 per cent. At the same time, the hours every recipient got from a home helper increased by 3.5 per cent. A consequence for the patient was continuity of care, while the number of home helpers with each patient was drastically reduced.

Similar arrangements with a shorter working day at full pay have been organised in two wards in Södertälje Hospital, the home help services in Åkersberga and a nursing home in Blackeberg, all close to Stockholm. In all three cases, a 40-hour week was scheduled, with some flexibility at the beginning and end of the day. Part of the 40 hours, however, included preventive health care for employees (physical exercise or simply walking in the woods in groups, while discussing how to organise the work of the autonomous group). While reports from these experiments have been positive, the Stockholm county health authority has been unwilling to embark upon further projects. The changing labour market seems to explain some of this reluctance.

Failed negotiations

The willingness to adopt flexible arrangements depends to some degree on the kind of job, as is clearly illustrated by a case from the Karolinska University Hospital in Stockholm. At the hospital there are two neighbouring paediatric clinics. One is a neo-natal clinic, the other a clinic for cancer patients. The neo-natal clinic has a workload which is very unevenly distributed over the year (births peak in spring) and both employer and personnel are interested in a flexible working arrangement. A proposal was made to schedule the work according to the work load and have longer spells of leisure when there are fewer patients. As a *quid pro quo* a reduction of yearly working hours was offered.

A schedule was being worked out when the employees of the cancer clinic protested and challenged the arrangement. This clinic normally has a very stable work load. A negotiator from the Stockholm local branch of SKAF was invited. As a rule, any local agreement has to be signed by a representative of the national union, and he (it is almost always a male, with a background in the technical service, implying day work, or in mental care, where schedules tend to be rigid) sided with the cancer clinic – there was to be no flexible working time arrangement.

A young national union officer, responsible for organisational development in health care administration, was called in by the other side, who invoked the arguments of the union's own discussion guide ''On working hours''. These attempts were to no avail. The traditionalists were not willing to give way, even when it was suggested that the neo-natal clinic could introduce flexible working hours as a research project that could be evaluated later by both parties. The effort failed even though it was directed at providing better quality care under more humane conditions, with a possible shortening of the annual working hours as an extra bonus. Union members in the neo-natal clinic blamed the union for the failure, and some of them quit paying their union dues.

Physicians' working hours

Another major controversial issue relating to working time, has been the regulations applying to medical doctors. Almost all Swedish physicians are salaried and under union contract. A special clause exempts doctors from the normal procedures for scheduling work. According to the Working Hours Act, employees may work a total of 19 hours per day, including pauses (between 5.00 a.m. and 12.00 midnight). Taking into consideration pauses, the total number of working hours may amount to 17.5. According to this regulation, physicians' working hours are scheduled as ''eight hours of active duty followed by 10 hours of stand-by'' (''jourtjänstgöring''). This may, however, be exceeded.

The collective agreement states that: "Regular working hours for physicians are assigned weekdays between 7.00 a.m. – 9.00 p.m.".[2] All other hours are covered by doctors on duty or on call. The latter, compared to other groups in the health sector, receive generous compensation either economically or with time off.

Exceedingly long periods on duty have been cited as a factor impairing the quality of work a doctor is able to perform, but for many years the Medical Association refused serious discussions. If doctors, like nurses, could be placed on a shift schedule, the Landstingsförbund claims, this would be less costly in terms of pay and also provide improvements in the organisation of work. Some small steps to remedy this problem have been taken in recent national agreements. The demand by employers that physicians' schedules should include shorter but more frequent calls on duty or stand-by time, has been accepted with some caution. Under the new agreement there is a general provision that doctors, too, should accept a share in shiftwork.[3]

Results of alternative arrangements

Naturally the results of alternative working time arrangements vary with the type of changes introduced. Unfortunately the study made by the Landstingsförbund does not differentiate between arrangements, when analysing views with regard to the new alternatives. However, at the aggregate level, the study shows that a majority of the head nurses interviewed believe that the quality of care has improved. Interestingly, they also see more satisfied personnel as the most significant outcome (30 per cent). Other benefits mentioned include advantages in improved staffing, more time for patients, etc.

When specifically addressing the economic issue, an equal number say either that "the economy has improved", or "it has not changed". Eleven per cent believe it might have been negatively affected. Different changes have naturally had different outcomes, which is also seen in the responses as to whether staffing has increased (29 per cent), decreased (18 per cent), or remained unchanged (52 per cent). A reasonable guess is that the more positive answers reflect the experience with flexitime and similar arrangements, while the improved shift schemes for weekends have demanded a higher staffing level, which in effect seems to be the reason why that specific trend is now being reversed. The Landstingsförbund no longer seems to want to talk of less, but rather of more frequent work on Saturdays and Sundays, as shown in Chart 9.2.

Two-thirds of all clinics expect to continue with new working time arrangements. Flexitime is the most frequently cited forthcoming reform, but the more advanced forms of flexible work, such as time banks, annual working time or personal schedules, have been cited with approval by one clinic in four. This trend is strongly endorsed by the employers. The trade unions are somewhat more ambiguous, but on the whole they too welcome the new flexible working time arrangements, as long as the employees have a reasonable say in how the work is scheduled.

The performance of the health care system, especially in the case of surgery, has greatly improved through the new schedules. The inefficient use of operating theatres became a national scandal, when a newspaper disclosed that the facilities were used five to six hours rather than eight hours a day. Unwillingness to allow overtime at the end of

Chart 9.2. **Plans for further working time arrangements in Swedish clinics**
Percentages

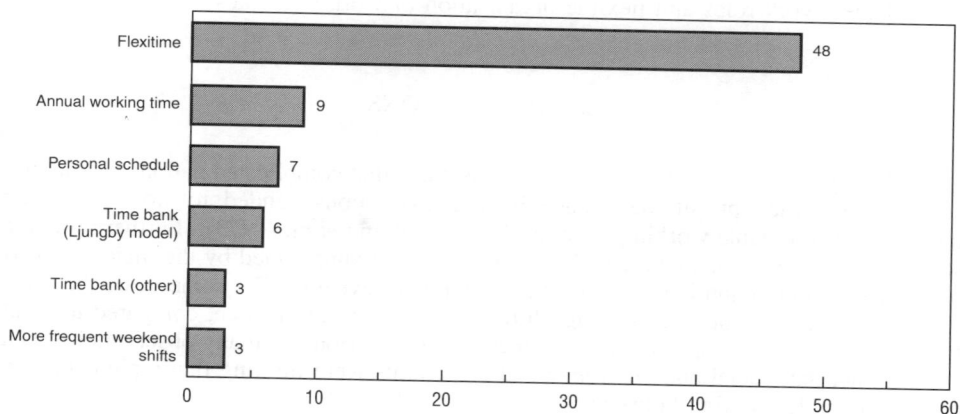

Category	Percentage
Flexitime	48
Annual working time	9
Personal schedule	7
Time bank (Ljungby model)	6
Time bank (other)	3
More frequent weekend shifts	3

Source: Landstingsförbundet (1992).

the day, should the operation take longer than expected, often inhibits operations after 3.00 p.m. or even earlier on Fridays. Greater flexibility in working time arrangements shows much promise in allowing expensive capital equipment to be used more effectively and has been an important factor behind improved productivity. As has been seen above, the outcome of alternative arrangements can be quite favourable, especially when using personal scheduling and time bank schemes.

The Landstingsförbund is actively promoting projects of this kind today. By organising conferences, publishing booklets, etc. it is trying to facilitate local initiatives. One major conclusion to emerge from the projects which have been evaluated is the need for computerised support for logging time and providing both the employer, employees and trade union locals with relevant aggregates of information. One of the reports published by the Landstingsförbund offers the following view on new working time schedules:

"Work satisfaction increases and work stress decreases if employees themselves can adapt working time to their lifestyles and needs. Irrespective of whether financial or personnel resources are scarce, it is essential that working time is used effectively. With flexible arrangements the work load is more evenly distributed and staffing is related to the amount of work which needs to be done [Landstingsförbundet (1992), p. 7]."

The health sector is faced with some of the most difficult and demanding challenges in the labour market, in making jobs more attractive and more acceptable socially. During recent years some highly innovative projects have developed, based on more flexible time arrangements. But to fulfil their potential, these projects need to be supported by technology, adapted work roles and flexible organisation of work schedules.

E. CONCLUSIONS

Already in the 1970s, the observation was made that complicated nation-wide labour contracts and the oppositional stance by national unions, tended to slow down the introduction of flexible working hours in Sweden [Elbing *et al.* (1973)]. Furthermore, the scheduling of work was one area which was left largely unaffected by the major reforms of co-determination and labour legislation in the late seventies. For some years the issue was much in the public eye, although little was achieved in practice, compared to what took place in other European countries over the same period. To many observers it was a striking fact that social and environmental constraints were limiting the implementation of more flexible working hours in Sweden.

Some commentators have suggested that the extensive social welfare arrangements, such as child day care, sickness benefits, extended parental leave, etc., all reduce the need for individuals to adjust their time budget through flexible working hours [Ronen (1981)]. This situation is apparently now changing, mainly for two reasons. One is the economic pressure for a more efficient production process, in the health sector as well as in the overall public sector and elsewhere. The second is political pressure: the non-socialist coalition government formed in 1991 is emphasizing deregulation, free choice, privatisation and competition in the public sector, as part of its programme "to put an end to all Swedish idiosyncrasies" [Barkan (1992)].

With an unprecedented increase in unemployment – from a few percentage points to almost double digits in three years – the trade unions would find it difficult to resist the new arrangements aimed at making work more effective even if they wanted to. The union membership is divided in their views on alternative time schemes. On the one hand, there is a sizeable body of senior officials who feel that the individual will always suffer when dealing with the employer without full support from his/her union. On the other hand, there is a young and vocal group of feminist employees, who demand a shorter work week and also believe flexible arrangements will help female workers deal with their dual roles in society. A growing number of men support the women's position, expecting that it would also encourage more egalitarian roles in the family.

Employers, public as well as private, are vigorously promoting a policy of decentralised work arrangements, with flexible working time as a prime goal. The situation raises the question as to how effectively employees will be able to balance their own needs with those of the employers, especially in a labour market recession like the one now being experienced in Sweden. The results of the projects reported from the health sector suggest that there is a need to develop some framework for local co-determination which might even out power differences.

It is equally important that norms be established at the local level as to what is fair and reasonable, who should have a first choice of his/her individual working hours, etc. In the experiments reported here, some norms of this kind did emerge which considered not only work-related issues but also the social situation of fellow workers. Little is yet known about the full impact of highly flexible work arrangements on the work culture, the cohesion of the work group, competence and training and, in the case of the health sector, the needs of patients. But it seems clear that the organisation of time is not an issue independent of other questions of management and job design. The rigidity of traditional work organisation is one issue which health personnel insist needs to be counteracted, if flexibility is to have a real meaning for them.

The trade unions' demand for a shorter working day does not, at least at present, seem to have a bright future. Increasingly people are turning to other arrangements to facilitate the harmony of work and family life or leisure. Clearly there is pressure from the rank and file to develop alternative working time arrangements. The initiatives surveyed in this chapter indicate a wide variation from simple and pragmatic forms of personal scheduling, to the more elaborate and sophisticated thinking behind the time bank.

If one is to take a less rosy view of the future, recent changes in the Swedish welfare policy systems make some of these reforms particularly timely. It can make economic sense to organise for child care by developing a personal work schedule, or to use the flexibility option when a child is ill or personal business demands attention. Under the new health insurance rules in Sweden, benefits are paid only from the third day of illness, while previously they were paid from the first day. Thus while not meeting the social ideals promoted by the trade unions, it is likely that flexible arrangements might help people cope at a local level, during a period of scarcer resources and strong pressure to improve performance in the health sector.

The impetus behind time banks and similar ideas is that one should not have to be at work when one is not needed there. Traditionally, saving time is primarily an employer interest. With the new arrangements, there can also be an incentive to the employee, as illustrated in the time bank experiment. During temporary workloads the employer can call in personnel at a lower cost than usual, while the employee can benefit from time off during slack periods.

Notes

1. Rules concerning physicians come under the BOL 90 agreement, while those for nurses and nursing assistants are covered by AB. The parties can enter into local agreements which, on certain specific issues, can derogate from the provisions in the national contract.
2. BOL 90, paragraph 5 C.
3. The agreement also refers, obliquely, to the right of doctors to working hours not deviating too much from those of other groups with a similar position in society (BOL 90).

Bibliography

BARKAN, J. (1992), "End of the Swedish Model?", in *Dissent*, Spring, pp. 192-198.

ELBING, A.O., GADON, H. and GORDON, J.R. (1973), "Time for a human time-table", in *European Business Review*, No. 39, Autumn, pp. 46-54.

LANDSTINGSFÖRBUNDET (1991), *Individuell datorstödd arbetstidsplanering*, Stockholm: Landstingsförbundet.

LANDSTINGSFÖRBUNDET (1992), *Enkät om arbetstidsförändringar*, Stockholm: Marknadsindikator.

PERSONALEKONOMISKA INSTITUTET (1991), *6-timmars arbetsdag med 8-timmars betalning. En personalekonomisk kalkyl på hemtjänsten i Kiruna*, Case-study No. 91:1.

RONEN, S. (1981), *Flexible Working Hours, An Innovation in the Quality of Working Life*, New York: McGraw Hill.

SALTMAN, R.B. and VON OTTER, C. (1992), *Planned Markets and Public Competition*, Buckingham: Open University Press.

SKAF (1989), *Enkät om arbetstider*, Stockholm: Svenska Kommunalarbetareförbundet.

SOU (Statens offentliga utredningar) (1989), Arbetstid och Välfärd, SOU 1989: 53.

SOU (Statens offentliga utredningar) (1992), Årsarbetstid, SOU 1992: 27.

STOCKHOLMS LÄNS LANDSTING (1992), Första året med vårdavtal och befolkningskontrakt, Rapport No. 2; "Sätt vårde på vården".

VÄSTRA SJUKVÅRDSDISTRIKTET (1992), *IVA-projektet, Ljungby*, Landstinget i Kronoberg, mimeo.

Chapter 10

PROCEEDINGS OF THE OECD EXPERTS' MEETING ON FLEXIBLE WORKING TIME ARRANGEMENTS: THE ROLE OF BARGAINING AND GOVERNMENT INTERVENTION

by

by Gerhard Bosch and Peter Tergeist

A. INTRODUCTION

A meeting of experts on the subject of "Flexible working time arrangements: the role of bargaining and government intervention" was held on 3 and 4 May 1993 in Paris at the seat of the OECD. The participants included representatives of governments, trade unions and employer associations from various OECD countries as well as the authors of eight national reports and a synthesis report, all of which have been included in the present volume. The meeting was chaired by Dominique Taddei, Professor of Economics at the University of Paris-Nord.

In preparation for the meeting, the OECD had commissioned eight national reports (from Canada, France, Germany, Italy, Japan, the Netherlands, Sweden and the United Kingdom) on flexible working time arrangements in three different industries (health care, retail trade and metal industry). The synthesis report highlighted both the differences and the common trends revealed by the national reports.

The OECD's purpose in this project was not to document global and quantifiable trends in the evolution of working time, but rather to investigate their qualitative effects on industrial relations and collective bargaining. To this end, the reports were to highlight the interests of both employers and employees in respect of new flexible working time arrangements and to describe the processes by which new time arrangements are negotiated, against the background of legislative provisions.

Industrial relations in the eight countries differ substantially in certain fundamental characteristics (*e.g.* rate of unionisation, extent of state intervention in working time issues, centralisation vs. decentralisation of bargaining), while the industries selected for special study also vary widely in structure (private vs. public sector, services vs. manufacturing, male vs. female-dominated, high-wage vs. low-wage industry). This combination of national and sectoral reports provided a sound basis for dealing with the broad scope of the conference theme.

The discussion at the meeting was divided into debates on the three industries under investigation and on two general issues, namely the role of statutory regulation and the extent to which employer and employee interests in flexible working time arrangements diverge or converge.

B. THE OPENING SESSION

The opening session began with a presentation by Mr. Peter Scherer (Head, Social Affairs and Industrial Relations Division) who pointed out the OECD's interest in a better understanding of rigidities and flexibilities in the labour market. Working time patterns were increasingly diversifying. As a result of the increasing capital intensity of their investments, it was in companies' interest to extend operating hours in order to adjust rapidly to fluctuations in demand. The modern workforce, on the other hand, was concerned with a more "individualised" balance between work and private life. As a result, employees had divergent interests that might even conflict with each other. As consumers, workers might well be in favour of longer shop opening hours which would, however, require other workers to adjust to new flexible working time patterns. There was a long-term need, said Mr. Scherer, to schedule working hours in ways that ensured economic efficiency while at the same time responding to individual worker preferences.

Mr. Olivier Drague, representing the OECD's Business and Industry Advisory Committee (BIAC), saw the flexibilisation of working time as one way of helping to solve the employment problem. Firms could use it to increase their productivity and competitiveness. He had no difficulty in envisioning a compensatory reduction in working time, although this would need to be coupled with company restructuring. Mr. Jean-Claude Pichenot, representing the Trade Union Advisory Committee (TUAC), believed that current high levels of unemployment made it essential to redistribute the available work in creative ways in order to boost the level of employment. He pointed, among other things, to the high level of overtime. While it seemed that an extension of operating hours in capital-intensive sectors was unavoidable, its implications for individual working hours were to be negotiated at industry level.

The *rapporteur* of the meeting, Mr. Gerhard Bosch, who also authored the synthesis report submitted to the meeting (see Chapter 1 of this publication), briefly outlined his most important conclusions from the national studies. In order to understand the various forms of flexible time arrangements described in the reports, a distinction had to be made between societal effects, strategy effects, sectoral effects and the impact of the long-term structural changes affecting all industrialised countries.

In all countries under consideration, working time patterns were becoming increasingly individualised, while female labour force participation was rising. At the same time employers were being affected by important structural changes. On the one hand, they were trying to extend the utilisation times of expensive capital equipment and on the other to replace expensive forms of working time organisation with cheaper ones. Although these common trends had a strong impact upon the organisation of working time, the differing structures of industrial relations and the wide variations in the collective agreements and legislation governing working time meant that working time arrangements in the countries in question differ considerably (societal effects). The most important differences between the countries referred, first, to the existence of legal or collectively agreed and generally applicable minimum conditions and, second, to the existence or otherwise of an effective plant-level system of employee representation. In many countries, the rapporteur noted, it is the weakness of representation structures at plant level that constitutes the real stumbling block in any attempts to flexibilise working time.

Furthermore, very different strategies *vis-à-vis* new working time arrangements were being followed in the various countries, industries and firms, ranging from the introduction of a legal entitlement to parental leave to the pursuit of *laissez-faire* policies (strategy effects). Finally, Mr. Bosch outlined the importance of sectoral effects: flexibility of working time has different meanings in manufacturing industry and the service sector. In manufacturing, firms can reduce costs by extending operating hours, which puts them in a position to offer their employees attractive compromises when it comes to the fixing of new working time arrangements. In the labour intensive and often poorly unionised service sector, on the other hand, new working time arrangements are used primarily to reduce labour costs, which may lead to unattractive arrangements for employees, with compensation tending to be much less generous than in manufacturing.

C.   THE SECTORAL STUDIES

Health care

The second session discussed the country and sectoral studies submitted to the meeting. A first round was devoted to issues of working time flexibility in health care. This segment was introduced by Peter Scherer and Peter Tergeist from the OECD Secretariat, followed by commentaries by the authors of two national reports, Mr. W. de Lange (Netherlands) and Mr. C. von Otter (Sweden), and by a general discussion.

Mr. Scherer and Mr. Tergeist referred to the low prestige of the nursing professions in particular and to the recruitment problems experienced by hospitals, and asked whether new working-time arrangements might provide a solution. There was currently an increasing demand for a more efficient provision of public health, and flexible working time arrangements might well play an important role in this regard. The Swedish time bank model, as outlined in the national report on Sweden, was considered to be a useful and innovative approach towards reconciling the divergent interests of hospitals and their employees, and hospitals might be encouraged to introduce such models. However, health care already belonged to the industries with the highest share of non-standard working time arrangements, and the move toward a "leaner" manpower organisation in hospitals might lead to an increasing precariousness of employment relationships in this sector, as, *inter alia*, the text on "on-call" arrangements in the report on the Netherlands appeared to show.

With reference to his report on the Netherlands, Mr. de Lange noted that there was little tradition of trade union activity in Dutch hospitals. However, this had now changed, and part-time workers had acquired the same rights as their full-time colleagues. After this success, trade union efforts in collective bargaining would be concentrated on further restricting the number of on-call contracts which was currently limited to 4 per cent of working hours. When working time had been reduced in the past, government-imposed budget restrictions had meant that hospital managements had simply increased work loads. As a result, trade unions were now opposed to further reductions in working time. Mr. de Lange agreed with the observation that the prestige of nursing professions was very low, resulting in serious recruiting problems. Solutions to this problem would consist of either granting higher wages or making working time arrangements more attractive, or a combination of both.

Mr. von Otter, co-author of the report on working hours in the Swedish health care system, spoke of the "empowerment of the patient" as a pioneering change. Patients now expected nursing care of higher quality, while at the same time cost restrictions had increased. "Lean" workforces had to react to diverse demands for their services by accepting more flexible working time arrangements. Because of rising unemployment, Swedish hospitals were not currently experiencing recruitment problems. He continued by describing experiments with "time banks" and similar schemes that try to better adjust the presence of personnel to the actual workload. He reported that sickness absenteeism had decreased drastically at hospitals that had introduced alternative working time arrangements. The time bank model functioned only if each work team contained representatives of the various categories within the workforce (*e.g.* those with and those without children). In that way, it was possible to reconcile both the diverging interests of the various groups of staff and those of employees and management.

The subsequent discussion focused particularly on the problems of part-time work. A great deal of attention was directed towards the various definitions of part-time work, with reference being made to discussions at the ILO on a possible recommendation or convention on part-time work. Some participants emphasised that part-time work was not in itself at all flexible. Many part-time employees were women with children who were available for work only at certain times. Furthermore, part-time work was not homogeneous. It ranged from stable, self-selected employment to precarious marginal jobs. The Austrian delegate referred once again to recruitment problems. Working time reductions had, he said, led to increased staff shortages in hospitals, which was why part-time working could not be encouraged. Referring to data from Eurostat, the chairman observed that in several European countries fewer children were being born on Sundays and asked whether it was the interests of employees or of patients that primarily determined working time arrangements. The Australian delegate also considered it necessary to investigate whether flexible working hours actually improved the quality of care.

Retail trade

The discussion of the country studies continued with the retail trade industry. The debate centred on the issue of shop opening hours on the one hand, and flexible methods of labour utilisation on the other. This segment was introduced by Mrs. Karen Ekenger from the Swedish Employers Confederation, followed by commentaries by the authors of the country reports on Canada (Mrs. Poulin-Simon), France (Mr. Lallement) and Italy (Mr. Gasparini), and by a general discussion.

In her introductory remarks, Mrs. Ekenger emphasised three points. First, increasing international competition required the flexibilisation of working time arrangements. Second, negotiations on working time should take place at as decentralised a level as possible. Third and finally, working hours ought to be allocated in such a way as to match them with shop opening hours and operating hours more generally; for example, modern delivery requirements meant that firms were becoming increasingly integrated into just-in-time systems.

Mrs. Poulin-Simon, co-author of the Canadian report, stressed that negotiations on working time in Canada were already completely decentralised. The retail sector was little unionised and the regulatory framework, either through collective bargaining or legislation, little developed. With a share of part-time in total employment of around 45 per cent nationally, the concept of "normal working hours" in retail trade was gradually losing its meaning. Companies use part-time employees, mostly under contracts of unlimited duration, to respond to the weekly fluctuation of business and to increasing pressures to open on Sundays. In addition, part-time workers are less costly, since their terms and conditions are not usually pro-rated to those of full-timers.

Mr. Gasparini, author of the Italian report, stressed the extraordinarily important role played by small shops in Italy. Until a few years previously, working time and opening hours had been the same in order to protect small shops. Permission had only recently been granted for opening hours to be extended to up to 70 hours per week. This had led to a decoupling of working time and opening hours. One consequence of this had been the introduction or extension of team work and part-time work.

Large-scale retailers had undoubtedly taken the lead in promoting and guiding the flexibility process, without, however, extensively relying on precarious forms of employment; there is, for example, no temporary work run through agencies, and little recourse to fixed-term contracts. Finally, regional regulations were becoming increasingly important. In Lombardy, for example, shops could now open in the evening on 110 days a year. The trade unions had been successful in negotiating certain benefits in return, mainly attractive shift arrangements but also reductions in working time.

Mr. Lallement, in commenting on his report on the French retail trade, noted that over the last decade French statutory regulations governing working time had tended to encourage flexible working arrangements. For example, shop opening hours on Sunday have recently been liberalised, in particular for stores selling very broadly defined "cultural goods". Since the 1960s, the number of supermarkets and hypermarkets had been increasing continuously, and these large shops were seeking to adapt their staffing levels as closely as possible to fluctuations in customer flows. In the majority of stores, the main method of managing these staffing adjustments was the increasing and simultaneous use of part-time employment and overtime. As a general rule, the work force in the larger retailers is young, mobile, female and relatively low paid.

A central theme of the subsequent discussion was the consequences of extended opening hours for employment levels and employment conditions. A representative from the Business and Industry Advisory Committee saw them as a particular opportunity for small firms. By contrast, a member of the TUAC delegation noted the fact that there were no regulations in French law prohibiting shops to open around the clock. The delegate from the United Kingdom reported on studies concerning the impact of Sunday trading which found that, while the number of people employed would increase slightly, the total amount of labour input would decrease. A similar study for France, according to Mr. Lallement, found that a total withdrawal of the ban on Sunday opening would result in long-term job losses, due to the ensuing concentration and rationalisation process. The Austrian representative saw the consequences as ambivalent: in his country, extended opening hours had created extra demand, largely because of the great importance of tourism. The same had been observed in Canada in the areas bordering the United States.

A second topic of discussion was the diverging interests of employees, firms and consumers. In Germany, both firms and employees have rejected any extension of shop opening hours, although for different reasons. Employees wanted to avoid any increase in unsocial hours, while many firms feared an increase in costs without any corresponding rise in demand. It was reported that in Sweden, on the other hand, employees seemed satisfied with the working time associated with longer opening hours. However, the higher costs incurred by retailers had led to price increases. There were clearly considerable national differences in the payment of night and weekend shifts, which might account in part for the differences in attitudes.

Winding up the debate, Mr. Scherer expressed his opposition to the simplistic view that demand would remain unchanged if shop opening hours were extended. He concluded that legislation and collective bargaining had to tread a fine line between providing extended choice and a higher quality of life for society as a whole and avoiding any deterioration in the quality of the working life of those who work in the retail industry.

Metal industry

The third industrial sector discussed during this session was metal manufacturing. This segment was introduced by Mr. J. Kreimer de Fries from the German Confederation of Trade Unions, followed by commentaries by the authors of the country reports on Germany (Mr. R. Trinczek) and the United Kingdom (Mr. P. Blyton), and by some remarks by the Japanese attaché for Labour and Social Affairs, Mr. H. Matsuura, who spoke on behalf of the author of the Japanese national report (Mr. Sasajima).

In view of current high levels of unemployment, Mr. Kreimer de Fries saw a continuing need for collective working time reductions. If working time were reduced, operating hours could be extended without creating any social problems. Two-shift systems in particular were socially acceptable. Working time should not be regulated solely by the demand for productivity gains: improving the quality of life should also play a role. For example, it was important to discuss flexible working hours in terms of improving employees' "sovereignty" over their time budgets.

Mr. Blyton, presenting his report on the United Kingdom, started out by noting that while much of the preceding discussion dealt with *atypical* working patterns, these were not necessarily *flexible*. He had taken an approach where flexible working hours implied varying employees' working time to meet some kind of business fluctuation. Referring to the situation in the United Kingdom, he observed that flexible working time arrangements were mainly an employer-dominated area, their main interest over the last decade having been to restrict "job control unionism" and to reduce non-productive work time, *e.g.* through the introduction of "bell-to-bell" working. In view of the current weakness of the trade union movement, employees' requirements for flexible working hours were of little significance. Overtime remained the most important source of working time flexibility for employers. Low wage-rates meant that employees, too, had considerable interest in working overtime.

Mr. Matsuura, in his comments on the Japanese situation, stressed his country's intended move towards the 1 800-hour working year and noted the importance of labour/management dialogue in flexible work time scheduling, as was discussed at length in the national report on Japan by Mr. Sasajima.

Mr. Trinczek, author of the report on the German metal industry, spoke of the extended opportunities for flexible working hours that had been negotiated in the German metal industry in the past decade. Firms, however, seemed to make little use of them; they tended rather to stick to tried and tested forms of work time scheduling. As a rule, firm-level negotiations on new working time arrangements took place within a cooperative atmosphere. The recession had made powerful works councils more willing to cooperate.

In the general discussion that followed, the Belgian delegate also reported that legal opportunities for organising special weekend shifts were hardly used and that firms were rather conservative in their approach to flexible working hours. Mr. Drague agreed that the actual number of employees working under innovative working time arrangements, such as staggered hours or weekend shifts, was quite low. Firms generally adopted a very gradualist approach to change; in order to advance the process, an adequate range of choices had to be made available to them.

D.   THE ROLE OF STATUTORY REGULATION

The third session of the experts meeting was devoted to the discussion of general issues. Introducing the discussion on "The Role of Statutory Regulation", Mr. Tergeist pointed out that the legal regulation of work time scheduling varies widely in extent between countries, with only maximum weekly hours, weekly rest periods, annual leave and public holidays regulated virtually everywhere. Pressure for legal regulation in this area came from various directions: concern for general welfare and quality of life, health and safety considerations, productive efficiency and international competitiveness, and concern for work sharing and employment stability.

While many governments were trying to provide more legislative flexibility, Mr. Tergeist observed, regulations had often not kept pace with changes in practice. Indeed, the differentiation of working time patterns was a challenge to the normative capacity of legal rules and regulations which generally laid down uniform measures for the establishment of fairly standardised "normal" employment relationships. As a result, some governments were tempted to tolerate practices that violated the letter of the law, while others had begun to allow exceptions upon conclusion of a collective agreement.

In the discussion that followed, several delegates, such as those from Germany, Ireland and the Netherlands, outlined current plans for new working time legislation, with all of them allowing for derogations based on a collective agreement. Against the background of the French experience, the chairman pointed out that governments could help to make working and operating hours more flexible by offering companies tax incentives and by creating advisory institutions such as the Agence nationale pour l'amélioration des conditions de travail (ANACT).

There followed a discussion on the current state of supra-national working time regulation by the European Community (EC) and the International Labour Organisation (ILO). The EC representative reported on the current state of the draft directive entitled "Certain aspects of the organisation of working time", while the ILO delegate discussed the provisions of the new Night Work Convention of 1990 relative to those of the old Night Work (Industry) Convention of 1948, which had now been denounced by a number of countries. The chairman warned of the risk of contradiction between EC and ILO regulation and observed that the regulation of working hours at EC level was important, in order to prevent distortion of competition. Mr. de Lange noted that this might be true for the EC member states but that it did not address the issue of competition with Japan and the United States, both of which, as was generally known, had much longer working hours. A final point in the discussion on statutory regulation was the relationship between flexible working hours and child care and the possibility of introducing legislation to restrict "unsocial hours" for parents with young children. On the latter point, Mr. Bosch warned of the negative consequences such legislation might have on the hiring of women workers.

E. DIVERGENCE OR CONVERGENCE OF EMPLOYER AND EMPLOYEE INTERESTS

A Panel Discussion followed on the subject of "Working Time Flexibility: Divergence or Convergence of Employer and Employee Interests?", with contributions by Mr. Kauppinen from Finland, Mr. Martin from France, Mrs. Paoli-Pelvey from the ILO, Mr. Drague for BIAC, Mr. Botsch for TUAC, and Mr. Scherer from the OECD Secretariat. Mr. Kaupinnen stressed the importance of achieving sustainable growth that could offer both increases in productivity and an improvement in the quality of life. This was, however, difficult to achieve. In times of economic boom, the interests of employees predominated, while the opposite was the case in times of slump. It was necessary to achieve continuity through the application of generally binding regulations and to take working time out of competition. If no limits were placed on the flexibilisation of working time, societies would find themselves in a permanent and unproductive state of tension.

Mr. Martin analysed the different points of view of firms and their employees in respect of working time. In his view, it was necessary to achieve "win-win" compromises. This was becoming increasingly difficult in times of economic crisis. Mr. Botsch voiced a concern that too much of the debate on flexible working hours focused on annual hours schemes. Employees' requirements in respect of work time scheduling could not be satisfied through such schemes. Their working time requirements varied over the life cycle. This was why any analysis of employees' interests in flexible working hours should also take account of the various ways of scheduling working time over the entire life cycle (parental leave, gradual retirement, training leave, sabbaticals). One of the most important forms of work time scheduling from the point of view of employees was still the reduction of working time. With a total unemployment figure of almost 40 million in the OECD countries, the redistribution of scarce work had to remain on the agenda.

Mr. Drague summed up the position held by many participants when he noted that the issue of divergent/convergent interests in relation to working time arrangements should no longer be tackled in terms of antagonist power relations and that the "social climate" could only improve if individuals were given greater opportunities for choice. In his concluding remarks, Mr. Scherer pointed out that the debate on interests in the scheduling of work time should not focus solely on those of employees and employers, but should also take account of those of the customer.

F. CONCLUDING REMARKS

In conclusion, the rapporteur summarised the discussion that had taken place over the two days of the conference. He saw dangers in an ideological approach to flexible working hours. Even rigid working time had its own logic. Japan, for example, had very rigid working hours but was, at the same time, highly competitive. It would be disastrous for economic development if the deregulation of working time arrangements was seen by firms as an invitation to stop planning.

The globalisation of the world economy and increasing international competition were undoubtedly exerting a growing influence on work time scheduling at national level. In manufacturing industry, decisions on plant location were being increasingly taken on the basis of the opportunities for utilising expensive machinery for as long as possible. As a result, there was great pressure in the manufacturing sector to relax national regulations restricting operating hours (*e.g.* bans on Sunday working). However, this pressure was less intense when industries were tied to a particular location. Thus in the retail trade, for example, national traditions in respect of shop opening hours would presumably be maintained, while capital intensive manufacturing industries would probably see the emergence of world-wide standards for operating hours.

There was a risk that developments in manufacturing and services were following different paths. In certain parts of the service sector (*e.g.* the retail trade), the following vicious circles could be observed: increased costs incurred through longer opening hours – increasing competition – low unionisation – lack of industry-wide or national regula-

211

tions – substitution of expensive working time arrangements by cheaper ones – recruitment problems. By contrast, in the manufacturing sector, at least in capital intensive industries, there were many examples of virtuous circles: decreasing unit costs as a result of extended operating hours – strong unionisation – improvements in pay and working time arrangements – no recruitment difficulties. In order to make new working time arrangements both economically efficient and socially acceptable, vicious circles had to be broken and replaced by new time arrangements that are advantageous to both employers and employees.

212

MAIN SALES OUTLETS OF OECD PUBLICATIONS
PRINCIPAUX POINTS DE VENTE DES PUBLICATIONS DE L'OCDE

ARGENTINA – ARGENTINE
Carlos Hirsch S.R.L.
Galería Güemes, Florida 165, 4° Piso
1333 Buenos Aires   Tel. (1) 331.1787 y 331.2391
Telefax: (1) 331.1787

AUSTRALIA – AUSTRALIE
D.A. Information Services
648 Whitehorse Road, P.O.B 163
Mitcham, Victoria 3132   Tel. (03) 873.4411
Telefax: (03) 873.5679

AUSTRIA – AUTRICHE
Gerold & Co.
Graben 31
Wien I   Tel. (0222) 533.50.14

BELGIUM – BELGIQUE
Jean De Lannoy
Avenue du Roi 202
B-1060 Bruxelles   Tel. (02) 538.51.69/538.08.41
Telefax: (02) 538.08.41

CANADA
Renouf Publishing Company Ltd.
1294 Algoma Road
Ottawa, ON K1B 3W8   Tel. (613) 741.4333
Telefax: (613) 741.5439
Stores:
61 Sparks Street
Ottawa, ON K1P 5R1   Tel. (613) 238.8985
211 Yonge Street
Toronto, ON M5B 1M4   Tel. (416) 363.3171
Telefax: (416)363.59.63

Les Éditions La Liberté Inc.
3020 Chemin Sainte-Foy
Sainte-Foy, PQ G1X 3V6   Tel. (418) 658.3763
Telefax: (418) 658.3763

Federal Publications Inc.
165 University Avenue, Suite 701
Toronto, ON M5H 3B8   Tel. (416) 860.1611
Telefax: (416) 860.1608

Les Publications Fédérales
1185 Université
Montréal, QC H3B 3A7   Tel. (514) 954.1633
Telefax : (514) 954.1635

CHINA – CHINE
China National Publications Import
Export Corporation (CNPIEC)
16 Gongti E. Road, Chaoyang District
P.O. Box 88 or 50
Beijing 100704 PR   Tel. (01) 506.6688
Telefax: (01) 506.3101

DENMARK – DANEMARK
Munksgaard Book and Subscription Service
35, Nørre Søgade, P.O. Box 2148
DK-1016 København K   Tel. (33) 12.85.70
Telefax: (33) 12.93.87

FINLAND – FINLANDE
Akateeminen Kirjakauppa
Keskuskatu 1, P.O. Box 128
00100 Helsinki

Subscription Services/Agence d'abonnements :
P.O. Box 23
00371 Helsinki   Tel. (358 0) 12141
Telefax: (358 0) 121.4450

FRANCE
OECD/OCDE
Mail Orders/Commandes par correspondance:
2, rue André-Pascal
75775 Paris Cedex 16   Tel. (33-1) 45.24.82.00
Telefax: (33-1) 49.10.42.76
Telex: 640048 OCDE
Orders via Minitel, France only/
Commandes par Minitel, France exclusivement :
36 15 OCDE

OECD Bookshop/Librairie de l'OCDE :
33, rue Octave-Feuillet
75016 Paris   Tel. (33-1) 45.24.81.67
(33-1) 45.24.81.81

Documentation Française
29, quai Voltaire
75007 Paris   Tel. 40.15.70.00
Gibert Jeune (Droit-Économie)
6, place Saint-Michel
75006 Paris   Tel. 43.25.91.19
Librairie du Commerce International
10, avenue d'Iéna
75016 Paris   Tel. 40.73.34.60
Librairie Dunod
Université Paris-Dauphine
Place du Maréchal de Lattre de Tassigny
75016 Paris   Tel. (1) 44.05.40.13
Librairie Lavoisier
11, rue Lavoisier
75008 Paris   Tel. 42.65.39.95
Librairie L.G.D.J. - Montchrestien
20, rue Soufflot
75005 Paris   Tel. 46.33.89.85
Librairie des Sciences Politiques
30, rue Saint-Guillaume
75007 Paris   Tel. 45.48.36.02
P.U.F.
49, boulevard Saint-Michel
75005 Paris   Tel. 43.25.83.40
Librairie de l'Université
12a, rue Nazareth
13100 Aix-en-Provence   Tel. (16) 42.26.18.08
Documentation Française
165, rue Garibaldi
69003 Lyon   Tel. (16) 78.63.32.23
Librairie Decitre
29, place Bellecour
69002 Lyon   Tel. (16) 72.40.54.54

GERMANY – ALLEMAGNE
OECD Publications and Information Centre
August-Bebel-Allee 6
D-53175 Bonn   Tel. (0228) 959.120
Telefax: (0228) 959.12.17

GREECE – GRÈCE
Librairie Kauffmann
Mavrokordatou 9
106 78 Athens   Tel. (01) 32.55.321
Telefax: (01) 36.33.967

HONG-KONG
Swindon Book Co. Ltd.
13–15 Lock Road
Kowloon, Hong Kong   Tel. 366.80.31
Telefax: 739.49.75

HUNGARY – HONGRIE
Euro Info Service
Margitsziget, Európa Ház
1138 Budapest   Tel. (1) 111.62.16
Telefax : (1) 111.60.61

ICELAND – ISLANDE
Mál Mog Menning
Laugavegi 18, Pósthólf 392
121 Reykjavik   Tel. 162.35.23

INDIA – INDE
Oxford Book and Stationery Co.
Scindia House
New Delhi 110001   Tel.(11) 331.5896/5308
Telefax: (11) 332.5993
17 Park Street
Calcutta 700016   Tel. 240832

INDONESIA – INDONÉSIE
Pdii-Lipi
P.O. Box 269/JKSMG/88
Jakarta 12790   Tel. 583467
Telex: 62 875

ISRAEL
Praedicta
5 Shatner Street
P.O. Box 34030
Jerusalem 91430   Tel. (2) 52.84.90/1/2
Telefax: (2) 52.84.93
R.O.Y.
P.O. Box 13056
Tel Aviv 61130   Tél. (3) 49.61.08
Telefax (3) 544.60.39

ITALY – ITALIE
Libreria Commissionaria Sansoni
Via Duca di Calabria 1/1
50125 Firenze   Tel. (055) 64.54.15
Telefax: (055) 64.12.57
Via Bartolini 29
20155 Milano   Tel. (02) 36.50.83
Editrice e Libreria Herder
Piazza Montecitorio 120
00186 Roma   Tel. 679.46.28
Telefax: 678.47.51
Libreria Hoepli
Via Hoepli 5
20121 Milano   Tel. (02) 86.54.46
Telefax: (02) 805.28.86
Libreria Scientifica
Dott. Lucio de Biasio 'Aeiou'
Via Coronelli, 6
20146 Milano   Tel. (02) 48.95.45.52
Telefax: (02) 48.95.45.48

JAPAN – JAPON
OECD Publications and Information Centre
Landic Akasaka Building
2-3-4 Akasaka, Minato-ku
Tokyo 107   Tel. (81.3) 3586.2016
Telefax: (81.3) 3584.7929

KOREA – CORÉE
Kyobo Book Centre Co. Ltd.
P.O. Box 1658, Kwang Hwa Moon
Seoul   Tel. 730.78.91
Telefax: 735.00.30

MALAYSIA – MALAISIE
Co-operative Bookshop Ltd.
University of Malaya
P.O. Box 1127, Jalan Pantai Baru
59700 Kuala Lumpur
Malaysia   Tel. 756.5000/756.5425
Telefax: 757.3661

MEXICO – MEXIQUE
Revistas y Periodicos Internacionales S.A. de C.V.
Florencia 57 - 1004
Mexico, D.F. 06600   Tel. 207.81.00
Telefax : 208.39.79

NETHERLANDS – PAYS-BAS
SDU Uitgeverij Plantijnstraat
Externe Fondsen
Postbus 20014
2500 EA's-Gravenhage   Tel. (070) 37.89.880
Voor bestellingen: Telefax: (070) 34.75.778